D1609835

Vodún

CONTEMPORARY ETHNOGRAPHY

Kirin Narayan and Alma Gottlieb, Series Editors

A complete list of books in the series
is available from the publisher.

VODÚN

Secrecy and the Search for Divine Power

Timothy R. Landry

PENN

UNIVERSITY OF PENNSYLVANIA PRESS

PHILADELPHIA

Published by
University of Pennsylvania Press
Philadelphia, Pennsylvania 19104-4112
www.upenn.edu/pennpress

Printed in the United States of America
on acid-free paper

10 9 8 7 6 5 4 3 2 1

Library of Congress Cataloging-in-Publication Data

Names: Landry, Timothy R., author.
  Title: Vodún : secrecy and the search for divine power / Timothy R. Landry.
  Other titles: Contemporary ethnography.
  Description: 1st edition. | Philadelphia : University of Pennsylvania Press,
    [2019] | Series: Contemporary ethnography | Includes bibliographical
    references and index.
  Identifiers: LCCN 2018020815 | ISBN 9780812250749 (hardcopy : alk. paper)
  Subjects: LCSH: Vodou—Economic aspects—Benin—History—21st century. |
    Secrecy—Religious aspects—Vodou. | Control (Psychology)—Religious
    aspects—Vodou. | Tourism—Benin—History—21st century. |
    Tourism—Religious aspects. | Ethnology—Benin.
  Classification: LCC BL2470.D3 L365 2019 | DDC 299.6/75—dc23
  LC record available at https://lccn.loc.gov/2018020815

To my parents, Catherine and Tim

To my brother Kevin, my sister-in-law Kim,
and my nieces Dakota and Logan

CONTENTS

A NOTE ON ORTHOGRAPHY AND STYLE

Throughout this book I intentionally blur the boundaries between Fonland and Yorùbáland, two ethnic territories found in present-day Nigeria and in the Republic of Bénin. I chose to do this for several reasons: (1) I seek to dismantle the long-standing scholarly and colonial associations that have connected Yorùbáland to Nigeria only; (2) I aim to re-create the multiethnic and transnational space of Ouidah, Bénin, as it exists on the ground; and, finally, (3) I hope to engage with the long-standing literature on Yorùbá religion, especially Ifá divination, while still attending to the ways in which Ifá divination is practiced by both Yorùbá and Fon peoples in southern Bénin. Even so, I attempted to provide local names and religious concepts in both the Fon and Yorùbá languages, using linguistically correct diacritical marks, while placing the emphasized language (which tended to shift from conversation to conversation during my fieldwork) first, and the deemphasized language second. Moreover, I prefaced Fon words with "Fon" and Yorùbá words with "Yr." for additional clarity (e.g., Fon Fá; Yr. Ifá). In these ways, I hope that scholars of both Bénin and Nigeria, and of both Fon and Yorùbá speakers, might find the research I have presented here useful. The only exception to my use of diacritical marks is in my repeated use of "Fon." I chose not to write "Fon" using the correct diacritical marks (Fòn) so as to remain consistent with existing scholarly literature. By contrast—and, again, following scholarly precedence—I use diacritical marks when I write "Yorùbá."

While "Vodún" is more accurately known as *vodúnsìnsen* (spirit worship) and its adherents described as *vodúnséntɔ́* (those who follow the spirits' taboos), for simplicity I name the religion as "Vodún" and the religion's followers, drawing on French, as "Vodúnisants" instead of using the more problematic English terms "Vodúnists" or "Voodooists." Following these conventions, I use "Vodún" to represent the religion as it is found in West Africa; "Vodou" to represent the Haitian variant; and "Voodoo" to show when I am indexing the stereotypical and often racialized African religion within non-Africans' imaginations. To indicate when I am speaking about the religion, I capitalize "Vodún," and when I use the word to mean "spirit" or "divinity," I write *vodún* with a lowercase "v."

In addition to these stylistic choices, when possible, I have changed the names of certain ritual ingredients and altered the order in which ritual events occur. This was done to protect ritual secrets and to prevent my work from being used as a "ritual manual" by spiritual seekers. In this same vein, I have used pseudonyms for all individuals and most place-names, including the name of the village (Fátòmè) in which I worked. I have, however, maintained the actual names of all major cities and historical figures.

Vodún

Introduction

> Vodun has survived by adopting and then adapting
> foreign elements. . . . The converging point of Vodun's
> "open-endedness" and "globality" is its pulse. That pulse
> is sustained by Vodun's flexible structure, its refusal to
> become stagnant, and, as a consequence, its ability to
> incorporate what it needs from local and global sources.
> —Rush 2013: 5

"Let's go, Tim! Daágbó Xunɔ̀ wants to see us," Marie, my research assistant, shouted as she pushed open the gate to the compound that I shared with her family.

"Oh, okay! I am coming!"

I had been waiting to see Daágbó for nearly two weeks. For many who live in the coastal city of Ouidah, Daágbó is recognized as the supreme chief of Vodún in Bénin. While his actual power and political reach are contested, receiving his blessing to conduct my research and hearing his perspective were important to me.[1] I hurried around the house and stuffed into my brown leather messenger bag my Moleskine notebook, a pen, a bottle of lukewarm water, and a few gifts I had purchased for Daágbó in anticipation of this meeting.

In just a matter of minutes, Marie and I hopped onto the backs of two motorcycle taxis en route for Daágbó's palace. As was customary, we arrived with a bottle of gin, 2,000 CFA (West African francs), and a handful of kola nuts. We were asked to wait for Daágbó in a long rectangular room wherein the supreme chief frequently held audiences with guests and dignitaries. The full length of the left wall was painted with an aging dynastic mural on which Daágbó Xunɔ̀'s predecessors since 1452 were represented. Lined up against each side of the room were more than twenty chairs for the priest's visitors. At the back of the room, sitting in front of the doorway that leads to Daágbó's private residence, stood his throne and a low rectangular coffee table on which Daágbó kept a tattered spiral notebook, a bottle of gin, four small etched glasses, and two cellular phones.

"Why is Daágbó considered the supreme chief of Vodún?" I whispered to Marie while we waited.

"A long-ago grandfather of his was a magical whale who had the power to turn into a man. As a man, the whale took many wives and had lots of children. Daágbó is descended from the whale's human children, and so he owns the sea [*xù*]. The sea is where all the other *vodún* [spirits] come from. So, we believe all vodún live here in his palace."

"Does everyone recognize him as the supreme chief?"

"No, not everyone. But a lot do," Marie responded.

After sitting patiently and chatting with Marie for more than half an hour, Daágbó emerged from behind the wooden beaded curtain that separates his private living space from the palace's public meeting room. We greeted each other. I offered him the gifts Marie and I brought for him, and he recipro-cated by pouring us two small glasses of gin.

"Welcome to Bénin," he announced. "Why are you here?"

"I would like to learn about Vodún," I responded. "I want to understand how Vodún is spreading throughout the world."

Daágbó took a sip of gin, smiled, and said, "Vodún spreads because it works."

"Can everyone benefit from Vodún?" I asked.

"Yes, Vodún is for everyone. People come to Bénin from all over the world to learn about the spirits. The spirits are for anyone who can protect them."

Daágbó was right: Vodún had become a global phenomenon. The fragile, but flexible, spirits and the secrets that safeguarded them could be found almost anywhere in the world. Today, it would be difficult to find a global city not occupied by *Vodúnisants*. While the religion's amorphous and flexi-ble nature has undoubtedly been one of Vodún's strengths, it has also not been without its challenges. As media, film, literature, and public discourse show, Vodún is a West African religious complex that has developed a prob-lematic celebrity and a global presence due to a series of interrelated his-torical events (McGee 2012). From the sixteenth to the nineteenth century, millions of enslaved West Africans were forcibly removed from their homes and sent to European colonies in Cuba, Brazil, Haiti, and the United States. In these places, new religions, such as Lucumí, Candomblé, and Vodou, formed out of the mixtures of European, Caribbean, and West African religious practices.

In the late 1920s and early 1930s "Voodoo" was propelled into the Western imagination by U.S. literature and film. William Seabrook's 1929 publication of *The Magic Island* and the 1932 release of the film *White Zombie* profited from racist, pejorative, and exaggerated images of black magic, skull-laden altars, bloody sacrifices, and staggering zombies. Where literature presented adherents of religions such as Buddhism as the enlightened "Oriental" other, African religious practitioners were represented as illogical, bloodthirsty idol worshipers. By the late 1960s, a few U.S. black nationals traveled to West Africa for initiation into Vodún and *òrìṣà* [Yr. spirit, god, or divinity] worship in order to reject Christianity's structural whiteness and to empower themselves, through ritual, with African spiritualities (e.g., Clarke 2004). At the same time, Cuban Americans who could no longer return to Cuba, because of the U.S.-Cuban travel embargo, began visiting West Africa in search of initiation into spirit cults that mirrored those found in the Afro-Cuban religion of Lucumí. Then, by the late 1980s—as the U.S. New Age movement continued to surge—middle-class, white, U.S.-based spiritual seekers began traveling to West Africa looking for divine power while also rejecting the politics of what they called "organized religion" (see Clarke 2004: 4–16). Since then, the Béninois state has teamed up with the United Nations Educational, Scientific, and Cultural Organization (UNESCO) to promote the country's "Voodoo culture" as an international commodity, thereby inspiring travel agencies to market Bénin as the "cradle of Voodoo," and some local tourism offices, such as the one in Ouidah, arrange initiations for foreigners who wish to become Vodún priests, devotees, and diviners (Rush 2001; Forte 2007, 2010; Landry 2011). Influenced by, and in some cases even supported by, these national trends, Daágbó and his predecessor—along with many other Béninois Vodún priests—have welcomed countless American and European spiritual seekers to Bénin (e.g., Caulder 2002). It is indisputable that Vodún's international presence is on the rise and the religion's global relevance is becoming increasingly more evident. This constellation of global events inspired this book.

As is illustrated in Daágbó's claim that "Vodún is for everyone," I explore the ways in which Béninois enhance Vodún's global appeal and contribute to the religion's multinational success. Since the late twentieth century, practitioners of African religions have enjoyed a greater Internet presence; spiritual tourism in Africa has been on the rise; African religions and spiritualities have enjoyed new global expansions; and African immigrants have contributed to the burgeoning religious diversity of some of the world's most cosmopolitan cities. This ethnography is first and foremost a look at the ways in which African religions, such as Vodún, have begun to expand in new directions with the support of recent trends in spiritual tourism. However, it is also an exploration of contemporary Vodún, a religion that was born in the West African rain forest but has begun to thrive in new places around the world. That is to say, this book is not meant to be an ethnography of foreign Vodún practitioners as much as it is an ethnography of Vodún within today's globalizing world. Vodún is becoming more popular in local, national, and transnational arenas—especially as spiritual markets, encouraged by processes of religious secrecy, serve to legitimize the transnational practice of Vodún. Vodún's growing reach across national, ethnic, racial, and class lines makes the religion the perfect example of an indigenous religion gone global, where according to Daágbó, the spirits exist for "anyone who can protect them."

Defining Vodún

While "vodún" is the progenitor of the English word "Voodoo," the religion in reality is nothing like what we have seen in movies such as *The Serpent and the Rainbow* or *The Skeleton Key* or, most recently, in the television series *American Horror Story: Coven*, where Papa Legba, the ever-important Haitian spirit (*lwa*) of the crossroads, was depicted pejoratively as a cocaine-snorting demon who demands the ritual sacrifice of babies. There is no doubt that African religions and their adherents have suffered profoundly from U.S. and European racist conceptualizations of Africa that have proliferated in film, media, and political discourse (see Barthkowski 1998). As Adam McGee points out, because Voodoo "is coded as black, presenting voodoo in scenarios that are belittling, denigrating and, most especially, *aimed to evoke terror* is a way of directing these sentiments at blacks without openly entering into racist discourse" (2012: 240). Yet despite these challenges Vodún and its Caribbean derivatives continue to thrive.

Far removed from Hollywood's racist imagery, Vodún is a religious system in which its devotees seek to achieve well-being in the world by focusing on the health and remembrance of their families (see Brown 2001). At the most basic level, "vodún" is a word from the *gbè* languages of the Niger-

Congo language family, and it translates best as spirit, god, divinity, or presence. Before transnational traders, colonial powers, scholars, and Christian missionaries came to Bénin, Vodún was known simply as *vodúnsínsen* (spirit worship) and its adherents were described as *vodúnséntɔ́* (those who follow a spirit's taboos). In precolonial Fonland, spirits—whether they be local or foreign—were all vodún. To the Vodúnisants, the spirit world truly offered limitless possibilities. Until colonialism, Vodún was not identified as a monolithic religion that could be placed in contrast to the Abrahamic religions. In fact, before Western involvement in West Africa, Vodún was best understood as a social system made of countless spirit and ancestor cults that existed without religious boundaries.

Vodún is part of an interconnected globalizing religious complex that I call the "African Atlantic forest religions." The West African and West African–derived forest religions include religions such as Vodún, òrìṣà worship, Sevi Lwa (Haitian Vodou), Lucumí (Santería), and Candomblé. These religions are characterized by their long-term connections to both West Africa and the Americas as a result of the transatlantic slave trade; the centrality of the forest in their cosmologies as one of the religions' primary "key symbols"; and their emphasis on ritual secrecy, spirit possession, and divination (Ortner 1973). African Atlantic forest religions have been active participants in globalization for more than four hundred years and have begun to establish themselves in urban centers such as New York City, Paris, Montreal, Miami, Chicago, and Houston. In these spaces, practitioners of the African Atlantic forest religions collaborate among themselves and draw from long-established traditions such as Christianity, Islam, and Western Occultism (P. Johnson 2007). In the city, human diversity causes religious boundaries to blur, as adherents of religions such as Vodún become increasingly multinational and multiracial. For these reasons, throughout the book, when analytically meaningful, I draw periodically on examples from the entire African Atlantic forest religion complex while retaining my primary focus on how Fon Béninois and foreign practitioners practice a religion they now call Vodún.

Even as I define Vodún, it is important to accept that Vodún is remarkably indefinable. As a religion, it has been described as a "vortex" and a "sponge," as being "open-ended," forever "unfinished" (Rush 1997, 2013), and intrinsically "eclectic" (cf. Mercier 1954: 212n4; Blier 1995; Bay 1998, 2008; Rush 2013: 10–11). Dana Rush has argued convincingly that the religion's remarkable abilities to absorb foreign gods, customs, and ideologies "were not just grafted onto a particular Vodun world view, but rather were the sustenance of the world view itself" (2013: 11). Vodún is a religion where Yorùbá divinities, through war or marriage, become new spirits for the Fon (Le Hérissé 1911; Mercier 1954; Blier 1995; Bay 1998, 2008; Law 2004; Rush 2013); where Jesus Christ becomes a vodún (Rush 2013); where Hindu gods can represent the spirits (Drewal 2008; Rush 2013); where Qur'anic script becomes a source of immense magical power; and where Islam inspires the worship of new witch-fighting spirits, such as Tron or Tinga (Tall 1995; Rush 2013: 78–86). Vodún is simply inexplicable. Highlighting this reality, Rush has suggested correctly that "an operable understanding of Vodun is based on the acceptance that, in order to make sense of Vodun, one must acknowledge that it cannot be fully made sense of" (2013: 56). Along with Rush, I accept that Vodún is seemingly defined by its obscurity. I make no attempt to restrict one's understanding of religions such as Vodún by struggling to define them. Instead, I embrace the religion's absorptive nature as a way of chronicling the ways in which Vodún has become increasingly important to a growing number of people across the globe.

Power, Secrecy, and Globalization

Vodún is a religion that has begun to build on the African Atlantic world as it includes new migrations, new expansions, and new localities. Religion, according to Gertrud Hüwelmeier and Kristine Krause, has thrived in today's world "because globalization provides fluid transnational networks that help transport religious messages from local to global audiences" (2010: 1). This ethnography is, in many ways, an examination of how religious messages and secrecy are transformed by Béninois practitioners through ritual and economic exchanges into experiences that have become increasingly more salient to a growing number of people with various backgrounds.

Nearly fifteen years ago, Ulrich Beck (1999) defined globalization as a "dialectical process" that involves "social links" while also "revaluing local cultures" and promoting "third cultures" that must provide an "extension of space; stability over time; [and] social density of the transnational networks, relationships, and image-flows" (12). All these criteria, according to Jacob Olupona and Terry Rey (2008), have been fulfilled by indigenous Yorùbá religion, as Yorùbáland has expanded to include not only West Africa but also Brazil, the Caribbean, and the United States. Many scholars have attended to the ways in which African and African diasporic religions have localized and been reimagined in new transnational spaces (e.g., Barnes 1997; Brown 2001; Murphy and Sanford 2001; Clarke 2004; D'Alisera 2004; Richman 2005; Olupona and Rey 2008; Parish 2011; P. Johnson 2013; Rey and Stepick 2013; Beliso-De Jesús 2015; Carr 2015; Pérez 2016). However, few ethnographies have examined the globalization of African religions from the perspective of Africans and through an analysis of events and ritual encounters that occur not in the religions' new territories but on the African continent itself.

To fill this gap, I focus on spiritual tourist encounters in Bénin. In so doing, I argue, the transnational flow of African religion is encouraged by secrecy—a social force that anthropologists have long seen as restrictive and one that reinforces local notions of power and authority between the secret holders and the secret seekers (e.g., Bellman 1984; Beidelman 1997). Secrecy thrives in a social paradox. For secrecy to retain its social power, the very experience that is meant to be kept from public consumption must be, at least on occasion, revealed. To put it another way, "secrecy must itself be performed in a public fashion in order to be understood to exist" (Herzfeld 2009: 135). In Vodún there is not a shortage of public performances of secrecy. Tourists often see brightly colored Egúngún (ancestral) masquerades dancing in the streets, or they feel pushback from Vodún practitioners when they want to take pictures of shrines or even visit certain spirit temples. Vodún's culture of secrecy is conspicuous, even to foreigners. As one becomes more intimately acquainted with the religion it becomes even clearer that ritual secrecy embodies tremendous social power. To be initiated into Vodún is to "find the spirit's depths" (Mɔ̀ hùn dò), to be initiated into the secret ancestral Egúngún society is to become a "bride of secrets" (awosì), and to divulge the secrets of the spirits is to "break" or "shatter" the spirit beyond repair (gbà hùn). In the sacred forest, ritual allows for the depths of the spirits to be simultaneously exposed safely and made vulnerable through revelation (see Chapter 2). Through initiation, secrecy becomes the social shell that protects the spirits and the initiates who now know each other's depths. The secret then becomes "an 'adorning possession' made more potent because its exact nature is unknown" (Newell 2013: 141) to those who seek the hidden.

As many anthropologists have shown, the secret itself is often less important than the processes of secrecy. Through what Michael Taussig called "active non-knowing" (1999: 7), Béninois often feign their knowledge of the spirit's "public secrets" until they too are initiated and therefore given the social authority to reveal what is, ironically, "generally known, but cannot be spoken" (5). Béninois understand, and even draw power from, this paradox. To them, initiation provides them with the embodied authority and the right to admit to know publicly the spirits' secrets. However, foreign spiritual seekers, who lack the habitus of their Béninois counterparts, struggle with this social reality. Without the required social networks from which secrecy draws its meaning, foreign spiritual seekers tend to focus on the secret itself. During the initiation of Christopher, a white American man in his thirties, into the secret Egúngún society, it was obvious that he was incredibly disappointed when René, his initiator, revealed to him that the society's ancestor masquerades were animated not by the ghostly ancestors as everyone claimed publicly but by men. Once this public secret was revealed to him, one could see his face flush with anger. He glared down at the forest floor and then up at me.

"Are they kidding? This is what I paid for? I paid $500 to learn something I already knew! Is this a joke?" Christopher asked, under the cover of English.

He later confided in me that he thought his initiators were lying to him and that "there must be something" they were not telling him and that he felt as though he was being "scammed." By this time, I had been initiated into the Egúngún society myself (see Chapter 2), and I had watched Jean initiate his own sons and nephews. Each of these initiations mirrored Christopher's experience precisely. There was no doubt that Christopher received a proper initiation. Yet there was little I could do to convince him. Christopher's perception of his initiators was already tainted by long-standing, racist, postcolonial politics in which Africans are imagined to be "corrupt" and "untrustworthy." The "silent power" Christopher carried with him as a result of his own racialized "unspoken authority of habit" (Comaroff and Comaroff 1991: 22) made it nearly impossible for him to appreciate the initiation he was allowed to undergo—and his initiators knew it.

When I asked René why he was comfortable revealing secrets to foreign spiritual seekers like Christopher, he shrugged and replied, "He doesn't live here. What is he going to do with what I teach him?" In this way, Béninois are able to redefine power as they initiate foreign spiritual seekers into systems that foreigners may not be fully equipped to understand. As a Béninois Vodún priestess one told me, "I can teach a white person how to be possessed by the spirits but it'll never happen."

In a similar way, Jung Ran Forte has argued, "Because of the substantial lack of knowledge, Westerner [initiates] are somehow less effective than Beninese ones. . . . Whites are not allowed to be possessed during public ceremonies, at least in Benin, when gods 'mount' human bodies, as during the confinement in the convent there is not apprenticeship of the modes of possession" (2010: 134). As both my and Forte's Béninois informants reveal, there is a sense among some Béninois that foreign initiates may lack the social and embodied power to participate fully in particular rituals. For them, foreigners simply lack the habitus or embodied memory to undergo ritual events such as spirit possession.[2] Regardless of these sentiments, or perhaps because of them, foreigners tend to focus less on effectively undergoing possession and more on successfully undergoing initiation. Before, during, and after initiation, foreign spiritual seekers commonly attempt to use their economic and racial power to coerce Béninois into revealing religious secrets. In Christopher's case, he eventually offered René an extra 100 USD to "tell him the real secrets"—but was told unapologetically, "Christopher, you already know them all."

While power, such as that exhibited by Christopher, often reveals itself as an oppressive and coercive force, in the case of Vodún's global expansion, my research confirms Michel Foucault's claim that power is also creative and productive. Béninois have creatively turned the tables on historic power relations, not just through their control of secrecy, but also through their willingness to charge foreign spiritual seekers large sums of money to learn secrets that even uninitiated Béninois typically already know. Because foreign spiritual seekers are not a part of the local community, where the "active milling, polishing, and promotion of the reputation of secrets" (P. Johnson 2002: 3), or what Paul Johnson called "secretism," acquires its social meaning, it is often assumed that foreigners can do little social harm with the secrets they are given. Nevertheless, it does not take long for foreign initiates to realize that the promotion of secrecy and the subsequent community that secretism helps to create, both in Bénin and in their home countries, are important to their success as priests and to the validity of the ritual secrets and powers that are entrusted to them.

Christopher found himself in a conundrum. Despite his claims of being "scammed," he could not disavow his initiator without discrediting his own status as an initiate, and he could not reveal the secret, regardless of how inconsequential he found it to be, without diminishing the economic and esoteric significance of the initiation he sought to provide to others in Vodún's global religious market. Instead, all he could do was reemphasize the authority given to him by the initiation process to other foreign spiritual seekers, thereby inadvertently reifying the transnational social value of secrecy over the secret itself. Christopher discovered what his initiators already knew—secrecy establishes community.

As secrecy creates global Vodún communities, foreign initiates in particular speak about the value of West Africa as an important symbolic place in their religioscape (e.g., Appadurai 1996). Many foreign spiritual seekers, even after being initiated into Haitian Vodou or Cuban Lucumí, travel to Nigeria and Bénin for initiations, arguing that West Africa is where "real Voodoo," "real secrets," or "true spiritual power" is found. For these tourists, Bénin and Nigeria have become symbols that authenticate their practice and imbue their own positions as priests with social power and authority.[3]

Since the 1990s, in an effort to escape Nigeria's perceived political instability and as a result of a strong marketing push by the Béninois government, an increasing number of spiritual tourists have begun traveling to Bénin for the same initiations, ceremonies, and spiritual powers they once traveled only to Nigeria to receive. Upon arriving in the Béninois side of Yorùbáland, spiritual tourists once again encounter the "Nigeria is more authentic" trope, but this time by Fon- and Yorùbá-speaking Béninois who themselves see Nigeria as the "origins" of many of the rituals, ceremonies, and cults in which spiritual tourists have become interested (e.g., Fá/Ifá, Egúngún, Orò). Indexing this perception among local Béninois, one Yorùbá man told me, "Nigeria is where the real power is. That is where all these spirits came from. That is where the real secrets live."

Discussions of authenticity and power among Béninois practitioners often centered on acè, the Fon and Yorùbá concept of "divine power." I would hear "Yorùbá oracles have more acè than Fon oracles!" or "Fon magic has more acè than Yorùbá magic!" Acè (Yr. àṣẹ) has been explored by many scholars (mostly of Yorùbá speakers) who have described acè in various ways. Àṣẹ has been defined as "a supernatural force that can cause an action to occur" (Clarke 2004: 317); "the notion of power itself" (Barnes 2008: 181); "divine power" (Babatunde 1985: 98); "spiritual essence" (Drewal 1998: 18); and, perhaps most poetically, as "that divine essence in which physics, metaphysics and art blend to form the energy or life force activating and directing socio-political, religious and artistic processes and experiences" (Abiodun 1994: 319). Àṣẹ's function is as dynamic and mysterious as its identity, described as a force that can be "impregnated" into or "absorbed" by objects (Doris 2011); àṣẹ pertains to the identification, activation, and utilization of all innate energy, power, and natural laws believed to reside in all animals, plants, hills, rivers, natural phenomena, human beings, and òrìṣà (Abiodun 1994: 310).

Àṣẹ's usefulness is said to depend on "the verbalization, visualization and performance of attributive characters of those things or beings whose powers are being harnessed" (Abiodun 1994: 310). An important factor in initiations, divination sessions, prayer, ceremony, and even in the continuation of life, acè/àṣẹ is a dynamic combination of the principles of both animism and animatism. All of the definitions given above are accurate—but, like the incomprehensible nature of acè/àṣẹ, all are insufficient. Thus I do not attempt to offer a definition as such of acè/àṣẹ, as that would be, by acè's very nature, impossible. Instead, I hope to contribute to our ever-growing comprehension of acè/àṣẹ by paying special attention to how acè/àṣẹ affects the process of religious secrecy, and initiates' understanding of their validity as priests, especially in the context of spiritual tourism.

In Bénin, acè was described to me in two ways, and while using French, Fɔngbè, or Yorùbá. In one sense, acè is perhaps best described as spiritual "power" (*pouvoir*). Here, Béninois would affirm that initiation, for example, imbues one with the "power" of the vodún, or that some Nàgó (Yorùbá) spirits have more power than Fon spirits, or that some spirits embody powers that are too intense for the uninitiated or the unprepared.[4] Conversely, acè was described to me as a way of understanding one's spiritual "right" (*droit*) or "jurisdiction" (*juridiction*). In this sense, Fá diviners would argue that priests of other spirits, for example, do not have the right to read the sacred signs (dù/odù) of Fá, or that newly initiated priests do not yet have the right or the power to initiate others. However, even as I bifurcate our understanding of acè into power versus right, in all these cases one's right is given as a result of one's power—thereby affirming the important relationship between a priest's right and power to act in Vodún. It is this acè, or the right and power to initiate, to create spirit shrines, and to perform divination, that many spiritual tourists seek. Acè is the spiritual force that, when installed into one's body by initiation, transforms ritual actions and religious material culture (e.g., bodies, carvings, charms, divination tools, masquerades, shrines) into powerful and meaningful expressions of an initiate's new identity and authority as a practitioner. As I will show throughout the book, spiritual tourists travel to West Africa to have their bodies become secrets by being imbued with the spirits' acè so that they may then transport the spirits across oceans, housed in sacred objects and sacred bodies that have been transformed ritually by acè. Simply put, acè becomes Vodún's spiritual—and secret—commodity.

As both a spiritual power and a social right, acè is bought and sold on Vodún's globalizing market. Béninois and international Vodún practitioners alike seek and obtain acè through transformative ritual processes, and they continue to confirm acè's influence daily through ceremonial action such as prayer, the pouring of libations, and animal sacrifice. As Vodún's most cherished commodity, the local and international flow of acè is controlled through secrecy. Acè, like secrecy, is shared, embodied knowledge. Paradoxically, acè is contained within every living thing on earth. However, acè must be bestowed by another who has already been given acè.

Among Béninois, and between them and foreign spiritual seekers, access to secrecy and authentic forms of acè is hotly contested. The historical struggle for regional supremacy between the Fon and Yorùbá peoples manifests in local discourses of power and authenticity—each, at times, laying claim to having access to the most powerful or the most authentic religious secrets or spirit cults. For spiritual seekers such as Christopher, the power that is inherent in "real secrecy" is what is most valuable. Along with consecrating his initiation experiences as authentic and spiritually powerful, ritual secrets serve to validate his status as a priest, regardless of what he truly believes about the secrets he now knows. Like the Ivorian *bluffeurs* described by Sasha Newell, who are "known for the illusion of wealth they produced rather than what they actually possessed" (2013: 139), Christopher and other foreign spiritual seekers must perform the religious power of the secrets that was revealed to them during their initiations. In both cases, validity becomes "a performative speech act" in which secrecy gives "the objects consumed their imaginative potency, the invisible possibility of authenticity" (148).

Like the vodún who are believed to live at the crossroads, spiritual tourist encounters find meaning at the crossroads of power, secrecy, and globalization. Through the creative manipulation of power, both Béninois and foreign spiritual seekers negotiate access to secrecy, which in turn creates "fluid transnational networks" that have helped to transport Vodún "from local to global audiences" (Hüwelmeier and Krause 2010: 1).

In both local and global spaces, a ritual is efficacious because of the acè it confers; a ceremony is powerful because of the acè it maintains; objects and bodies are authenticated by the acè they contain; and the spirits are made important by the acè they bestow—and all of these ritual possibilities are protected, empowered, and made possible by secrecy.

Understanding Spiritual Tourism in Bénin

Since the Béninois government began to make a concerted effort to attract foreign tourists to Bénin in the 1990s, tourists from a wide range of nationalities and racial identities have come to Bénin for what one might call "Voodoo tourism." While the Béninois government originally sought to attract Haitians with the slogan *"Bénin-Haïti: Tous du même sang"* (Bénin-Haiti: All of the same blood), its initiatives instead began to attract tourists from all over the world. From my experience, most of the tourists I met were from the United States, France, or Brazil, although Forte mentions having encountered foreign spiritual seekers who were "from France, Italy, Austria, and Germany" (2010: 141). Most of the spiritual seekers I knew came to Bénin alone or in pairs, and they self-identified as white, while, with a few exceptions, the African Americans I met tended to travel in larger groups focused on Bénin's slaving past (e.g., Bruner 2005; Reed 2014). For specificity, I have been explicit about the racial identities of the spiritual tourists I mention throughout the book. However, Béninois tend to classify all non-Africans, including African Americans, as *yovó* (Fon) or *òyìnbó* (Yorùbá)—meaning "white person" or "outsider." As Kamari Clarke has noted, "Many Nigerian Yorùbá . . . insist on black American exclusion from Yorùbá membership, citing the popular trope that the transport of black people as captives to the Americas and the many generations of acculturation they endured led to the termination of cultural connections between Africans and African Americans. For this reason, black Americans . . . no matter what their complexion, are often referred to as *òyìnbó*" (2004: 14). For these reasons, I never observed a difference in the ways Béninois treated or initiated African Americans, Euro-Americans, or Europeans. To my Béninois informants, all foreigners, regardless of their ancestry, enjoyed "a particular class status, cultural standing, education level, and outlook" (Pierre 2013: 77) that connected them all historically to whiteness.

While I believe that it would be enriching to unpack the different ways European, Euro-American, and African American foreign spiritual seekers internalize their initiation experiences through their own racial lenses and in juxtaposition with each other, that analysis is beyond the scope of this book.

Because I focus on the ways in which Béninois have contributed to Vodún's global expansion, I have decided to do as they have done, so I consider all foreign spiritual seekers to be foreigners—regardless of their race—with similar relative economic and national privilege.

In seeking to provide an ethnographic account of Vodún that attends critically to foreign involvement in the religion, I struggled to find a word to describe those diverse individuals who were traveling to West Africa to become initiated. On the one hand, "tourist" seemed too insubstantial. To many of the foreigners with whom I spoke, "tourist" did not quite capture their sincerity or, in their words, the "sacredness" of their trip. As one American man expressed, "I am here to become a priest. Not to visit a tourist trap."

On the other hand, "pilgrim" seemed to imply that foreign spiritual seekers were traveling to Bénin to confirm established religious beliefs or to find physical relief from hardships, pain, or worries (Turner and Turner 1978). But for many foreign initiates, their trip to Bénin marked their first steps into Vodún. They were looking for what Alan Morinis called a "place or a state that [they] believe to embody a valued ideal" (1992: 4). Their initiation experiences are cultivated in their imaginations long before they arrive in Bénin. By reading voraciously, interacting with other future and past initiates on Facebook, and searching YouTube for any videos that might reveal a small glimpse of the rituals they seek to undergo, spiritual seekers achieve a sort of revelation and a longing for West Africa and the secrets that are protected by the forest. In this sense, they are pilgrims. But they are also true neophytes. They arrive speaking little to no Fɔngbè or French and they have a clumsy understanding of basic cultural rules and social norms. Unlike what one might expect from pilgrims, they do not come to Bénin in search of solutions or remedies or even to confirm their trust in the spirits. Instead they come hoping to find new ways of relating to the divine.

Like C. Lynn Carr (2015), who examined what she called "cultural newcomers" to Lucumí in the United States, I found that many foreign spiritual seekers came to Vodún looking for religion. They yearned for a sort of Durkheimian effervescence (1965 [1912]) that simultaneously brought them closer to the divine but further from Western Christian conservatism (e.g., Fuller 2001). Despite the religious foci of foreign spiritual seekers' trips to West Africa, describing them as pilgrims seemed just as deficient as calling them tourists. Indeed, for many of them, the domain of the tourist and that of the pilgrim had begun to blur in meaningful ways (e.g., Badone and Roseman 2004). Or, was it that, in the words of Victor and Edith Turner, "a tourist is [always] half a pilgrim, and a pilgrim [always] is half a tourist" (1978: 20)? Indeed, I prefer to think about a tourist and a pilgrim as two points on a spectrum upon which individuals can meaningfully move as they search for religious experiences that are, to them, "really real" (Geertz 1973).

Foreign spiritual seekers and West African Vodúnisants often mobilize one term over the other; understand them as concentric experiences with a great deal of overlap; or reject either category all together. It is in these moments of creative contestation, where pilgrim and tourist, insider and outsider, initiate and noninitiate coalesce, that I argue the "really real" is found. It is where religious ownership gets hashed out. It is where access to secret religious knowledge and beings is negotiated. It is where the entrée into desired moments of religious effervescence is realized. It is where Vodún becomes global. Throughout the book I use the terms "spiritual tourist" and "foreign spiritual seeker" interchangeably out of convenience. In this way, I avoid the pilgrim-tourist divide but retain the precision I need to discuss how foreign and Béninois Vodúnisants interact and work to transform Vodún into a global phenomenon.

Ouidah and Its Historical Legacy

While spiritual tourism in Bénin might be a relatively new phenomenon, the history of foreign involvement in Vodún spans more than three centuries. I chose Ouidah as the ideal locale to examine Vodún's global reach because of the city's long-standing position as a multiethnic and multinational port; its 350-year connection to the Americas; and Vodún's centrality to Ouidah's landscape. Ouidah rests on the shore of the Republic of Bénin, the former West African "Slave Coast," and on the coast of the present-day Bight of Benin along the Gulf of Guinea. With a population of approximately 92,000 people (as of 2012), Ouidah is a modest but vibrant town. Yet, despite Ouidah's relatively small population, its particular precolonial, colonial, and postcolonial histories have made the city an important cosmopolitan player in Africa's long-term global flows (cf. Hannerz 1990). As one of West Africa's largest former slave ports, Ouidah has occupied an important international geopolitical space for nearly 350 years.[5] The former kingdom of Xwedá, from which present-day Ouidah drew its name, was conquered in 1727 by Agajá, the fourth ruler (axɔ́sú) of Dahomey.[6] As a result, Dahomey took control of Xweɖá and the smaller kingdom of Savì—which lay seven kilometers to the north of Ouidah. Today, in part because of Ouidah's political past, the town has become an ethnically rich area where one can find people who identify as Ajǎ, Gùn, Xweɖá, Maxí, Fon, and Yorùbá (Nàgó)— most of whom are Fɔ̀ngbè speakers. In addition to Ouidah's local diversity, the city has also been influenced greatly by its historical connection to Portugal and Brazil. In 1818, Francisco Felix de Souza, a Brazilian man born to a Portuguese father and a Native American mother, aided Gakpe, the Dahomean king's brother, in a coup d'état, which resulted in Gakpe taking the throne from Adándózàn (r. 1797–1818). Gakpe then took the name "Gezò" (r. 1818–58) and became the ninth—and most infamous—ruler of Dahomey (Bay 1998: 166–78). From 1820 until his death in 1849, de Souza sold African slaves to European buyers on Gezò's behalf.

In 1835, during the height of Gezò's reign, the Brazilian region of Bahia experienced a slave uprising that led to the "Great Revolt" (also known as the "Malê Revolt").[7] In the aftermath of the failed revolt, the Brazilian government deported back to West Africa those people of African descent who were suspected of having inspired the revolt. According to Robin Law, "the re-emigration then continued on a more or less voluntary basis through the rest of the nineteenth century" [and] "in the immediate aftermath of the rebellion . . . one party of 200 free blacks were deported from Bahia . . . to Ouidah" (2004: 179–80). This large influx of returnees to Ouidah from Brazil—and, for different reasons, from other lusophone countries such as Madeira, São Tomé, and Angola (Law 2004: 185–90)—greatly, and permanently, influenced the social and political lives of the people of Ouidah. For example, Portuguese architecture, with its distinctive "shuttered windows, ornate mouldings, colonnades and verandahs" (Law 2004: 187), still decorates the landscape, and descendants of Francisco Felix de Souza still inhabit Ouidah today.

An increase in the Portuguese and Afro-Brazilian presence in Ouidah was not the only cultural change that was supported and encouraged by the reemigration of ex-slaves from countries such as Brazil. Because Yorùbá captives had made up a large majority of Africans who were sent from Bénin to Brazil, Ouidah experienced an upsurge of Yorùbá-speaking peoples returning to the area. This, coupled with an influx of domestic Yorùbá slaves who worked for households such as that of the de Souza family, further added to Ouidah's unique ethnic and national diversity. The incorporation of these diverse peoples into the kingdom of Dahomey points to the "Fon propensity to embrace and adopt influences from many directions: Europe by way of the Atlantic coast, Akan areas to the west, Yoruba-speaking lands to the north and east, and to a far lesser extent, Islamic West Africa to the north" (Bay 2008: 4).

As far back as documented history reveals, Fon society has always been one of inclusivity, absorption, and flexibility—a mentality that continues into the present, as Béninois become important players in the transnational and global flow of African religious ideologies such as Vodún. Contributing to Vodún's expansion, Ouidah has been marketed as the "spiritual capital of [Bénin] with a thriving and lively Voodoo culture" (Butler 2006: 114), and it is highlighted on a "Cradle of Voodoo" tour provided by Explore, a British "adventure travel" company, as the home of Bénin's "ancient snake cult." Because of Ouidah's long-standing and sometimes tumultuous relationship with the West, its position as an international and multiethnic border zone, coupled with its centrality to "Voodoo tourism," makes the city the most compelling space in Bénin to observe the interplay between local religion, international tourism, and processes of globalization and transnationalism.[8]

Ouidah and Its Contemporary Importance

Despite Bénin's current interest in spotlighting its Vodún heritage as a marketable international commodity, Vodún has not always enjoyed this national prestige. In 1890 the French invaded Dahomey and formally dethroned Gbèhánzìn (r. 1889–94) in 1892; after two years of hiding, Gbèhánzìn surrendered to the French in 1894, officially making Dahomey a French protectorate. After forcing Gbèhánzìn and his family into exile onto the West Indian island of Martinique, French officials installed their puppet king, Agoliágbò, as Dahomey's twelfth and final local ruler. In 1898, Agoliágbò subverted French authority by objecting to an annual tax. The French reacted in 1900 by forcing Agoliágbò into exile in the Congo, and the kingdom of Dahomey was subsequently abolished.

Sixty years after France took control of Dahomey from Gbèhánzìn, Dahomeans were able to negotiate their full independence from France on August 1, 1960. After some years of political and economic turmoil, in 1972 Mathieu Kérékou gained control of Dahomey through a military coup d'état. Kérékou began making swift and exacting changes to Dahomey, including a 1973 ban on "all [Vodún] ceremonies for the duration of the rainy season" (Joharifard

2005: 23). Two years later, the Kérékou regime began forbidding the "wearing of traditional ceremonial clothing" and "ultimately required anyone holding a [Vodún] ceremony to acquire explicit authorization from local government officials" (23). In addition to these restrictions, the cloistering of Vodún initiates (an important part of Vodún initiations) was made illegal, animal sacrifice was tightly regulated, important secret societies were banned, and sacred forests were destroyed (Joharifard 2005). Following these regulations, in conjunction with Kérékou's broad "war on Vodún" (Elwert-Kretschmer 1995; Strandsberg 2000; Joharifard 2005), in 1974 Kérékou announced that the country would adopt a Marxist-Leninist style of government, and in 1975 Dahomey was renamed the People's Republic of Bénin.

After fifteen years of communist rule, in 1989 Bénin's Marxist-Leninist government was abandoned and the country began transitioning to democracy, which, in 1990, led the National Assembly to choose Nicéphore Soglo as Bénin's prime minister. In 1991, Soglo became Bénin's first democratically elected president in a multiparty election. President Soglo swiftly lifted Bénin's anti-Vodún laws and began working with international organizations such as UNESCO, the International Centre for the Study of the Preservation and Restoration of Cultural Property, and the Getty Institute to build and design La Route des Esclaves, a historically informed journey beginning at Francisco Felix de Souza's former home and ending on the beach, where international visitors could explore Bénin's slaving past (Forte 2007; Araujo 2010; Landry 2011). Vodún quickly became a second focus as the new democratic government planned "Ouidah '92: The First International Festival of Vodun Arts and Cultures." The festival, which occurred February 8–18, 1993, was such a success that Bénin's parliament established "National Vodún Day," which has been celebrated on January 10 of each subsequent year (Araujo 2010: 146). As Forte points out, "The historical conjuncture of the early 1990s and the opening of the country to an international audience have added new meanings and significances to . . . 'traditional' religious practice. The numerous cultural events organized during this period and the heritage projects sponsored by international agencies have transformed Vodun into a cultural artifact, a national heritage and tourist commodity" (2007: 132).[9]

Of course, for much of the global North, Africa has always been a disposable commodity (e.g., Rodney 1981; Bond 2006). From its people to its art, and now to its indigenous religions, Africa has long been a gold mine from which Africans themselves have rarely profited. In 1984, the sociologist Bennetta Jules-Rosette observed that "the international art market depends upon the Western demand for 'exotic' souvenir and gift items and the assumption that they should be procured abroad" (1984: 192). Over the past quarter-century, that claim has met an unexpected expansion in Bénin—where, surprisingly, the "market" identified by Jules-Rosette now includes religious practice. Since the early 1990s, with the help of local spiritual leaders, the government of Bénin has positioned its indigenous religions as a new type of consumable art, with initiation into those spiritual traditions the ultimate "souvenir . . . procured abroad" (192). Thus Americans of varying ethnic and racial backgrounds now travel to Bénin (and elsewhere in Africa) in search of "spiritual enlightenment," constituting a new mode of travel that some scholars have called "spiritual tourism" (e.g., Geary 2008; Coats 2011).

Vodún, Ethnography, and the Critical Politics of Race

The emergence of spiritual tourism in West Africa has not come without its challenges. As international tourists travel to Bénin and Nigeria for initiation into Fon and Yorùbá esoteric traditions, the processes and legacies of racialization become increasingly visible. Reflecting what I consider to be the pervasive power of race in dynamic tourist encounters between international spiritual tourists and local Fon-speaking Béninois, I chose not to devote an individual chapter to racial politics. Instead, in the same ways that racial politics are interlaced through all aspects of postcolonial Africa, I wove my analysis of race—especially as it relates to the experience of power and social inequalities—throughout each chapter.

Bénin, like all contemporary West African nation-states, is, at least in part, the product of its former colonizers. French is the national and official language, and class and governance have been mapped neatly onto Western models of democracy, government, and mobility (cf. Lugo 2008). Bénin's contemporary struggles with global racial inequities and international structures of "white supremacy" (Mills 1998) have been shaped greatly by many factors: Bénin's legacy as a former French protectorate (1894–1904); fifty-six years as a French colony (1904–60); the effects of a French-orchestrated

coup d'état of two former kings; twelve years of postindependence political and economic struggles (1960–72); a fifteen-year Marxist regime led by
Mathieu Kérékou (1972–89), who sought to distance Bénin from the control of its former colonizers; and more than twenty-five years of various
forms of neocolonialism as international institutions such as UNESCO
support Bénin's desire to market its indigenous religions and its slaving
past to an emerging neoliberal spiritual economy (Rush 2001; Araujo 2010;
Landry 2011).

    With these historical legacies in mind, I have positioned "spiritual tour-
ists," who travel to Bénin and Nigeria to participate or become initiated in
religions such as Vodún, as products of the Western world—where "whiteness" runs supreme, or as Charles Mills has argued, where "European domi-
nation of the planet . . . has left us with the racialized distributions of economic,
political, and cultural power that we have today" (1998: 98). My own whiteness continuously shaped my experiences in Bénin. At times it complicated
my desire to participate in Vodún, while at other times the power and global
capital of my racial identity uncomfortably opened doors that would have
otherwise been closed (e.g., Harris 1993).

    Regardless of their own racial identities—be they European, Brazilian,
Euro-American, or African American—tourists were consistently categorized as a yovó (white foreigner), which, in this context, always means
"privileged" (Pierre 2013).[10] In all cases, when foreign spiritual tourists and
Béninois negotiated access to religious secrecy, the tourists' whiteness and
the Béninois' blackness were always on the table, as it were, as they each
discussed the cost and accessibility of initiation (Dominguez 1993). While
Béninois typically conceptualized Western tourists (who may or may not be
phenotypically "white") as "rich," Western tourists in effect (if uncon-
sciously) frequently framed Béninois (and other Africans by extension) as
"exploitable"—people who, because of their perceived poverty, should be
selling access to rituals, ceremonies, and art objects for well below what
their white counterparts were charging back in the United States and Europe.

    The mapping of one's race onto other aspects of one's life (e.g., wealth)
has been observed elsewhere by Jemima Pierre, who notes that "Whiteness
is the recognition that racialization occurs both in tandem with and *in excess*
of the corporal. In other words, race (in this case, Whiteness) articulates with
racialized-as-White bodies, all the while moving beyond such bodies and
expressing itself in other representations of itself—such as culture, aesthet-

ics, wealth, and so on" (2013: 72). The pervasiveness of race and the structural effects of racism and global white supremacy throughout the African world have been thoughtfully documented (e.g., Rodney 1981; Fabian 1983; Harris 1993; Mills 1998; Hesse 2007; Pierre 2013). It is, therefore, not my intention to provide a detailed analysis of race, of blackness, or of racialization in Bénin. Rather, I aim to use the trope and social reality of race, and its relationship to the social capital of power, to understand more fully the social and global significance of spiritual tourism, transnationalism, and the multiracial consumption of the African Atlantic forest religions—especially as these religions become increasingly global.

To complicate the issue further, in a theoretical space so deeply shaped by critical race theory, I believe that overly spotlighting postcolonial racial politics and racial inequities of power may provide a final analysis that is simply too obvious. On the one hand, current scholarship on the subject is invested rightfully in positioning religions such as Vodún and òrìṣà worship as globalizing and even nascent "world religions" (Olupona and Rey 2008). On the other hand, there is a reactionary tendency to mark European and Euro-American spiritual seekers as active participants in racist neocolonialism and cultural appropriation.

There is no doubt that analyses of racial, postcolonial, and neocolonial politics should be central themes in an African ethnography. However, we must also recognize that if African religions are to be global and urban then they will inevitably become multiracial. Being excessively critical of European and Euro-American involvement in religions like Vodún and òrìṣà worship ignores an important ethnographic fact—Africans themselves are encouraging foreign involvement. And so an important dichotomy is born: to decry European and Euro-American involvement in African religions is to constrict forcibly African religions back to the proverbial African village. However, to allow European and Euro-American involvement without critique is to permit willfully and perhaps even encourage new forms of colonialism, where even African religions can be consumed by an empowered white world. In reaction to this epistemological challenge, in the following chapters I employ a critical research strategy that attends to postcolonial and neocolonial racial politics while also, for the first time, taking European and Euro-American involvement in Vodún and òrìṣà worship to be serious West African expansions that have been encouraged by West Africans themselves.

My Approaches to Anthropology and Vodún

The secrets that enable the giving and embodiment of acè are revealed only after a certain amount of time and after much trust is established. As I delved deeper into Vodún's culture of secrecy, it became clear that I needed to focus primarily on one location. For this reason, most of the research for this book was conducted in the coastal town of Ouidah, Bénin, and its surrounding areas. To gain comparative insight and to explore why and when spiritual tourists chose certain places to become initiated, I supplemented my time in Ouidah with short research trips to Abomey, Savalou, and Cotonou.

In Ouidah, I spent much of my time living with Marie, my long-term research assistant, and her family. Marie is a woman in her early fifties who was born into one of Bénin's Afro-Brazilian families and raised Catholic. In 2008, to the chagrin of her mother, Marie left Catholicism behind and became an initiated priest of Tron. Because she speaks Fɔngbè, French, and English fluently, she has, over the past decade, received more than twenty spiritual tourists who were interested in becoming initiated into Vodún. Apart from being one of the most prolific Vodún guides in Bénin, her language skills have also allowed her to conduct regular secular tours for large tour groups, churches, universities, and diplomats. Through Marie, I was able to meet many of the spiritual seekers and tourists whom I will discuss throughout this book.

Often with Marie's assistance, while in Bénin I used both formal and informal research methods. To experience Vodún in context, I participated in hundreds of Vodún ceremonies, initiations, and festivals. My own initiation as a Fá diviner allowed me to maximize these field moments by permitting me to participate in ritual dance, singing, and sacrifice—including during those secret rituals, frequently held deep in the sacred forest, that were limited to initiates. I supplemented these experiences with thirty-five structured interviews, split almost evenly among men and women, in which I collected life histories, explored individuals' opinions about foreign involvement in Vodún, and developed an understanding of how people maintain religious secrecy despite increased foreign interest. After seventeen months of interviews, countless conversations, and experiences of Vodún both as an observer and as an initiate, I concluded my research with a formal survey. For this portion of the project, I surveyed 125 respondents of different genders, ethnic identities, and religious affiliations. By ending with a survey, I was able to confirm my suspicion that, in the case of Vodún, religious secrecy has become an emerging global commodity.

While I gleaned a great deal of information from these research strategies, following a long tradition in anthropology, most of my contact with Béninois and foreign Vodún practitioners was conducted informally over meals and drinks, while hanging out deeply or during religious events. In this way, I was able to take advantage of serendipity and the natural flow of conversation while remaining as unassuming as possible. These more intimate moments with Vodún practitioners of all types helped me to appreciate the profoundly personal reasons that people have to devote their lives to the spirits and why Vodún's global reach has become more present than ever. Hearing their stories and walking with new initiates into the sacred forest showed me that my personal and academic journey into Vodún was not so different than theirs.

Like many of the individuals I write about in this book, I was a child when Vodún and its acɛ̀ began to interest me. When I was twelve I spent hours huddled up in the corner of my parents' closet reading my grandfather's tattered copy of *Gumbo Ya-Ya*, a 1945 collection of Louisiana folktales. My small hands always thumbed straight to the appendices where a collection of "superstitions" lay buried by more than five hundred pages about Creoles, Cajuns, ghosts, and music that I was too young to appreciate. Reading about "love powders" made from hummingbird hearts (p. 539), garlic bundles to relieve toothaches (p. 534), and peach leaves to cure typhoid (p. 535) piqued my young imagination. This early interest in African religion eventually led me to Haitian Vodou. While conducting fieldwork in Haiti (2003–5) I became initiated as a Vodou priest (*houngan asogwe*). My initiation into Haitian Vodou marked the beginning of my long-term enthusiasm for intimate research methods, including apprenticeship as a mode of observant-participation, that I carried with me to Bénin where I became a diviner's apprentice (Coy 1989; Keller and Keller 1996; Landry 2008; Lave 2011).

The decision of an anthropologist to become an apprentice is supported by a long-standing disciplinary tradition that dates back at least to Zora Neale Hurston (Hurston 2008a [1935], 2008b [1938]) and more recently to Judy Rosenthal (1998: 12) and Paul Stoller (Stoller and Olkes 1987). Like many of my predecessors who straddled the precarious line between observer and participant, I too was forced to grapple intimately with important issues such as postcolonial racial politics, cultural appropriation, and even my own belief or trust in the spirit world—all of which I examine throughout

the book. Yet, despite the challenges, apprenticeship enabled me to experience Vodún, and especially Fá divination, from the "inside"—albeit not
exactly as a local person would. Also I could explore the strategies that local
Fá diviners employ to teach complex religious practices and belief systems
to foreign initiates. When one gives in to the possibility of belief, I argue,
religious apprenticeship can provide an ontological glimpse into the spiritual
worlds of devotees. However, it does not come without its challenges.

Stoller, who served as a sorcerer's apprentice among the Songhay in
Niger, discussed some of the issues surrounding religious apprenticeship. In
a 1987 memoir that he cowrote with Cheryl Olkes, he asked, "How far can
we go in the quest to understand other peoples? Is it ethical for ethnographers to become apprentice sorcerers in their attempt to learn about sorcery?" (xii). I grapple with this and related questions throughout the book
as I juxtapose my position as a Euro-American anthropologist living in
Bénin and studying to become a diviner to those of other initiates—both
Béninois and foreign.

As happens with many would-be initiates, my quest for an initiator did
not come without difficulties. Béninois friends steered me to different Fá
diviners, often invoking their personal relationships as evidence for their
diviners' authenticity and power. Conversely, I was also told to avoid certain diviners (usually indicated to me by name) who were said either to be
drunkards, to perform Fá divination "only for the money," or to be frauds and
therefore powerless.

Thankfully, although having just arrived in Bénin, I did not have to find
my new mentor alone. André, a forty-seven-year-old Béninois man I met
through a mutual friend two years prior to beginning my research, helped me
find the right diviner. A few weeks after he offered to help me find a teacher,
he was ready to tell me about the man he had found. Émile was in his late
forties and had been an initiated Fá diviner for more than fifteen years. He
practiced the Fon version of Fá and was well known in the area. He had
many clients largely due to a radio show that he hosted on a local station
where he gave spiritual advice to callers. The diviner seemed perfect—he
was knowledgeable and quite established.

I immediately told André that I would be interested in meeting Émile to
discuss the possibility of working with him during my stay in Bénin. However, André told me that he did not want the two of us to meet until the day
of my initiation ceremonies—yet André would not reveal his reasons.
Because I had never heard of anything like this happening, I was suspicious

of André's motives. Several days later—after many lengthy and persuasive conversations—my suspicions were confirmed when André admitted to me that he did not want Émile to know I was "white and rich." He believed that if Émile knew I was a white American, he would want to charge me double—or maybe triple—his normal fee and "capitalize on my wealth."

I found myself in an uncomfortable and ethical conundrum. Should I allow André to continue with his plan? Or should I insist that he reveal my identity to Émile? After changing my mind at least a dozen times, mimicking the choice of a typical spiritual tourist, I ultimately decided to go along with André's plan. One month later, Émile and I met at midnight to begin the ceremonies that would make me a Fá diviner. As André and I had anticipated, Émile was upset. Émile announced, quite publicly and loudly, that he would have asked for a higher fee if he had known that I was white. Nevertheless, Émile agreed to continue with my ceremonies, and over the next several hours we became much more comfortable with each other. He was proud of what I accomplished and eager to tell his friends that he had initiated his first yovó. I began my time with Émile as a "polluting presence"— one whose skin color, and all that my white skin symbolically represented, marked me as an outsider. By the end of my ceremonies, my "difference" had lessened, but it was clear that it would never vanish. Unfortunately, my apprenticeship with Émile was short-lived. He lived more than an hour away from Ouidah and, while I attended several of his ceremonies and even some of his future initiations, I needed a teacher who lived closer.

After searching for several months, a longtime friend introduced me to Jean and the village of Fátòmè, near Ouidah. When I met Jean, he instructed me that, in order to work with him, I would need to redo my initiations and convert my personal Fá from the Fon Fá to the Nàgó version. Interested in the differences between the two systems and eager to work with Jean, a *babaláwo* (Yr. Ifá diviner) with experience working both with Béninois and with foreign students, I agreed. This began my fifteen-month intensive apprenticeship that operated on a near-daily basis and continues today over the telephone.[11]

I was Jean's fourth foreign initiate but the only one who was able to stay and work with him for an extended period of time. Over the course of my time with Jean, he taught me fragments of his spiritual truths. He taught me how to construct shrines; how to recognize and invoke each of Fá's 256 binary signs that embodied Fá's corpus; and how to perform divination for myself and others. Even so, there were certainly ceremonies and magical recipes that Jean held from me just as there were things that he taught me freely. One evening over hot tea, Jean admitted to me that there were things— special medicines and charms—that he would teach his children only. It was clear that some barriers could only be overcome by kinship. "Some things are only for my sons," he noted. I agreed with—and even appreciated—his sentiment.

After spending just a few months in Fátòmè, Jean formally accepted me as his apprentice. Within a few days of working with Jean, he took the Fá I received earlier from Émile and converted my Fá from the Fon system to the Nàgó system.[12] Doubtless, local practitioners benefit economically as the clients always pay the priest performing the conversion for his time and expertise. However, having participated in both systems, I understood such a process is required for reasons that extend beyond economics. The Nàgó ceremonies take more time, require more sacrifices, and are more involved. It is easy to see why some local people might feel that the Nàgó system is a more potent manifestation of Fá; even as an outsider I caught myself— perhaps stereotypically—favoring the complexities found in Nàgó Fá.

After working with Jean for only a couple of weeks, it became clear to me that becoming a Fá diviner, over being a devotee of any of the other spirit groups that are worshiped by Fon and Yorùbá peoples, would bring advantages. As Jean taught me, Fá diviners tend to have a broad general knowledge of all the spirits, so they can adequately advise their clients of necessary ceremonies and even perform basic sacrifices and offerings to a wide array of spirits on their behalf. In addition, their roles as Fá diviners often facilitate relationships with many different priests, temples, and practitioners—most of which were made available to me, thanks to Jean.

Jean and I began working together only two days after he agreed to serve as my mentor. "I want you here ready to work at 8 a.m.," he said. "We have a lot to go over while you are here." Over the next couple of days I reviewed a faded photocopy of *La Géomancie à l'ancienne Côte des Esclaves* by Bernard Maupoil (1943), which I had borrowed from a local Vodún practitioner just a few weeks earlier. I thumbed through Maupoil's formative work on Fá divination and used other locally published sources to test my ability to recognize perfectly the 256 different patterns (Fon, dù/ Yr., odù) of Fá that are elegantly interpreted when a diviner, seated on a straw mat, casts a "divining chain" (Fon, *akplè*/ Yr., *òpèlè*) onto the floor. The complexity of the 256 signs of Fá left me overwhelmed even before my apprenticeship began—but my anxiety also added to my excitement.

On the day we were to begin working, I arrived at Jean's home eagerly, fifteen minutes early. I was ready to begin, but Jean had other plans. He left me to sit on a low cement wall where I waited for him for nearly three hours. I quickly learned that my training would be on his terms. I was always expected to be punctual, and he never was; his position as teacher and elder, and mine as student and child, was always clear. As the people in Fátomè became my close friends, I learned to appreciate the time I spent in the village waiting for Jean to decide to include me in his day. Once I released my contemporary U.S. expectations of what an education should be—or how time should function—I realized the time I spent waiting in the village, seemingly far removed from lessons in divination, was just as important to my training as was learning how to pray, move, and act as a diviner would— a lesson I suspect Jean knew all along. During these times I learned about the prevalence of witchcraft, and I watched children pretend to perform divination with small seeds that they found on the ground. Eventually, I came to appreciate these moments as important backdrops to my formal lessons in divination.

Seeking Divine Power

Secrecy has contributed to, and even encouraged, Vodún's global expansion. More and more, foreign spiritual seekers are becoming initiated and participating in the country's growing Vodún tourism industry. As these numbers grow, an increasing number of Béninois Vodún practitioners, faced with the promise of economic success and international networks, have begun to reveal and market Vodún's secrecy. In Chapter 1, "Touring the Forbidden," I examine the politics of spiritual tourism in Bénin by showing how and why foreign spiritual seekers negotiate access to Vodún. By interacting with two British tourists, Michelle and Christine, who disappointedly felt little resistance when visiting a "Voodoo village"; with Luiz, a Brazilian man, who did all he could, and failed, to learn how to construct one of Vodún's more sought-after and dangerous shrines; and with Marcella, an African American woman who was determined to disrupt Vodún's long-standing rules and become initiated into a men's-only spirit cult, I document the religious secrecy and the resistance one faces as one attempts to observe or experience Vodún's secret objects, and also how religious experiences are authenticated for foreign spiritual seekers.

Many tourists come to Bénin hoping to participate in Vodún by observing rituals or purchasing religious objects. There are, however, those select few tourists who come to Bénin for the sole purpose of initiation. In Chapter 2, "Receiving the Forest," I turn my attention to the initiations of both Béninois and foreign spiritual seekers. In this chapter, I begin to show why foreign involvement in Vodún should not be simply dismissed as a form of cultural appropriation or neocolonialism. Through ritual, Béninois merge both foreign and Béninois initiates with the forest and install spirits (vodún) in the bodies of both white and black spiritual seekers. Challenging colonial structures of power, the ritual provides Béninois with a meaningful space to, in effect, turn the tables on long-established structures of power by ritually colonizing the bodies of foreign spiritual seekers with African spirits and occult forces. Through this experience, foreigners are validated as Vodún practitioners as their bodies are imbued with what I call an "occult ontology," or those hidden ways in which one's being is transformed through mobile ritual secrets and religious commodities. Throughout the chapter, I draw on my initiation as well as the initiation of Jean's son, Auguste, into the cult of Fá, the oracular spirit of knowledge. Through this process, as initiates move slowly and deliberately through an object's or place's social aura of secrecy, they become inoculated ritually to the social dangers and risks that come with being exposed to a ritual secret too soon. By slowly taking the secret into one's body, even if unintentionally, and inscribing one's successful encounter with a ritual secret onto one's body by shaving one's head, undergoing ritual baths, and by wearing special beads, one's body undergoes ontological changes as it is transformed into a secret itself that can then be marketed within the emerging Vodún global marketplace. In this way, I join other anthropologists in arguing that it is the process of secrecy—and not necessarily the secret itself—that holds social importance. While secrecy is often thought of as a restrictive social force by which access to information is controlled, by focusing on what Johnson called "secretism," I begin to lay out my argument: that it is paradoxically through secrecy that Vodún has become global.

After someone is successfully initiated, he or she often begins collecting objects from Vodún's rich material repertoire. In Chapter 3, "Secrecy, Objects, and Expanding Markets," I delve more deeply into the secret international Vodún market in which religious art, artifacts, and ritual paraphernalia are all sold to interested agents—including spiritual tourists trying to practice Vodún authentically in their home countries. I examine the importance of emerging technologies, especially Facebook, in the spreading of this market, and how local Béninois and Nigerian entrepreneurs have begun to profit from Vodún's increased transnational efficacy. Examining this emerging market leads scholars to grapple with the ethical, and sometimes legal, challenges surrounding the buying and selling of secret religious artifacts, and how these objects factor into the wider discussion of authenticity, especially as Vodún locality shifts from somewhat bounded "culture areas" in West Africa to more fluid transnational spaces around the world.

An influx of spiritual tourists who are purchasing religious objects and becoming initiated into Vodún has encouraged both foreigners and Béninois to question what it means to believe. In Chapter 4, "Belief, Efficacy, and Transnationalism," I walk the reader through my own journey with belief as I struggle, despite my initiations, to believe in the spirits and in witchcraft. In so doing, I explore the analytical value of belief in Vodún and consider how spiritual tourism and emerging capitalist markets have begun to transform Vodún's beliefscape. Drawing on the ways in which Vodún in Bénin has connected belief to notions of efficacy, both Béninois and foreign practitioners actively negotiate their belief in the spirits. For some, their belief in Vodún and fear of witchcraft have led them to a belief in Christ, where protection from malevolent forces comes without the need to provide expensive offerings and rituals to the spirits. For others, Vodún's transnational presence has opened the possibility of believing in spirits that they previously rejected in order to attract international clientele and monies. These changes, I argue, have led belief and transnationalism to creatively absorb additional layers of meaning, thereby simultaneously strengthening and transforming the ways in which belief and efficacy are understood by foreign and Béninois Vodúnisants.

People from different national, racial, and ethnic backgrounds have come to believe in Vodún. Their involvement in the religion has led to the global commodification of ritual secrecy. With secrecy limiting tourists' access, while paradoxically rendering the experiences they have in Bénin as more authentic and more coveted, secrecy becomes the primary social mechanism by which Vodún expands. In Chapter 5, "Global Vodún, Diversity, and Looking Ahead," I show how Vodún's commodification has both enriched and complicated the religion's global expansion. By examining the politics of cultural appropriation and cultural borrowing, I complicate the process of cultural appropriation and ultimately show that the complexity surrounding these practices is never an all-or-nothing proposition. Instead, I argue that, when mediated by local interested agents, the transnationalization of West African religions such as Vodún is only Vodún's next step in its already long journey across space—a journey that, as Rush (1997) has argued, defines Vodún and encourages its continued local and global vibrancy.

This project owes a great deal to the legacies of scholars such as Melville J. Herskovits (1938, 1971 [1937]) and Pierre Fatumbi Verger (1995a, 1995b), who realized early on that practitioners of West African religions have long been important actors on the global stage. Herskovits in particular argued that cultural flows have the potential to transcend distinct continental divisions. Throughout this book, I build on the prescient approach of these earlier researchers by emphasizing both the challenges and benefits that are tethered to Vodún's current multinational and multiracial development. While Vodún's recent expansion is incredibly messy, filled with contradictions, and deeply enmeshed in postcolonial and racial politics, the religion has proven to be incredibly resilient. Indeed, Vodún has shown, time and time again, that the religion thrives within these contested spaces, where politics and power seem insurmountable.

CHAPTER 1

Touring the Forbidden

The reproduction of Vodun cults is increasingly becoming
dependent on external tourism . . . as incomes deriving
from religious service cannot alone sustain communities
and their religious life. Vodun priestesses and priests take
advantage of the opportunities that cross their paths and
take up the challenge that the initiation of foreigners or
the participation in tourism activity might carry.

—Forte 2010: 141

The untold story of Vodún's contemporary expansion begins with a rise in what many Béninois simply call "Voodoo tourism." Ouidah's tourists typically follow a well-worn script. Most of them visit the Python Temple, where Dangbé, the python spirit, is served;[1] King Kpassé's sacred forest, which is the seat of the vodún known as Lǒkò;[2] and the slave route (La Route des Esclaves) that was established in the early 1990s with support from the United Nations Educational, Scientific and Cultural Organization (Landry 2011) and other foreign governments (especially Germany and France). While these three destinations form a "must-see" triumvirate of tourist sites in Ouidah, other places such as the palace of Daágbó Xùnò, the so-called supreme chief of Vodún in Bénin, are also becoming popular, as tourists become increasingly adventurous, following the advice of tour books about Bénin (e.g., Butler 2006), and as more Vodún priests and temples make themselves available to tourists in the hopes of earning extra money.

The average tourist is content to have a photo taken with a snake from the Python Temple wrapped around his or her neck; to walk through Kpassé's sacred forest to see a permanent exhibition of Vodún-inspired art sculptures erected in the early 1990s for "Ouidah '92: The First International Festival of Vodun Arts and Cultures" (Rush 2001); or even to hike the 2.5-kilometer sandy road from Ouidah's center to the beach where some one million Africans boarded ships bound for the Americas during the transatlantic slave trade.[3] However, for a minority of other tourists scripted activities are not enough. These tourists commonly speak of "adventure" or "going off the beaten path," a desire to experience "the real Bénin" or, for many, "real Voodoo." For them, it becomes important to capture a special photo of restricted or secret Vodún ceremonies, temples, or people that would lend "authenticity" to their "African adventure" or to their "frightening brush with Voodoo." Some of these "adventure tourists," as they often call themselves, seek out diviners to learn of their futures or to understand more clearly their pasts (e.g., Rosenthal 1998: 168–69; Clarke 2004: 239–56; Forte 2007: 134–36); some even strive to become initiated into one or more of the Vodún cults found in southern Bénin. As indigenous religions and international travel intersect in Bénin, a constellation of local and global forces has begun to push Vodún practices along several dimensions at once, impelling local and foreign peoples to collide. To chronicle these changes, in this chapter, I explore the ways in which tourism develops simultaneously alongside Vodún in Bénin. In this way, I deprovincialize religions such as Vodún that are frequently seen as being restricted to their locale and that play a decidedly "other" role in most Westerners' imaginations. To illustrate the transnational practice of Vodún, I focus both on the politics of travel, attending especially to international visitors who wish to become initiated or use the "secret powers of Vodún" to gain control of their lives, and on how these themes contribute to Vodún's transnational flow.

Understanding the Local Political Economy of Vodún

Spiritual tourists complain regularly about the cost of ceremonies, initiations, and even religious paraphernalia such as beads, special bird feathers, and other supplies needed to construct shrines for the spirits (see Landry 2016). Coupling the rising costs associated with livestock and other ritual supplies with a long-established precedent within Vodún linking money and religion (cf. Ogundiran 2002), spiritual undertakings such as initiations can be costly. Tourists may pay more than locals for the privilege of initiation, but local practitioners also pay relatively large sums of money to seek advice from diviners, to become priests, and even to placate—or thank—the spirits. Sometimes the financial expenditure is great—even for Béninois practitioners. Over a period of six months, Marie paid over 4.5 million CFA for her initiation ceremonies, her priestly regalia (such as expensive beads and prayer instruments), and the construction of a small temple attached to her house devoted to Tron, her new *vodún*.[4] While Marie's expenses were exorbitant, there exists an established and vibrant local spiritual economy whereby the costs associated with Vodún vary from paying only 100 CFA to receive divination to the high costs paid by Marie. However, most local costs fall between these two extremes and often come with a promise from the spirits that any money spent on Vodún will be returned exponentially. Even with spiritual promises of return, the day-to-day expenditure on Vodún can be daunting for many local residents. Working with Jean, I observed more than a dozen of his divination clients each pay in excess of 50,000 CFA for small ceremonies or sacrifices prescribed by Fá to regulate a given problem or issue. In addition, I watched five of Jean's Béninois clients each pay more than 250,000 CFA for beginning-level initiations, and in one case a local man from Cotonou paid Jean 1 million CFA to receive the powerful and dangerous vodún known as Gbǎdù.[5]

In a country in which the average per capita income is around 1,500 USD (in 2011 dollars), most people cannot afford to initiate. Nevertheless, many people engage in Vodún's religious economy in smaller ways. When praying at a shrine, it is customary to leave a small amount of money (usually 50–100 CFA) for the spirits. During ceremonies, people will often press money on the foreheads of good dancers and drummers to show their appreciation for their contribution to the ceremony.[6] The amount given in this situation varies from 50 CFA to 10,000 CFA, depending on the giver's actual—or perceived—wealth. When the community perceived individuals to be rich, they would often give more than they could comfortably afford to avoid being shamed.

While some Vodún priests have other ways of making money, the vast majority of the priests and priestesses I met took care of their families from the proceeds they made from serving the community as religious specialists. In the case of Jean, he had clients who came to him from all over southern Bénin and Togo. A day rarely passed when Jean did not perform divination, ceremony, or ritual for either a client, a member of his family, or a resident of Fátòmè. His proficiency in Fá divination attracted people regularly and helped him to develop a solid reputation as one of the best diviners in the area, and he was one of the few who could accurately construct Gbӑdù, the female vodún who is believed to be the source of Fá's power. Jean's reputation even reached into Cotonou (an hour's drive from Ouidah) and found its way into the lives of foreigners living in Bénin who needed a diviner's assistance.

During my time in Fátòmè, Jean was visited by half a dozen foreign clients (French, American, and Brazilian) seeking his help—which ranged from a simple consultation to complex requests for initiation into Fá or other spirits found at Fátòmè. With a steady stream of both local and international clients, Jean made a good living. His wealth allowed him to build a massive two-story cement home, provide additional homes for his four wives, keep his adolescent children in school, and support his community in times of crisis. Aside from being an important diviner in the community, Jean also filled the role of the family's vǐgán (literally, "the chief of the children").[7] As the vǐgán, Jean served as a liaison between the members of his family, the family head, and his father, the village chief (togán).[8] In this capacity, he resolved disputes between villagers, and he decided when the village's elders needed to become involved. Jean's political power, along with his spiritual obligations and ritual skill, came with a great deal of responsibility and communal pressure.

The community benefited greatly from Jean's success, as he frequently agreed to initiate young men in the village in exchange for work—often paying the cost of these ceremonies out of his own pocket. With a steady influx of clients, meat from the sacrifices he performed on a daily basis was always available, and Jean shared this meat with his community. Keeping in mind the taboos that keep women from consuming the meat of animals sacrificed to Gbӑdù, or men from consuming the meat of animals sacrificed to a diviner's sacred staff of office (fásén), Jean made every effort to distribute meat evenly and fairly to the three major lineages who lived in Fátòmè.

From paying for ceremonies with money or labor to paying for divination, leaving money at shrines to pray, and even giving exceptional dancers, singers, and drummers money in appreciation for their work and their acè, money is clearly an important component of Vodún. Whether in the form of contemporary currency or as cowrie shells, money is a dominant symbol found in almost all Vodún ceremonies and rituals—as it is among many other religious systems across West Africa (e.g., M. Johnson 1970a, 1970b; Bascom 1980; Gottlieb 1995; Gregory 1996; Şaul 2008). In many ways, the use of money in Vodún indexes the client's power and spiritual success. Prayers to the vodún almost always include requests for financial wealth—and therefore the accumulation of wealth and the public display of one's wealth during ceremony and ritual. Whether it is in the clothes and beads a priest wears or in his or her ability to give larger sums of money to the dancers, singers, and drummers, money serves as evidence of one's spiritual power and favor with the spirits—and, by extension, of one's power as a priest.

With the dominance of vodún such as Dàn (the serpent spirit of riches), Mamíwátá (the mermaid spirit of abundance), and Yalódè (the Yorùbá river spirit of material wealth), it is easy to see a cultural preoccupation with money and its accumulation. Indeed, money has become an important symbol of spiritual prowess and evidence of favor from the spirits, marking the rich as spiritually connected and the poor as spiritually incapable.

While money dominates the symbolic repertoire for Fon and Yorùbá peoples, many tourists come to Bénin and Nigeria unaware of these important cultural structures and symbolic forces. A tourist's lack of awareness of the symbolic power of outward wealth is further complicated by false imaginings, usually spurred on by U.S. and European media, that Africa is "cheap." When the long-established economy of Vodún collides with U.S. and European imaginings of Africa, tourists are often left feeling exploited, while locals are often convinced that international spiritual seekers are trying to coerce them into revealing their cultural secrets for a pittance.

Tourist and Local Imaginings of the Other

These feelings of exploitation—felt, ironically, by both tourists and locals—are a result of a long colonial history that is deeply intertwined with contemporary manifestations of racism, power, privilege (Rodney 1981), and processes of "othering" (Bond 2006). On the one hand, spiritual tourists feel as though they are being exploited financially because they often sense that they are required to pay more than what a local resident might expect to pay for the same ceremony. On the other hand, local residents feel Western tourists are trying to gain access to secret religious powers for little to no money so that they can then return home to sell the information to others and become even richer.

One evening, while talking with Jean and his family, a young Béninois man in his twenties told me, "We can't teach everything to white people. We can't give them all our secrets. If we do, they will take those secrets and fight us with them." Echoing a similar sentiment, another young Béninois man in his late twenties told me, "We can't just initiate any white person. We have to be selective. White people are smart. They are always thinking about how to do things better. Black people only think about how to make quick money. But white people like to improve on things to make money. If we give them Vodún, they will make Vodún better and take our culture away."

Both of these troubling statements illustrate the devastating power that colonial regimes have had on personhood and consciousness in southern Bénin, and how spiritual tourism has the potential to develop into a form of neocolonialism. Local fears that "white people" will improve on Vodún, or that "white people" may take Vodún's secrets and turn them against Vodún's historical custodians, are felt by many Béninois. Indeed, many of my informants spoke of Vodún as their "last real weapon" that they could use to fight off a "foreign invasion." Sadly, many local people imagine foreign visitors to be smarter, richer, and more focused on the future.

Opposed to these views are tourists' impressions that access to Vodún should be "given to anyone who seeks it." While some priests, such as Daágbó, reinforce this notion by arguing that "Vodún is for the world," tourists often come to this realization on their own without local promptings. Many tourists I spoke with argued that "Vodún is a religion, not a culture," or that "Vodún, like Christianity, is a religion for the world and should be accessible to anyone who seeks to learn." I never met a Béninois priest who denied Vodún's international presence or value. However, many tourists I encountered neglected to appreciate the cultural system to which Vodún belongs; it often seemed that they were trying to pry Vodún from the cultural hands of Béninois in order to propel it into the global and international arena for anyone to practice, learn, and even transform. These politics have made access to Vodún a significant point of contention between Béninois *Vodúnisants* and foreign spiritual seekers, where access to restricted religious knowledge is often discussed vigorously.

In Bénin, individuals most commonly negotiate access to Vodún while in consultation with a diviner. In these moments, potential initiates are informed of the rituals they may or may not undergo and are provided with general advice as they take their first steps into Vodún. One such man was Luiz, a forty-three-year-old Brazilian man, who in 1990 was first initiated into Candomblé, an Afro-Brazilian religion with roots in the West African forest. During this trip to Bénin, Luiz hoped to become a diviner. His encounter with a Fá diviner typifies many pre-initiation discussions. While consulting Fá, the oracular spirit of knowledge, Luiz and Thomas, a well-known Fá diviner in Ouidah, negotiated the cost of initiation and access to cherished religious secrecy. When I asked Luiz why he chose to come to Bénin, he said, "I came to Bénin to experience Candomblé's source. The Ketu [Yorùbá] spirits are important to us. This is where they come from." Like most of the Brazilian spiritual tourists I encountered, Luiz emphasized those spirits in Candomblé that belong to the Nagô-Jeje *nação* (nation). These spirits, which are characterized by a historical connection to Yorùbá (Nagô) or Gbe (Jeje) cults, can still be found thriving in Bénin today (P. Johnson 2002).

Seeking to revitalize existing relationships with his spirits and possibly bring new spirits back to his family in Brazil, Luiz asked Marie to help him to find a respected diviner. Within a few days Marie had arranged for Luiz to meet with Thomas, a diviner and priest of Sakpatá (the vodún of the earth and of smallpox) who lived in Ouidah.[9] Within a few days of making the arrangements, Luiz, Marie, and I made our way to Thomas's house. Luiz was filled with anticipation.

"I hope he gives me good news. I really want to become a diviner. I want to bring Odù [Gbǎdù] back to Brazil with me. Do you think he can do all of this? Do you think he can help me?"

"We will see," Marie offered quietly.

"*Kɔkɔkɔ!*" We announced ourselves as we walked into his compound.

"*Kúabɔ̀!* Welcome! Come in. Wait outside on the bench," a disembodied voice shouted from inside one of the four temple structures. After ten minutes, Thomas emerged from the temple and greeted us customarily with a bottle of *soɗabì* (a strong, locally distilled palm liquor).

"You're here to consult Fá?" Thomas asked, looking at Luiz.

I had met Thomas before. He looked to be in his late thirties and was respected for his proficiency with Fá divination and known as someone who could successfully fight witchcraft. Some even suggested the reason Thomas could fight witchcraft and divine so well is because he himself is a witch (*azètɔ́*).

Luiz answered, "Yes. I came to Bénin to receive *Fá*, and I want to know how to begin." Thomas opened a small cloth bag and pulled from this bag a divining chain (*akplɛkàn*) and a few divination indicators (*vode*) that are used to ask Fá direct questions.[10] Sitting on a straw mat with his back against a wall, Thomas poured a small amount of water onto the mat and began singing praise songs to Fá, welcoming the purveyor of all knowledge into our space. After a few moments, Thomas tossed his divining chain onto the mat to reveal Fá's message for Luiz.

"*Letè-Meji!*" Thomas announced. "You're right. Fá says you must become a diviner."

"Can you do that for me? Can I also receive Gbădù? Can I learn how to make Gbădù?" Luiz inquired in quick succession. Gbădù was one of the most secretive and most restrictive and dangerous spirits in Vodún. Many Béninois fear Gbădù for her association with *Mĭnɔna* (the primordial mothers) and witchcraft. Though exceedingly dangerous without proper initiation, Gbădù's worship promises unbridled protection from any number of occult and mundane forces. But Luiz, and almost every spiritual seeker like him, did not want to receive Gbădù for her ability to protect. Luiz needed Gbădù because her help is required to make new diviners. If Luiz ever wanted to initiate others authentically into Fá, he needed Gbădù in his home.

"Yeah, I can make Gbădù for you," Thomas responded. "But I can't show you how to make Gbădù. Not yet."

"Well, how much will the initiation cost me?" Luiz anxiously inquired.

"One million CFA," Thomas responded quickly as if he were anticipating the question.

Luiz's demeanor changed. He instantly went from exuding excitement and enthusiasm to being obviously melancholy and worried.

"How will I find 2,000 dollars?" Luiz asked me in English.

For Thomas this was the cost of entry into one of Vodún's most protected secrets. This cost was not unusual for foreigners. During my time in Bénin I watched Americans, Europeans, and Brazilians pay as little as 1,500 USD and as much as 3,000 USD for the same rituals Luiz was in discussion to receive. Local people often paid half these prices—but not always. Many Béninois explained to me that Gbădù was particularly expensive because of her immense power and because of her ability to make new diviners. Her required presence during Fá initiations made her a valuable international religious commodity.

Sensing Luiz's worry, Thomas leaned into him and whispered, "Don't worry. It's not expensive. You realize that with Gbădù you can make the money back after a few initiations? Vodún Gbădù will bless you."

"But I need to learn how to make Gbădù. Is there anything I can do to convince you to teach me?" Luiz begged, desperate to learn Gbădù's secrets.

"No, maybe next time you come—but not this time. She's dangerous. I need to trust you before giving you that much power. I need to know what you're going to do with it."

In a moment of desperation, Luiz retorted, "But how will I know that you didn't put cocaine in the shrine? I need to watch you make the shrine for my own protection."

Thomas shrugged and said, "There's nothing in Gbădù that will get you into trouble."

From Luiz's encounter one can see how spiritual tourists might attempt to gain access to Vodún's secrets. Luiz's case was quite representative of the dozens of interactions I experienced. The vast majority of the spiritual tourists I met made their entrée into Vodún through a diviner. During these encounters Béninois practitioners often delicately provide information to foreign spiritual seekers while simultaneously holding back religious secrets that they intend to reveal at a later date or guard indefinitely for their own families. Conversely, foreign spiritual seekers such as Luiz, motivated by their own anxieties, often tap into racist fears of Africa. In Luiz's case, he begged Thomas in a moment of desperation for permission to watch him construct Gbădù because he worried Thomas might add illegal drugs into the vodún during the shrine's construction. Having postcolonial, racist imaginings of a corrupt illicit Africa, many tourists I met expressed fears that Africans might construct shrines using marijuana, illegal animal parts (e.g., leopard hides or elephant ivory), or, in one case, even human remains.

Despite the challenges that these exchanges bring, an amicable conclusion in which Béninois teach some religious secrets to a foreign spiritual seeker while retaining others is almost always achieved. For Luiz, he was able to come up with the money for his initiation after a few weeks. He finally conceded that Gbădù would bless him and that he would be able to make his money back once he could do initiations on his own when he had returned to Brazil. Though he never learned how to make Gbădù, he received the shrine, and, despite his objections to being kept from viewing the shrine's construction, he and Gbădù made it to Brazil safely.

When one combines Bénin's colonial history with an influx of tourists seeking to learn and participate in a worldview that many Béninois feel is the last secret that they have as their own, it is no surprise that Béninois are cautious about whom they can trust and at what cost. These costs are, in some cases, reduced after a certain amount of time, but in other cases they may require tourists, who are for the most part inseparably members of the "Western world," to lubricate the social frictions generated by secrecy. Heightened by a long history of colonial and postcolonial interactions, other gestures are often economic in nature and beyond a simple promise.

Tourism and the Friction of "Authenticity"

Local tour guides often facilitate tourist experiences, including photographic access. These tour guides, who have learned what foreigners enjoy seeing, photographing, and experiencing, tend to congregate around hotels or tourist centers. One afternoon while resting in the beautiful gardens of one of Abomey's small hotels, I met Bernard, a local tour guide. Over the months, Bernard and I became good friends as we discussed the local tourism market, and he disclosed some of the requests that tourists had made of him. From hiring local sex workers to ensuring access to important Vodún ceremonies, Bernard had done it all. Over the years, he made his living by approaching hotel guests who he thought might be interested in local tours of the ancient palace buildings of Dahomey, one of Abomey's sacred forests, and even, on occasion, Vodún ceremonies. The hotel was particularly busy one July afternoon, and Bernard was making his rounds, explaining his services to all the tourists lounging around the hotel's manicured gardens. He finally approached two British women, both in their mid-twenties, who agreed to take Bernard up on his offer to visit some of the local Vodún temples—especially as he promised to take them to temples that were "rarely seen by outsiders." After sharing a few cold beers and talking about what the women might like to see, both Bernard and the tourists invited me to come along with them. I eagerly packed a small day bag and climbed onto the back of Bernard's motorcycle. The four of us left the hotel's gardens and rode off into the countryside for some twenty minutes. After a bumpy drive, we finally arrived at the place he called the "Voodoo village"—a small village at the edge of the forest that, according to Bernard, was known for Vodún.

Upon our arrival, people scurried about looking for chairs and fresh water so they could greet us in the customary way. Bernard explained to the villagers that we were interested in learning more about the vodún they worshiped. An old man came from a mud-brick home positioned across the courtyard. He shook our hands, led us into his temple, and showed us a series of wooden carved statues (bòcyɔ́) that were half-buried in the dry red, cracked earth. After offering little explanation of what we were looking at, he became irate that we were not taking pictures.

"Aren't [my vodún] good enough to photograph?" he asked through Bernard.

"Of course they are!" Christine, one of the tourists, responded. Then, while taking pictures, she looked at me and asked in English, "I thought we weren't supposed to take pictures of things like this. Is this place even real?"

"Let's watch and find out," I replied.

After a few moments of picture-taking, we were ushered into the next room, where the Vodún priest demonstrated how to pray and dance for the spirits. His prayers were unusually loud. He danced while holding two buffalo horns as if he were mimicking the way they would have grown had humans had horns. His display seemed to be a caricature of countless dances I had seen before. He was clearly performing and catering to foreign, perhaps racist, sensibilities. After his dramatic performance, he settled down into a small wooden chair, reached into a black cloth bag, and retrieved small balls of tightly spun red thread. "These are charms that will protect you from accidents," he explained. "I sell them for 5,000 CFA," he quickly added.

After his failed sales pitch, he took us to a small courtyard where he showed us more shrines, drawing our attention to one shrine in particular that hung from the branches of a tree. He explained that the shrine was "bloody" because he had just sacrificed a chicken to the nameless arboreal spirit that morning. The "blood" was red—very red, not brownish-red like dried blood often looks when applied to white cloth. The tourists never commented on the redness of the blood—perhaps it was just as they expected it to be—and I never pointed it out but it made me suspicious. As I internally struggled with this site's authenticity, the tourists discussed it openly.

"I don't think that place was real," Michelle stated.

"Why not?" I asked curiously.

"He didn't care that we took pictures. The shrines were too clean and the priest just wants to sell us charms! It looks like a scam to me. This place is like a theme park—it isn't real," Michelle concluded.

For Michelle and Christine, this site was too open and too free. To have what they would call an authentic experience, they wanted to be told that they could not take pictures. They wanted to be restricted. They wanted to experience and then negotiate their way through the social friction that secrecy generates. In the case of Vodún, foreign travelers hope to be met with just enough resistance to authenticate the experience but not so much so that access is denied completely.

I too had my suspicions, but I never confirmed or denied them to Michelle or Christine. After they had retired to their room that evening, Bernard and I met at the hotel bar for a drink. I asked him, "Bernard, just between you and me, that place you took us to today; was it real?"

"Of course! I don't bring tourists to fake places," he retorted, defending his choice.

Bernard was invested in the perceived authenticity of the site so that he could make a living. Yet tourists, myself included, were skeptical. Or perhaps part of the site was real and part was a fabrication created for tourists. Ethnographic moments such as this one have long inspired scholars to explore the relationship between tourism and authenticity (MacCannell 1999 [1976]; Urry 2002; Bruner 2005). Dean MacCannell is famous in tourism studies for his "backstage"/"frontstage" dichotomy (1999 [1976])—in which "real" culture is hidden backstage from tourists while they are allowed to participate in a frontstage version of local culture. Still others, like Edward Bruner, have attempted to eschew MacCannell's preoccupation with the authentic, calling it a "red herring, to be examined only when the tourist, the locals, or the producers themselves use the term" (2005: 5). What seems to be happening in the case of Michelle and Christine seems to rest between Mac-Cannell's model (all tourist productions are inherently "inauthentic") and Bruner's model (all tourist productions are inherently "authentic"). Michelle and Christine were not, at least from their perspective, given a "backstage" performance of "authentic" Vodún. The performance that we all experienced, whether staged or not, was an attempt to present to us the authentic "Voodoo" of our imaginations. Unfortunately, in this case, the Vodún priest failed to present a believable version of Vodún. His performance was not only lacking in resistance, but also a "hyperreality"—a caricature—of U.S. and European imagination (see Eco 1983 [1973]).

Divination, Cultural Brokerage, and the Marketing of Knowledge

Michelle and Christine's Vodún encounter had been devastating for them. Pointing to the priest's attempt to sell them charms, and to their absolute freedom of movement in the temple, for fifteen minutes they talked about how "inauthentic" or "fake" the temple seemed. Although Bernard spoke to Michelle and Christine in French—sometimes using me as a linguistic intermediary when their understanding of French proved inadequate—he intermittently spoke rudimentarily in English as well. Keying into Michelle's and Christine's body language, and picking up on their dissatisfaction from the English he was able to understand, Bernard suggested the women go see a "real diviner"—"one of the best," Bernard explained. Eager to move past their experience in the "Voodoo village," the women agreed ecstatically.

"It's just a short walk up the road," Bernard offered.

Over the next fifteen to twenty minutes, both Bernard and I explained to Michelle and Christine what they should expect from the diviner (bokɔnɔ). They began worrying about which types of questions they should ask him and which areas of their lives needed, and deserved, this kind of spiritual attention.

"Just let the diviner do his job. Don't worry about what you *should* ask—he'll know what you *need* to ask," I explained. They each looked at me and smiled in agreement as we continued down the narrow trail that led into the forest. After approximately ten minutes we arrived at the diviner's home. He was at least eighty years old and stood no more than 5'5" tall. He wore an old torn, khaki, uniform like outfit and carried his divining tools in a well-worn, faux-leather briefcase. He greeted us with a customary cup of water and began talking to us about the reason for our visit.

"The ladies would like to consult with Fá," Bernard explained.

The diviner handed Michelle a small nut and asked her to "talk to the nut" and "tell the nut all her worries." After softly confiding in the small nut, she set it down in front of the diviner, along with 2,000 CFA—much more than was customary. After the diviner said his opening prayers and lightly tossed his divining chain onto the ground in front of him, he began detailing Michelle's future while also providing solutions to the employment problems she was experiencing.

After just a few moments into her consultation, the diviner told Michelle, "You must receive a cleansing ceremony to ensure your future success." "You should also receive Fá and become an initiate," the diviner continued. After these two spiritual prescriptions, I stopped listening, as my mind began to drift more than two years into the past when I had received my first divination from a priest who did not know me from the next foreign client he may have seen. "You should become a diviner and a priest of Tron," the diviner had explained to me. At the time, I was unwilling to undergo the rituals—partly due to time and partly due to cost. But over the two years that had passed between my divination and Michelle's, several diviners had insisted that I undergo certain rituals—rituals that would have cost me more than 3 million CFA—rituals that I almost always refused. Michelle and I were not unique. While tourists were not always told that they should become initiated, most tourists I encountered who sought a diviner's guidance were told that they should undergo one ritual or another—all for large sums of money, and almost always for more money than local people would be expected to pay for the same spiritual intervention.

Diviners consistently serve as religious brokers—selling ceremonies or other spiritual services such as spiritual baths or charms (bǒ)—for local and foreign spiritual seekers alike. Divination is far more than having your future told and serves greater purposes than mere entertainment. For a diviner to be effective, he or she must provide his or her client with solutions to his or her challenges, or ways to reinforce and maintain blessings; telling clients that they are ill is of little use if the diviner cannot help them to heal. For Béninois, divination is about achieving well-being. Understanding the commitment not just to receiving divination but also to the treatment, many Béninois approach Fá (and other forms of divination) cautiously, as a trip to a diviner, much like a trip to the doctor, can cost them a great deal, once offerings and post-divinatory ceremonies and rituals are considered.

Although foreign spiritual seekers may be charged more for the same ceremony, Béninois certainly pay for the guidance, advice, and ceremonial intervention of ritual specialists. In fact, even among local people, a sliding scale of services exists—family members often enjoying ritual services at a greatly reduced rate, and middle- to upper-class Béninois pay a premium that approaches what tourists may pay.[11] Remarkably, Western spiritual seekers, all of whom have spent a great deal of money to travel to West Africa to become initiated, often balk at the cost of ceremonies, arguing that "Africa is supposed to be cheap."[12]

Nevertheless, attitudes about spending money during religious encounters are diverse across the tourism spectrum. As Luke Desforges points out, "Money seems to play an important role in the experience of [tourism] because of its role in the imagination of place" (2001: 362). Desforges provides compelling evidence that the ways in which a tourist spends (or does not spend) money may highlight how he or she might imagine the geopolitical situation of a destination. Yet, despite working in postcolonial Peru with British tourists, he completely avoids discussing how race or postcolonial politics affect the ways in which travelers imagine their destinations and the people who live there. In the case of spiritual tourists in Bénin, they wish to connect profoundly with indigenous West African religions such as Vodún. Many of them are seeking refuge in Vodún, and Africa more broadly, in reaction against the West and especially Western religion (Comaroff and Comaroff 2012).

Joyce, an African American woman in her fifties, traveled to Bénin to consider initiation into Vodún. After a few weeks searching for the right teacher-initiator, she left Bénin having received the beginning initiation into Fá and the encouragement she needed to make plans to return to be later initiated as a devotee to Mamíwátá. When I asked Joyce how she became interested in Vodún, she carefully responded, "I love ritual. I love how ritual makes me feel. I love being close to the divine. I love the sense of community that ritual gives me and how it connects me to those around me. But I despise what [Western] religion has become. I dislike the oppression, the judgment, and the hate. I am over all of it. Vodún allows me to have all that I love about religion without all the things I hate. Vodún is my sanctuary in a way that Catholicism can't ever be."

While critiques from foreign spiritual seekers such as Joyce have resulted from an honest and cogent critique of the misuse of religion in the West, there is also the danger of re-creating the classic racist trope of the "noble savage." Jean once told me, "When my foreign initiates come to Bénin they insist on sleeping here in the village—right here on the ground! They love eating the local food and learning about what it is like to live here." As this statement illustrates, spiritual tourists in Bénin often extol—and romanticize—the "village life" (see Piot 1999). Desforges and others (Frow 1991; S. Stewart 2007 [1984]; Jordan and Weedon 1995) have noted that "there is a strong case in which the folk, peasant, or working classes are singled out as holders of the true spirit of the place" (Desforges 2001: 358). Because the "peasant, folk, and working classes" are also associated with poverty and "traditional culture," Western spiritual seekers are also likely to see Vodún practitioners as unimportant players in the global economy. This association then leads many tourists, blinded by their own racial or national privilege, to frame those West Africans who are, in their eyes, the "holders of the true spirit" of Vodún as being "cheap," "affordable," and, by extension, exploitable.

Similarly, foreign spiritual seekers often complained to me in private conversations that "there is no way that this is what they charge their own families for these ceremonies." Their perceptions of a "cheap" and exploitable Africa are most certainly propagated by U.S. and European film studios, news agencies, and print journalists who often spread misconceptions that irrevocably link Africa to poverty, war, and corruption (e.g., Cheru 2010) and further implicate the West in Africa's continued political and economic difficulties (Rodney 1981; Bond 2006; Airewele and Endozie 2009). Disturbingly, as Western spiritual seekers travel to Bénin, and complain of the relatively small economic premium they are asked to pay for their initiations, African students attending U.S. universities are paying a massive premium for their educations. Yet these economic structures are hardly considered, let alone criticized, by most Americans seeking initiation into Vodún.

Despite these challenges, Vodún is most certainly "on the move" (Rush 1997: 1–3). As an increasing number of Western spiritual tourists seek new religions to replace those such as Christianity, many of them, inspired by an existing African presence in the Americas (e.g., Lucumí and Haitian Vodou), are turning to West Africa. Unfortunately, in their tendency to other, even if unknowingly, the very Africans from whom they seek to learn, spiritual tourists have a tendency to emphasize Africans' connection to the primitive and the traditional. Perhaps this is because, like in the important art movement of primitivism that began in the late nineteenth century, spiritual tourists are searching for "origins and absolutes—for unspoilt nature and uncontaminated humanity, for the paradise we (modern Westerners) have lost" (Jordan and Weedon 1995: 320). Ironically, the more they become involved in religions like Vodún—that is to say, the more transnational Vodún becomes—the less likely they are to find what it is they are looking for.

"I Want to Be Initiated": Tourism, Initiation, and Access to Secret Knowledge

Not all diviners prescribe initiation rituals just for the sake of making money—many of them explain to their clients, whether that person be Béninois or foreign, exactly what Fá says that their client needs to do to fix his or her problems or to maintain his or her blessings. Sometimes Fá's prescriptions are small, such as focused prayers; at other times Fa's prescriptions are elaborate, such as costly sacrifices or initiations. Either way, Fa's solutions are always based on a constant necessity for ritual intervention to remain balanced and cool (fífá) (Thompson 2011). While serving as a diviner's apprentice, I learned that all encounters, or consultations (*fákíkán*), with a diviner should lead to some type of ritual or spiritual medicine being prescribed. In fact, this constant need for spiritual maintenance has led some Béninois to reject Vodún in favor of Christianity—a religious practice that is often seen as "less worrisome and less expensive." However, most client-diviner encounters do not lead to a discussion of initiation, even if some do.

Although the initiation of foreigners into Vodún cults is new and still somewhat infrequent in Bénin, in some areas of neighboring Nigeria it is quite common (Clarke 2004). Even so, many Béninois and Nigerians, especially those who do not stand to gain economically from foreign initiations, are worried about tourists' motives. "I don't understand what [tourists] want. [Europeans] have taken everything else from us—do they really have to take [our secret religious knowledge] too?"; "Our culture is not for sale"; and "I don't trust [tourists]—they will figure out a way to turn this against us" were all reasons I heard from people who were leery of allowing tourists access to Vodún's world of secrets. Nevertheless, others expressed that "Vodún is for everyone, and everyone should have access" or "Tourist interest in Vodún gives me hope that my religion [Vodún] isn't as evil as I've been told by missionaries," thereby indexing some positive effects of foreign involvement in Vodún.

Troublingly, the perceived need for tourist interest in Vodún to provide hope to young Vodún practitioners implies that colonialism, neocolonialism, and even contemporary travel and a strong Christian missionary presence in Bénin have all contributed to the malignment of African spiritual traditions, especially "Voodoo," thereby positioning Vodún and other indigenous religions as "traditional, backwards, and superstitious" (Chidili 2007) while, for some, Christianity, and in some cases Islam, enjoys a more contemporary and progressive positionality. Regardless of one's position on Vodún, it is clear that local practitioners approach international tourists with their own preconceived ideas of what tourists are looking for—ideas that have been influenced greatly by West Africa's past and present relationship with the so-called Western world.

As many scholars have pointed out, postcolonial Africans have repeatedly been mistreated, forgotten, dehumanized, and discounted by the Western world (Mudimbe 1988; Comaroff and Comaroff 1993, 2012; Chidili 2007; Moreman and Rushton 2011). An awareness of this history, and a fear of once again being exploited and forgotten, has made some Vodún priests cautious about initiating foreign spiritual seekers. Because of Bénin's long and tumultuous history with France, its former colonizer, some priests, including Jean, refuse to work with French tourists, asserting, "they are nothing but liars and cheaters." Only when Jean was confident that I was not French did he agree to speak with me. Resistance to initiate foreigners is, at times, palatable to those tourists seeking access to Vodún's secret knowledge. While tourists often feel comfortable discussing these challenges among themselves—and with other foreign visitors like me—few of them actually confront the resistance directly with local priests. Instead, they begin a fascinating process that, following Anna Tsing (2005), I call "social lubrication."

Faced with the fricative aura generated by a religious secret—that is, the invisible, somewhat amorphous social field that permeates outward from a social secret—tourists rely on their social networks, often invoking the names of other foreigners who have successfully navigated the foreign initiation market in Bénin, or relying on local friends who may vouch for a tourist's integrity or sincerity. When I first arrived in Bénin, my initial encounters with prospective initiators were almost always managed by Marie, my research assistant and dear friend, who used her family's position in the community as well as her status as a Vodún priestess to assure some members of the Vodún community of my seriousness. Aware of my prior status as a priest (houngan asogwe) of Haitian Vodou, Marie often took it upon herself to introduce me as both an anthropologist and a houngan, so as to present me as a "believer."[13] Although my status as a houngan never granted me instant access to Béninois Vodún's secrets, locals often accepted it both as evidence of my "belief" in the spirits and as proof of my own determination to learn and embody the Vodún worldview.

As my social networks grew in Bénin, so did my ability to call on them when I needed to "lubricate" the "friction" that I experienced when trying to navigate actively the secret world of Vodún. These networks of intense social capital were afforded to me by my time in the field—something most tourists do not have the luxury of enjoying. Instead, many tourists invoke the power of money, the one commodity they know that most Vodún priests in Bénin want. I watched uninitiated photographers gain access to restricted temple interiors by paying large sums of money (sometimes as much as 1,000 USD), and I met tourists who paid to become initiated. I even observed some tourists using money to avoid some ceremonial discomforts, such as the shaving of one's head or forced confinement to the temple when new initiates learn how to "serve the spirits." Most of the tourists I met were middle-class, and they came from the United States, France, or Brazil. They came to Bénin to become initiated, and they were willing to pay. One such tourist was Mar-cella, an African American woman who was determined to be initiated into the mysteries of Gbǎdù, a cult traditionally restricted to men, telling me, "I will go home with Gbǎdù in my hands—even if I have to pay for it" (cf. Beliso-De Jesús 2015: 183–211). She used some of the same metaphysical arguments that I have heard circulate within the U.S. New Age movement for years. She believed strongly in the "cosmic power of the divine femi-nine" and even argued that "Gbǎdù rightfully belongs to women, anyway," citing her devotion to a seemingly generic "goddess" as evidence of her right to the mysteries of Gbǎdù. Additionally, she argued, "Gbǎdù is a woman herself! Did you know that? Can you explain to me why men are the ones who control her cult? Why would men have a monopoly of something that's clearly a woman's mystery?"

Gbǎdù is indeed a female divinity and seen as Fá's wife—although most noninitiated people I met did not seem to know this. However, when I asked male diviners about why women are not allowed access to Gbǎdù, most of them say that "Gbǎdù is a womb. Women don't have Gbǎdù because they don't need Gbǎdù. They already have Gbǎdù between their legs. Women and Gbǎdù are kept apart because they both have the power to create—keeping them away from each other ensures coolness, and bringing them together would only disrupt that."

When I posed the same question to Laura, one of Jean's wives, she said, "Gbǎdù is dangerous. I would never want to see her! If I did, I could no lon-ger become pregnant, and I might even die!" By contrast, Marcella never explained or understood Gbǎdù in this way—and, despite my knowing of Gbǎdù's "dangers" prior to meeting Marcella, I did not think it my place to explain Gbǎdù. Instead, I listened to her story over a cold drink at a noisy roadside *buvette*. To my knowledge, Marcella was never allowed to initiate into Gbǎdù—although I am not certain that a story of her success or failure is important when one explores the meaning of social lubrication when dealing with secrecy. For this discussion, what matters is that Marcella, like many others, attempted to become initiated. For Marcella, money was not enough to secure her initiation into Gbǎdù—the social resistance, in this case, was just too much. However, given enough time—and perhaps enough money—there is no telling what secret knowledge Marcella, and other women and men like her, might access.

If I have learned anything about secrecy in Vodún, it is that access is frequently negotiable, and the ways in which one gains access are always changing. This is true especially when new actors are introduced into what are effectively "social dramas," which is what Victor Turner (1996 [1957]) called rituals that allowed a society's "tension" and "strife" to be expressed and worked out. In the Béninois case of foreign initiation, the "ritual" has become the negotiation through which tourists hope to overcome their difference—in effect, their liminality—through the transformative ritual process of negotiation and social lubrication, such that, in the end, they would be incorporated (but not reincorporated) into Vodún as emerging social actors. Here, the ritual of negotiation, as a sort of "social lubrication," provides a space for spiritual seekers to be separated from their own national, racialized, and religious identities; if successful, they may then become incorporated (even if incompletely) into the world as Vodún priests, priestesses, and diviners.

Although Turner argued that "social dramas occur within groups of persons who share values and interests and who have a real or alleged common history" (1980: 149), in the case of Vodún, the social actors (Fon, Yorùbá, American, French, Brazilian, and others) all come from different histories. However, most foreign tourists, regardless of their nationality, share a common imagined, perhaps mythical, connection to West Africa and the African Americas that both validate and empower the creative ritual processes that are under way. As international spiritual seekers negotiate access to Vodún's body of secret knowledge, become initiated, and then return back home as newly incorporated members of a new global Vodún, they also inadvertently create a new African diaspora, a ritual diaspora, with explicit links to individuals and places in West Africa—a diaspora that is at once multiracial and multinational and supported by the social power of ritual.

Spiritual Tourism Supports Religious Expansion

Tourists travel from the United States and Europe to Bénin for a multitude of reasons. Some want nothing to do with "Voodoo," citing exaggerated fears of "demon worship" or "Satanism." But for many, Voodoo is the impetus behind their trip. For those people who travel to Bénin specifically to encounter Voodoo, Bénin offers a great deal, from breathtaking photographs and powerful religious objects to ceremonies sacred to the Fon and Yorùbá peoples living in southern Bénin and even the chance to become initiated into Vodún. Regardless of the degree to which they hope to participate in

Vodún, each of these tourists is required to navigate Bénin's social landscape and Vodún's ritualized secrecy. Some tourists are able to lubricate the needed social friction that is generated by processes of secrecy more successfully than others can, but the barriers that surround and protect Vodún's hidden knowledge of power are experienced by nearly every traveler who encounters Vodún.

Those international travelers who are successful at maneuvering through Vodún's culture of secrecy and complex political economy potentially join a new community, an imagined (Anderson 2006 [1983]) and established ritual community that constitutes a second diasporic layer that is anchored not by diasporic bodies (Gilroy 1993; P. Johnson 2007; Beliso-De Jesús 2015) but by ritual. Regardless of foreign spiritual seekers' racial or ethnic identity, they all participate in re-creating Africa back home in the Americas, and they actively, albeit perhaps unintentionally, remember Africa and its slaving past by interacting ritually with the long-established African diasporic community already living in the Americas. Maneuvering through the racial and economic politics of postcolonial Africa, each time a foreign spiritual seeker becomes initiated, he or she becomes a cocreator of Vodún's global expansion and the consequential development of a multinational Vodún marketplace, wherein initiations, specialized religious artifacts, and secret spiritual powers are all bought and sold. Tourist encounters and initiation are usually one's first step into Vodún's secret religioscape. As individuals negotiate access to secrecy, they place a social value on the resistance that surrounds ritual secrecy. In the next chapter, I turn my attention to the ways in which ritual may imbue bodies with occult ontologies that transform individuals into religious secrets and commodities (see Johnson 2002). Through a careful analysis of one's movement through the sacred, and highly secretive, forest, I will show how Béninois challenge existing structures of power by colonizing foreign bodies with African spirits. In so doing, they create spaces in which new initiates receive spirits and the sacred forest, thereby allowing for ritual secrecy to transform their foreign bodies into participants in Vodún's global expansion.

CHAPTER 2

===

Receiving the Forest

In a ritual, the world as lived and the world as imagined,
fused under the agency of a single set of symbolic forms,
turn out to be the same world.

—Geertz 1973: 112

A week before my initiation, Jean performed divination to ask Fá how to prepare for my journey into *fázùn*, Fá's sacred forest. As he had always done when consulting Fá, Jean sat on a straw mat with his back against the far wall of the ten-by-thirty-foot earthen building in which he received clients and performed rituals for Fá. In the spot where Jean sat for an incalculable number of consultations over the years, the mud wall had begun to lose its red-earth color, leaving behind a ghostly black image of Jean's shape.

"Sit here to my left," Jean instructed me, pointing to a low wooden stool.

After balancing my body onto the wobbly seat, I dropped 100 CFA into Jean's hand as a customary payment for the consultation. Almost immediately, Jean began to sing to call Fá forth. After a few moments, he tossed his divining chain, the *akplɛkàn*, onto the ground in front of him.

Diviners craft their akplɛkàn by stringing together eight halves of a tear-shaped nut that, when split in half, has one rounded side and one hollow side, which is marked by a woody ridge that runs down the center, from the top to the bottom of the nut. When a diviner throws his akplɛkàn onto the floor, it forms an upside-down U, with four segments on the left and four on the right— thereby revealing one of the possible 256 signs known as *dù*.

I watched intensely as Jean's akplɛkàn fell onto the smooth but cracked cement floor in front of him. The staccato rhythm created when the eight seed halves crashed against the surface echoed off the walls of the small enclosed room.

"*Trúkpè-Ablà!*" Jean announced.

Saying the name of the dù aloud makes the sign real—and, according to Jean, unchangeable. Before the dù's name is spoken aloud, Jean contended that the dù, and, therefore, the individual's destiny for which the dù was cast, was still fragile and uncertain. Speaking the dù's name brought the sign into being.

"Fá says that before your initiation, you must offer sacrifice [vɔ̃] to Sakpatá [the divinity of the earth, smallpox, and other eruptive diseases], Xɛbyosò [the spirit of thunder], and Dàn [the serpent spirit of riches and cool breezes]. These *vodún* will support you. They will make you strong. This is important," Jean explained with a seriousness in his voice that I had not heard before.

"Okay. What do I need to do?"

To answer my question, Jean once again turned to his akplɛkàn and began asking Fá about the details of the sacrifices I needed to perform.

"A Guinea hen for Sakpatá, a rooster for Xɛbyosò, and a white she-goat for Dàn."

No surprise here—I knew that all Fá initiations start with divination and the resulting sacrifices. For Jean, a devotee offering a sacrifice was a way to ensure that initiation candidates took their first steps into fázùn fully prepared and with the vodún's support.

Within a couple of days, I managed to purchase the prescribed animals, along with some palm oil, a dozen kola nuts, and a bottle of gin. Animals in tow, I walked proudly into Jean's cinder-block house and announced, "Jean, I am ready to make the sacrifices. I have everything we need!"

Within a couple of hours, Jean and I, along with a few of his sons and apprentices, were walking into the forest to perform my sacrifices. After we offered the birds to Sakpatá and Xɛbyosò, we started down the long forest path that led to Dàn. Within a few minutes, we arrived at Dàn's small, public grove. To the back of the forest clearing was an earthen mound that covered the leaves and other buried objects that were used to construct this shrine (see Landry 2016). On the mound, which protected Dàn's unseen powers, rested the visible portion of his shrine: eight terra-cotta pots. The ritual vessels were coated with years of offerings (Aronson 2007; Norman 2009). Dried blood and palm oil blended together on the surface of the pots, forming a thick black patina all over the shrine. Countless white chicken feathers and dried kola nuts had been left on the shrine and the forest floor, each indexing times that individuals came to Dàn—some with their pains, others with their joys. I was ready to offer a goat to Dàn and contribute to the ever-growing "unfinished" quality of the shrine (Rush 2010).

Romar, Jean's eldest son, offered a bundle of leaves to the white she-goat that I had led into the forest on a frayed hemp rope. The goat almost immediately took a bite of the leaves, thereby signaling Dàn's acceptance of the sacrifice. Before I knew what was happening, Romar picked the goat up off the ground, tied its leaf-filled mouth shut, and bound its legs together to keep her from kicking.

"Speak a message into the goat's ear," Jean coached. "Tell her what message you want her to bring to your ancestors."[1]

I leaned down and whispered a message into the goat's ear—a message of good wishes to my long-dead grandparents and to my uncle who had just passed away unexpectedly a few weeks earlier. I had been unable to travel back to the United States for his funeral, and this moment helped me to overcome feelings of guilt. It was a welcomed alternative to saying goodbye to him in person.

As I stood up, Jean jolted me from this personal moment with my remembered dead by placing a knife in my hand.

"Here," Jean said. "You need to learn how to do this if you're going to be a diviner."

I hesitated. I did not think I was ready to take the goat's life. I had, for the most part, grown up blissfully removed from the consequences of eating meat.

Using his finger, Jean made a slashing mark on the goat's throat.

"Just cut here. Do it quick," Jean instructed.

I took a deep breath and adjusted my grip on the knife. In a final act of hesitation, I rested the blade on the goat's throat for longer than Romar was comfortable.

"Just do it, Tim. Don't think about it," Romar shouted.

With Romar's encouragement, and under Jean's watchful gaze, I made one swift downward gesture with the knife and opened the goat's jugular. The goat was silent as her blood poured from the sacrificial gash and onto Dàn. In a moment of shock and awe, one could see the sunlight creep through the thick forest canopy and reflect off the wet blood that now covered the shrine in an almost luminescent red sheen. With the sacrifice complete and with Dàn fed, Jean took a moment to teach me his next lesson.

"Give Gŭ some red palm oil. Pour it onto the knife. You have to thank the metal."

With that, Gŭ—the vodún of metal and blacksmithing—had been honored, Dàn had accepted my sacrifice, and I had managed to show Jean that I could feed the spirits that he devoted his life to serving. Later that evening, we all consumed the goat and took Dàn's *acè* (divine power) into our bodies. I was now ready to be initiated.

Mathieu Kérékou, Bénin's Marxist-Leninist dictator who governed from 1972 to 1991, felt that expensive initiations, such as the one I was about to undergo, were a waste of money, time, and resources that would be better spent on the country's economic and cultural development. As a result, Vodún was made illegal, and priests—who held a great deal of social sway— were forced to conduct initiations in secret and under the threat of punishment. To reduce their risk of persecution, and to avoid abandoning the spirits completely, *Vodúnisants* began to shorten the length of their initiations from years, during which the education of the new initiation candidates occurred, to months, weeks, or even days (Elwert-Kretschmer 1995). In the early 1990s, Kérékou's anti-Vodún regime was replaced by a new democratically elected government that sought to relegitimize Vodún and market the religion to international tourists as one of Bénin's cultural treasures. Nevertheless, the effect that Kérékou had on ritual practice—and especially on initiation duration—was lasting.

Vodún initiations have been changing to meet national and now global political demands for quite some time. Initiations were shortened in reaction to Kérékou's and now tourists' demands; ritualized facial and body scarification have become points of contention and negotiation for both Béninois and foreign initiates who wish to be able to more easily participate in global markets; and both Béninois and foreign initiates have begun to request that shrines be constructed without the use of prohibited ingredients such as elephant ivory, leopard pelts, or human remains in order to avoid committing international crimes as sacred objects begin to move commonly across national and continental borders. While ritual secrecy has made it impossible to know what sorts of changes communism and spiritual tourism have had on ritual initiations, we can say with absolute certainty that Vodún is adapting seamlessly and comfortably to global demands.

Understanding the ways in which rituals adjust to accommodate both these new political agendas and a broadened interest from spiritual seekers requires not only a close look at ritual performance but also an analysis that attends to the ways in which rituals may transform cultural outsiders into religious experts. Since Arnold van Gennep's research (1909), and certainly by Victor Turner's time (1967), anthropologists' discussions of ritual have emphasized space. While my analysis of Vodún initiation rituals certainly considers the social power of space, especially as initiates move between the village and the sacred forest, I also reflect on the ways in which one's body takes on a ritual's social power through movement and action, long after one's initiation, and even enters new spaces that are best described as global. In the cases I present throughout this book, and especially in this chapter, my analysis is often complicated by the ways in which multiple subjects, often differing in nationality and race and experience, draw meaning from the same ritual—frequently, simultaneously.

Regardless of the initiate's national or racial identity, ritual initiation is, at least in part, about receiving what Emile Durkheim called a "moral educa- tion." In the case of Fá, during one's *rite de passage*, a new initiate learns Fá's secrets. He or she begins acquiring the necessary skills to be a diviner, and most importantly the acolyte takes on Fá's acè. Although analysts from Durkheim (1965 [1912]) to Beryl Bellman (1984) and T. O. Beidelman (1997) have primarily viewed initiation as a "form of education" (Beidelman 1997: 13), in the case of Fá, I am not convinced that knowledge acquisition is the most important part of the transformation that occurs during the initi- ate's short time in the sacred forest. While learning the spirits' dances, the spirits' language, and the right ways to feed and venerate spirits are all sig- nificant parts of one's initiation, I contend that an overall shortening of ritual duration had made one's education secondary to what matters, as the perfec- tion of these skills usually continues for years after one's actual initiation. As I will show, for both Béninois and foreign spiritual seekers, the most cru- cial parts of an initiation are those permanent, ontological changes that occur to one's body as the initiate *moves* slowly into the forest, undergoes bodily transformations, and *experiences* secrecy.

When one thinks of rites de passage in anthropology from an earlier gen- eration, one might have thought of Bellman's formative work on Poro and Sande initiation (1984) or Beidelman's analysis of Kaguru initiation in Tan- zania (1997), where, in both examples, young people undergo a change in state through which they learn how to be social adults. In other words, for these anthropologists, rites of passage have been understood to be those ritu- als that exist to "construct" and "perpetuate" one's collective and "imagined" ethnic identity (Beidelman 1997: 30–31). However, for practitioners of Vodún it has not been that simple since the eighteenth century. From roughly 1727 to 1823, the Fon kingdom of Dahomey was a vassal state of Oyo, the powerful Yorùbá kingdom to the east. As a result of Dahomey's tributary status, a great deal of religious exchange existed between the two empires. By the reign of Tegbesú (r. 1732–74), Dahomey's fifth ruler, Fá had entered Dahomey from Yorùbáland, leading the historian Edna Bay to suggest that Tegbesú was the first Dahomean king to have entered into Fá's sacred forest to learn of his destiny. By Gezò's reign (r. 1818–58), Fá had become well established in the royal palace, and two Yorùbá ancestor cults, Oró and Egúngún, had begun to find a new home in Fonland. The reach and absorption of Yorùbá rituals in Fonland continued to grow, as more and more people found power in their use. In fact, Bay points out, "even prominent Afro-Brazilian families in [Ouidah] note a transformation of their Luso-Catholic culture during [Gezò's reign], adopting [Egúngún] and Oro" (1998: 190).

And these are just a few examples. My point is that while initiation for many Béninois may reinforce their ethnic and gender identities, as observed by Beidelman, they are also not bound by these rules. Fonland is a place where Yorùbá rituals have become Fon rituals; where Luso-Catholic individuals have found great power by being initiated into Yorùbá ancestor cults; and where contemporary American and European spiritual tourists seek the same divine power as those Fon, Yorùbá, and Afro-Brazilian initiates before them, albeit for different reasons. Pierre Bourdieu has suggested that "ritual in general is not a matter of following rules" (quoted in Bell 1997: 78). Indeed, taking Bourdieu much farther, I might suggest that Vodún's social fabric is built on something closer to breaking rules. The religion's flexibility and absorptive qualities are precisely why the religion has been remarkably successful in global spaces (see Rush 2013). Vodún rituals are not built on fixed rules of engagement. Instead, they are built on rules of effectiveness—even when those ritual rules call for the conceptual expansion of relevant actors.

Bell has shown that Bourdieu "characterizes ritual as strategic practices for transgressing and reshuffling cultural categories in order to meet the needs of real situations" (1997: 78). The influx of American and European initiates into Vodún makes it easy to see how the "rules" of engagement have begun to expand, as Vodún becomes increasingly more popular among non-African spiritual seekers. Béninois have started to "reshuffle" their own categories of membership as they react to new trends in Vodún's global development. While new situations—such as spiritual tourism—have prompted Vodún to once again adapt, the religion has successfully overcome similar challenges in the past. For centuries, Vodún has expanded into new territories and absorbed practitioners from diverse backgrounds. "Immigrants, including war captives, often carried their vodun with them and installed them in Dahomey. Dahomeans were sometimes sent to neighboring areas to be trained as priests of new gods. Vodún even arrived as spoils of war" (Bay 1998: 22). Following such earlier models, as Vodún now emerges in new spaces around the world, practitioners must negotiate new social, legal, and environmental landscapes. Due to ritual's remarkable ability to remember and reorganize strategically, Vodún's rituals have become prime examples of the ways in which the religion changes to meet the "needs of real situations."

Despite Vodún's history as a religion that commonly absorbs new ritual parameters and therefore appeals to an ever-growing set of spiritual seekers, some scholars may still argue that the recent inclusion of non-Africans in the religion is nothing more than a form of neocolonialism from which white prac titioners profit. While their critiques should be taken seriously, it is equally important to recognize that rigid religious boundaries are a result of global Abrahamic religious supremacy and have never truly explained religions such as Vodún. The religion's flexibility has encouraged foreign involvement. As a result, the complete dismissal of foreign practitioners is not only politically reductive, but also contrary to Vodún's very existence and antithetical to the religion's long-established success. Realistically, it is important to acknowl edge that the initiation of foreign spiritual seekers is simultaneously the result of systematic African oppression (Rodney 1972) *and* Vodún's growth into a global religion. Vodún's current situation is one in which a growing number of both African and non-African-descended peoples are becoming interested. Through the ritualized and economic consumption of acè, ritual action has become the primary means by which Béninois encourage and manage Vodún's worldwide expansion, as initiation transforms people, regardless of their race or nationality, into religious agents.

To illustrate these points, in this chapter, I draw on Fá initiation rituals to show how one's body develops what I call an *occult ontology*, or an inalien able change to one's being that is often hidden to the initiate him- or herself. In this context, I use the word "occult" to draw meaning from its relationship to both *magical* and *hidden* worlds. From these two distinct but overlapping registers, ritual transforms initiates, "under the agency of a single set of sym bolic forms" (Geertz 1973: 112–13), by creating hidden or concealed changes to one's identity and therefore to the ways in which an initiated person exists in the world.

Today, identity and initiation have been complicated by a conceptual widening of geographic space. The development of transnational networks has made it so that it is no longer enough for anthropologists to see initiation in Africa as a way of creating and perpetuating bounded ethnicities (e.g., Beidelman 1997: 30–31). In postcolonial Africa, one's ethnic, national, and global identities have all begun to overlap and even compete for shifting value in one's life. My use of *occult ontologies* helps to manage the added intricacies that transnationalism brings to understanding ritual initiation in Vodún. For Paul Christopher Johnson, ritual provides communities with tremendous flexibility, thereby allowing them to reflect on new "horizons" and new ways to imagine belonging (cf. Anderson 2006 [1983]). In this way, ritual action has the power to transform bodies into what Johnson calls the "body-as-secret," during which "bodies are ritualized into secrecy by becoming themselves secrets" (2002: 103). Aisha Beliso-De Jesús takes a similar approach to Johnson with her notion of *copresences* in Santería. Copresences, according to Beliso-De Jesús, are the felt experiences of "various spirits, ancestors, and oricha that operate in transnational Santería communities from a broad range of material-immaterial beings that are increasingly moving through diverse Santería worlds" (2015: 7). Supported through ritual, copresences are anchored in "the complex multiplicity of racial spiritual embodied affectivity" (7) and, therefore, work to blur the ontological existence of African and Caribbean spirits and ancestors with the diasporic bodies of their devotees.

Clearly, Johnson and Beliso-De Jesús have contributed greatly to the ways in which Africanists and Caribbeanists might grapple with the complex relationships that thrive at the intersection of religion, race, and the embodied experience of diaspora. Nevertheless, globalization has begun to contribute to a broadening of African and African diasporic religions that now include an increasing number of practitioners who are not of African descent. Occult ontologies, therefore build upon these theories by unhinging African and African diasporic religions from the presumption that the religions' devotees *must* be from Africa or the Caribbean. Instead, occult ontologies allow me to discuss not how ritual helps one to make sense of their embodied connection to the "Black Atlantic" (Gilroy 1993), but rather how ritual helps to reimagine the past and construct new futures with West African religions and their Caribbean derivatives. Indeed, I argue that ritual provides the ideal space in which to explore the multiracial and multinational salience of religions such as Vodún. Similar to the ways in which Fon, Yorùbá, and Luso-Catholics used ritual to join previously foreign spirit cults, foreign spiritual seekers, some of whom may not be of African descent, are also transformed into religious agents and empowered by acè to become priests and authoritative figures in African and African diasporic religions.

In Vodún, the ritual transformation that one's being undergoes is not necessarily a result of having learned new, often secret information. Rather, it is brought on by moving ritually through secret spaces such as the sacred forest; observing secret objects such as shrines; and undergoing bodily transformations such as the shaving of one's head and ritual bathing (P. Johnson 2002). In this way, ritual helps individuals to develop occult ontologies that then empower them as Vodúnisants. Throughout this chapter, I will show how initiation candidates experience ritual secrecy; how those experiences change the occult ontologies of initiates; and how these changes support Vodún's global expansion as the religion encounters new situations and new social actors.

Vodún and the Power of Blood and Leaves

In Fɔngbè, the word for blood (*hùn*) and the word for divinity (vodún) are often used interchangeably, as is seen in the Fon words *hunxɔ̀/vodúnxɔ̀* (spirit temple), *hunsì/vodúnsì* (initiate; literally, "bride of the spirit"), or *hunnɔ̀/ vodúnɔ̀* (possessor of the spirit). Blood is as much a component of Vodún's social fabric as are the spirits and the ancestors themselves. No other ritual in Dahomean history proves this point better than the *xwetanú* (annual customs). Originally designed to be a time for individual families to honor their ancestors and spirits, and to pay respect to their heads of household, during King Agajá's reign (r. 1718–40), annual customs became a state-sponsored event. According to Bay, nineteenth-century accounts of the ritual "describe human and animal sacrifices, parades of the riches of the king, military demonstrations, political debates, and mutual gift-giving between the king and the population" (1998: 12). Today, even though a rich collective memory of human ritual sacrifice still exists, animal sacrifice has become the ritual standard. Blood sacrifice was, and still is, too important to the ways in which Vodún devotees understand their place in the cosmos to reject. On any given day in Bénin, one can watch as devotees nourish their ancestors and their spirits who live in Kútómè (literally, the "land of the dead")—an invisible world that is parallel to their own—with the blood of sacrificial animals. In Kútómè, as in the visible world, families maintain households and active relationships with each other and with the vodún (see Bay 1998: 22–24). Those in the living world need the spirit world to help them to maintain their destinies and to overcome life's problems, while the spirit world needs the living for nourishment. Without each other, the existences of the living, the dead, and the spirits would all be in jeopardy. For these reasons, Béninois Vodúnisants understand animal sacrifice to be required for all initiations. When I asked Jean, "Could initiations be performed without blood sacrifice?" Jean just laughed and said, "That's not Vodún." For Jean, as for other Vodún practitioners, Vodún and blood sacrifice do not just depend on each other—they are inseparable.

Despite the centrality of blood in ritual, the varied meanings reflected in animal sacrifice have begun to change, to meet the needs of a diversifying group of devotees and initiates. Animal sacrifice is a multivocal symbolic act that draws from the "totality of human behavior and experience" and from a growing variety of religious agents in order to affirm one's connections to their cosmologies and worldviews (Beidelman 1997: 543). There are those animals that are sacrificed ritually in order to incarnate a spirit into what English speakers might call a shrine or, more problematically, a fetish (Landry 2016). For example, to incarnate Lĕgbá, the spirit of the crossroads, a rooster that has been force-fed red palm oil is buried alive with other ingredients upon which Lĕgbá's distinctive mound is built. While sacrifices such as these follow ritual rules that at times make the animal's meat unavailable to consume, the animals help to make the spirits physically accessible by charging the spirit's acè, which is contained in an amalgam of secret objects.

As important as incarnating sacrifices are to Vodún, they are not performed every day, and they do not normally come with requests or pleas from the spirits' devotees. They exist to give life to a new shrine. Other sacrifices occur on a regular basis to nourish the spirits, the dead, and the living so as to maintain complex relationships between Kútómè and the earthly world. In these moments, when an animal is sacrificed and its blood is directed onto the vodún's material body (that is, the shrine), the blood nourishes the spirit's acè. In turn, the animal's meat nourishes the living community, thereby completing the reciprocal commitments between humanity, the ancestors, and the vodún. Blood sacrifice is fundamental. Each time an animal is sacrificed, the resulting distribution of blood (to the spirits) and meat (to the community) reinforces the value of kinship by unifying an individual's earthly and spiritual communities under a shared meal. Vodún is, at its core, a system that supports the health, value, and memory of one's family (Brown 2001), and ritual sacrifice is central to the ways in which these connections are expressed and maintained symbolically.

As Vodún becomes increasingly global, the religion and its rituals begin to take on new meanings for devotees who are becoming progressively diverse. A couple of U.S.-based practitioners have made attempts to reject animal sacrifice, citing their "spiritual evolution" away from needing blood or the "barbarism" of ritual sacrifice. Over the years, these individuals have managed to market their Americanized versions of West African religions to a large number of devotees who are willing to pay thousands upon thousands of dollars to avoid sacrificing animals during their initiations. To the critical observer, their attempts to eschew animal sacrifice reflect racist and neocolonialist histories whereby American and European people argue arrogantly that they know what is best for African religions. Béninois themselves have largely rejected these types of foreign spiritual seekers as "charlatans" because, for Béninois, abjuring animal sacrifice is incongruous to their understanding of the world, insofar as it simultaneously threatens their reciprocal relationships with their spirits and jeopardizes the social importance of family.

For their part, foreign initiates tend to perform sacrifice to appease the spirits, thank them for their influence, or entice the spirits to work on their behalf. Of the dozen or so rituals I have seen performed in the New York metropolitan area, the animals' meat was eaten only once. Foreign spiritual seekers often lack the skills to butcher the animals properly and frequently see the process as "too much of a hassle." Depending on the locale, most of the time, animal carcasses are simply left in the forest, on the side of the road, or thrown into shopping-center dumpsters; one U.S.-based group even tosses the bodies of their sacrificial animals into a large, thirty-foot-deep, lye-filled pit. In all these cases, the symbolic relationship that connects sacrifice to nourishment—not just of the spirits but also of the community—has been reimagined. While still an essential part of these rituals, blood thereby takes on new meaning. Retaining its symbolic power as a connective force linking the human and spirit worlds, blood also embodies the transnational ritual authenticity that foreign practitioners need both to attract clients and to participate effectively in Vodún's global marketplace. As one American initiate said, "Practicing Vodún without blood is just play. If I decided to do that, no one would take me seriously. I would never have clients."

Despite the variations, then, blood sacrifice contributes to the ways in which both Béninois and foreign initiates fundamentally make sense of the world—one through their relationship with the spirit world and family; the other through their relationship with the spirit world and capitalism. This difference, I believe, reflects the power that Abrahamic-centric definitions of religion have in the lives of European and American practitioners. For them, religion is, as Christianity has taught them, about their relationship with the unseen world—the realm of spirits, gods, and divinities. It is about appeasing those beings and influencing them to help you when you need them most. However, for Béninois, Vodún, like so many other African religions, blurs the boundaries between the sacred and the secular by focusing on one's relationship with their families and their communities, of which the spirits are a part. As such, it is no surprise that foreign initiates deemphasize those rituals that index the value of one's family in favor of focusing more explicitly on their personal relationships with the vodún.

Leaves

If blood sacrifice is the symbolic event that nourishes divine power, leaves are the objects that embody acè's limitless potential and serve as the building blocks for the spirits' power and material presence on earth. Perhaps Aaron, a Béninois Vodún priest, said it best when he told me, "Vodún is nothing more than a way of making the natural power of leaves immortal." Here, Aaron was indexing the spirits' prominent position as "natural energies" whose acè and full spiritual potential come from the surrounding environment.

Indeed, for many in Fonland, what Westerners might consider "supernatural" is squarely a part of the natural world. Because of Vodún's strong connection to local ecology, the religion is almost defined by the imputed supernatural power of leaves, zoological curios (e.g., African grey parrot feathers, turtle shells, and dried chameleons), and other naturally occurring objects such as meteorites, soil from the crossroads, and kaolin. While in Bénin, I found Vodún's connection to the environment to be a dominant theme, regardless of where in southern Bénin I happened to be. To manage the effects of international interest, Vodún's portability, flexibility, and global value were continually tested, as the religion's "natural world" enlarged transnationally to include urban spaces such as New York City.

Nevertheless, part of Vodún's international appeal is its adaptability to change—and leaves are an important element of that story. In Vodún, spirit shrines are made with plants. Leaves, when brought together with other objects and awakened with sacrifice, allow communities to create gods (Landry 2016). Foreign spiritual seekers often become obsessed with learning these ritual recipes. Indeed, Jean claimed that these new practitioners "focus too much on what leaves are needed to make vodún." I discovered this critique one evening, long after my initiation, when Jean was teaching me and one of his sons which leaves were necessary to incarnate Lĕgbá.

"We don't have these leaves back home," I said to Jean.

"That doesn't matter, Tim. Walk in your forest and discover the leaves you do have. Use divination to learn which leaves you need. You'll figure it out. Every place has its power."

With that simple statement, Jean explained to me why he felt foreign practitioners focused on the wrong questions. For Jean, "every place had its power," and part of being a good Vodún priest meant determining what those powers were, and how one might use them effectively. Of course, Jean was right. It struck me at that moment that Haitian Vodou, Cuban Lucumí, and Brazilian Candomblé were evidence of communities finding the power of their own land. For Jean, this is a point missed by many foreign spiritual seekers.

Whereas Jean is determined to serve the spirits in a way that works, foreign practitioners are concerned deeply with performing a ritual in a way that they imagine to be "authentic." Strict ritual consistency, even where it may not exist among Africans, allows foreign spiritual seekers to verify and, therefore, authenticate the "validity" of their product—that is, their own initiation. As a result, despite claims from people such as Jean that, when it comes to leaves, Vodún is spatially relative, foreign initiates go through considerable effort to cater to their clients, who often expect rituals to be performed in a way that they imagine to be authentically African. To achieve this, they may order special plants from a growing number of Internet sites; call their initiators to ask them to ship plants to the United States; and incorporate those leaves that are used in religions such as Vodou and Lucumí because, as one American initiate explained to me, "we already know they work."

Learning the hidden powers of forests—and especially of leaves—was a theme that emerged repeatedly. Jean was not the only individual I encountered who felt that the forest was key to Vodún cosmology. One day, while visiting Frédéric, a friend who lived in Abomey, he and I began talking about the power of leaves. Frédéric was a priest of both Sakpatá and Dàn. He was also a schoolteacher and an engineer. Frédéric and I often discussed his initial reservations about being chosen by Fá to follow his father as the family's Vodún priest, especially since he already had an established career outside of the spiritual realm. He admitted to me that before his initiation he worried what his professional colleagues might think of him. Feeling bifurcated by his responsibilities to his family's spirits and by his carefully constructed identity as an engineer, he often felt unable to discuss what he called "intellectual Vodún" with either his Vodún or professional colleagues. As such, he especially enjoyed having thoughtful conversations with me about the spirits and, particularly, the undiscovered potential of leaves. He supposed, for example, that people once had the powers of invisibility, translocation, and polymorphism, all granted through the careful combination of different leaves, but now, he believed, all these powers were relegated to the realm of witchcraft. Frédéric seemed to think that this shift occurred as "good people" converted to Christianity and Islam and jettisoned the powers that Vodún could provide. Even so, Frédéric claimed that through service to the vodún, by paying attention to one's dreams, or by the will of the tiny, spritelike spirits (*azizǎ*) reported to live in the deep forest, these powers can be recovered.

While Frédéric believes that leaves are key to unlocking tremendous powers, my walks in the forest with Jean were never about recovering lost spiritual abilities—although part of me wished that while in the forest we would stumble upon some azizǎ just as told in the stories, to be taught powers such as invisibility and teleportation that bend Western notions of physical science. But learning how to become invisible was hardly central to my personal or professional goals. More prosaically, before my initiation, I was faced with having to learn the local names of leaves, along with their magical, ritual, and medicinal qualities. When Jean and his nephew Eddie took me into the forest, we walked side by side—visiting sacred shrines, groves, and plants, sometimes walking through the dense forest and other times using a web of trails that marked the magical landscape around Fátòmè (Gottlieb 2008). During our time in the forest, Jean and Eddie rapidly pointed out some of the many leaves that are sacred to Fá. As we moved from leaf to leaf, I took photographs and quickly—and rather futilely—scribbled the local names as best as I could, along with overwhelmingly complex ritual descriptions of the ways each plant is used.

Trips into the forest did not always include fastidious note-taking. More often, our trips were to find the leaves that we needed to complete an upcoming ceremony or initiation. While these were ethnographically rich moments,

I always found the process frustrating, as some of the plants were hard to find, and still others came with multiple names (often in Fon and Yorùbá) that chaotically swirled in my head and never managed to coalesce into anything workable. Over the course of fifteen months, I managed to learn the names and occult properties of only several dozen out of hundreds of plants.[2] Learning the leaves and all their religious and medical correspondences was never my strength, and Jean knew it, but he was always gracious, as he recognized that not every student could be good at everything.

Despite these challenges, the powers of plants did not remain entirely elusive to me. One plant, known locally as *agbègbé*, occupies a prominent place in local Vodún discourse and had a profound effect on the way I approached and experienced my apprenticeship with Jean.[3] Agbègbé's roots are indiscernible, as the plant grows parasitically on other plants, wrapping itself around its hosts' branches. This quality frames the way in which Béninois, especially diviners, apply meaningful interpretations to the symbolic and occult power of agbègbé. A Fon proverb, "the agbègbé root-digger will never succeed" (*Agbègbékúntɔ́ nɔ́ mɔ̀ dò tɔ̀n ǎ*), highlights agbègbé's social and religious value, as the proverb teaches locals that seeking Vodún's metaphorical roots is a task in futility. Similarly pointing to the importance of agbègbé, the art historian Dana Rush has written, "Those who understand Vodun will never be found searching for the 'proverbial roots' of the agbégbé [*sic*] vine. Indeed, in approaching Vodun, it is best to put away the shovel, for Western logic does not work in a system that is fundamentally opposed to making any empirical sense" (2013: 45–46). Building on this notion, Fá diviners understand the agbègbé plant to be intimately linked to *Èjì-Ogbè*, the first and most important of the 256 signs found in the Fá corpus, and the sign that, like the indiscernible and therefore seemingly endless root system of the agbègbé plant, represents limitless opportunities.[4] Like agbègbé's roots that wrap around its hosts' branches, my experiences as a diviner's apprentice enveloped my fieldwork. As a foreign diviner, I was intimately involved in borrowing and "appropriating" cultural values, ideas, practices, and beliefs. The twists and knots highlighted both the challenges and rewards that were brought forth by my involvement in Vodún. In a way, I had become agbègbé.

Learning which leaves are purported to grant metaphysical powers such as invisibility is only part of what new initiates must master. They must also learn which plants, such as agbègbé, might reveal important social lessons and which leaves, when combined, can incarnate the vodún into shrines. Along with being fed sacrificial blood, all vodún that I encountered were also constructed by combining a number of secret, vodún-specific leaves. In some cases, such as with Lĕgbá, particular leaves are buried in the ground along with numerous other secret objects, forming the hidden body of the vodún in material form. In other cases, such as with Fá, sacred leaves are macerated in a barrel of water to make "vodún water" (*vodúnsìn*) that is then used to wash, and, therefore, create, new shrines and initiates alike. Either way, as Jean once told me, "Vodún does not exist without the forest."

My First Steps

Because leaves are the central component of nearly all Vodún rituals, it did not take long for me to begin to see the forest as one of the religion's most important cosmological symbols. When Jean or some of his apprentices wanted to venture into the forest looking for leaves, I was always eager to accompany them. I figured these long walks would eventually help me to understand the depth of the forest's power within Vodún's social fabric. One late afternoon, Jean asked me and his sixteen-year-old son, Auguste, to accompany him into the forest to search for leaves for an upcoming initiation. After no more than thirty minutes into the forest, Jean began collecting a leaf I did not recognize. Before I could ask him how one might use the leaf in ritual, he looked at Auguste and said, "After we initiate this man coming from Cotonou tomorrow, we should start thinking about doing your initiation before you go back to school."

"Are you ready to be initiated?" I asked Auguste.

"Yes! I will finally be able to eat acè with my father and brothers."

"There's more to it than that," Jean laughed.

Acè is also what Fon speakers call the specially prepared meat of those animals that have been sacrificed to Gbădù, the female vodún who is understood to be Fá's wife and who is one of the cosmic forces who gave birth to the universe. Only initiates—whose bodies have been prepared ritually— can touch, butcher, and consume the animals that have been killed over her shrine-body. For Auguste, being able to participate in these rituals certainly increased his spiritual power, but more importantly to him, it played a significant role in his becoming a man (cf. Bellman 1984; Beidelman 1997; Ferme 2001). The initiation ensured that he would no longer have to eat with the women and children. Now, even if only during ritual, he could eat with the men.

Auguste had been anticipating this moment for a few years, and Jean was ready to pass his legacy on to another one of his sons. Both Jean and Auguste were prepared to walk into the sacred forest together from which Auguste would emerge transformed.[5]

"I think I want to initiate you and Auguste together," Jean said, looking to me.

We had started to prepare for my initiation a couple of weeks before, but we had not yet settled on a date. I knew Jean liked to do initiations in small groups or pairs because it saved him time and minimized the number of animals that would need to be sacrificed. However, I was nervous to prove to Jean that I could recognize each of Fá's 256 binary patterns (dù) that are required for divination (see Bascom 1991). But I knew that I could not refuse Jean's offer. I did everything I could to suppress my fear. I looked at Jean and said, "Yes, if you're ready. I'm ready."[6]

Receiving Fá's Forest

On a Tuesday morning, just after sunrise, Auguste and I sat on the short cement wall that bordered the small cinder-block building that housed Fátòmὲ's Gbădù shrine. We each wore a large, loose-fitting shirt called a *boubou* and wrapped our waists in yards of multicolored cloth (*pagne*). After a couple of hours, Jean and the other diviners joined us and began to prepare to escort Auguste and me to the sacred forest.

Auguste and I were each handed a short fiber rope, which we were supposed to use to guide the young blonde she-goats that were tied to the other end. Before we were able to gain full control of the goats, a woven-fiber cage with four chickens and a rooster inside was precariously balanced on our heads. We were ready to greet the forest. Honoré, Jean's ninety-eight-year-old father, led the way as we all followed him, Jean, and ten or so other diviners into the forest. With each step, as we progressed closer to the secret, our bodies, unbeknownst to us, began to change. At that point, steps could not be untaken, and sights could not be unseen. As we approached the symbolic center of the spirits' divine power, our bodies had become part of the vodún's social world. We could hear the voices of the men who were singing Fá's praise. Their forest melodies were punctuated only by the clickety-clack of the small iron bells that hung from the *fásén* (Yr., Ọpá Ọ̀ṣun) that led our way. The fásén is a metal staff that stands four to five feet tall. Its top is capped with a six-inch metal disk and, in some cases, a forged iron image of a rooster.[7] The staff's shaft is adorned with a dozen or more cone-shaped bells and a metal hook that points upward, from which the heads of sacrificial roosters are hung as a constant reminder to death that he must stay away.[8] (See Figure 1.) Margaret Drewal and Henry Drewal have shown that the fásén "represents the power of the [diviner] to conquer death . . . [and it] acts as a weapon against death and other destructive forces" (1983: 65). Additionally, the fásén indexes the unification of the diviner and Fá as a single synergetic force that, when brought together through initiation, has the power to conquer death and adversity through divination. The fásén's power over death was exemplified as we advanced, stopping at each of the crossroads that we encountered so that the fásén's enduring power could chase away death from everyone present, and especially from Auguste and me, as our lack of initiation made us particularly vulnerable. After we passed through our third set of crossroads, it was clear that we had already experienced too much to turn back. With only the night's darkness and the depth of the forest ahead of us, the transformation had already begun.

Eventually, we found ourselves at the entrance of fázùn, Fá's sacred forest and Gbǎdù's current resting place. I noticed quickly that the trail that led into the forest was obscured by a blanket of shredded palm fronds (azàn). Azàn (Yr. màrìwò) serve as an "emblem of sacredness and warning" (Doris 2011: 86). The palm fronds separate the sacred forest from the everyday lived forest, thereby empowering the sacred forest with presence and the ability to affect the ways in which humans exist in the world (Kohn 2013). Put another way, the palm fronds give the sacred forest an ontology that is at once dangerous and transformative (Figure 2).

To the right of the path sat a small Lĕgbá figure in a sunbaked terra-cotta dish that was brought to this location only during ritual events (Figure 3). When Lĕgbá guarded the passageway into the forest, everyone knew that Gbǎdù was present, adding to the forest's power and danger. Before we could appreciate the forest's potency, Jean offered a rooster to Lĕgbá and poured water and orange Fanta at the grove's entrance, to ask Gbǎdù's permission to return the following day for our initiations. Breaking a kola nut (vì) into its four natural segments, Jean tossed the kola nut onto the ground and asked the forest if our offerings were accepted. Two of the kola nut's lobes landed facing down and two landed facing up, indicating a cool and balanced "yes" (see R. Thompson 2011).

Figure 1. The fásén, the initiatory staff of the Fá diviner.
Photograph by the author.

Figure 2. Azàn marking the entrance to the fázùn. Photograph by the author.

"Good!" Jean announced. "The offerings were accepted. We can come back tomorrow."

Auguste and I had both received confirmation from Gbǎdù—who, from a safe and unknowable distance, had agreed to accept us into her sacred grove. With each ritual movement—whether it be physical steps or ritual checkpoints—our bodies changed, as we were protected from the danger and risk that emanated from Gbǎdù. These ritual steps imbued us with the social capital that we needed to overcome the resistance that kept us away from Gbǎdù and the divine and social power she conferred. Only through ritual were we able to navigate through Gbǎdù's thick aura of secrecy that was designed, paradoxically, to resist our entrance. With permission given, we could return the following day.

This brief but important part of the initiation ritual effectively separates new initiation candidates from the community's noninitiates by bringing them to the forest's edge. The forest's secrets beckoned us and pulled at our curiosity. As Auguste and I peered into the dark forest, our liminality became

Figure 3. Lĕgbá at the entrance of the fázùn. Note the years'
worth of sacrifices and offerings that have accumulated on the shrine.
Photograph by the author.

clear. While ritual allowed us to stand where, until now, we had not been allowed to stand, the palm-frond curtain warned us against entering the forest completely. The secrets that were shrouded by the forest would have to wait. Until then, our imaginations would only contribute to the secrets' growing strength (Bellman 1984; Taussig 1999; Gottlieb 2000; Newell 2012). We had to admit that as badly as we both wanted to see Gbădù, we just were not ready. Our bodies were too vulnerable. We were ritually, and therefore ontologically, unprepared to go any further.

"Don't look into the forest too long! You'll both go blind. You're not ready to see Gbădù," Jean said, catching Auguste and me staring blankly down the path that led to Gbădù's inner sanctum.

Being initiated into Fá means undergoing those changes to our being that will allow us to move safely through Gbădù's dangerous aura of secrecy. The gradual steps toward the forest, the asking of permission to enter the forest, and the warnings against peering into the forest all coalesce to add value and social power to ritual secrecy in Vodún. Through a process that Johnson has called "secretism," or the "the active milling, polishing, and promotion of reputation of secrets" (P. Johnson 2002: 3), one can see that our slow but steady exposure to ritual secrecy empowered us and the spirits' social efficacy. Successfully negotiating one's way through ritual secrecy—but not necessarily knowing the secret—becomes the force by which Béninois authorize foreign initiates to act as priests as they are transformed into vessels for acè, or what Johnson called the "body-as-secret" (P. Johnson 2005: 184). In this way, an initiate's body—through a gradual and ritualized exposure to secrecy and divine power—is transformed not necessarily into someone with a new identity or status, but into a contained secret.

Our visit to the forest's edge prepared us to receive Fá's sacred palm nuts (fádékwín). The transformation that an initiate's fádékwín undergo during one's initiation parallels the ontological changes that are experienced by the devotee. That is to say, in Fá's case, both the devotee and Fá are initiated so that they may be imbued with both acè and spiritual authority. Successfully venturing into the sacred forest and completing the ritual ensure that both Fá and the initiate are transformed in ways that help them to realize their full potential as they become a part of each other's physical and spiritual selves.

The next day, at sunrise, Jean woke us from our sleep in Fá's house and asked us to confirm our desire to enter the sacred forest.

"Are you ready? Are you sure you want to do this?" Jean asked.

"Yes," Auguste and I responded, almost in perfect unison.

With our eyes still adjusting to the early morning light, Jean ushered us
into the ritual room he used in the village for Fá veneration. The two front-
facing windows were closed and tightly latched; only the door, slightly ajar,
allowed the sunlight to trickle into the dark room. Illuminated by a dusty
beam of light, I could see that the straw mat in the center of the room was
nearly covered with bundles of sacred and powerful plants. The heat combined with the scent of livestock and with the leaves' natural fragrances—
some sweet and some pungent—made it difficult to breathe. Against the
back wall, where light could scarcely touch, I could barely make out four
small, palm nut–filled terra-cotta dishes whose rounded bottoms caused
them to wobble against the slick cement floor. I was certain that these were
the palm nuts that would accompany Auguste and me into the sacred forest.

Romar, and a few of Jean's other apprentices, poured fresh well water
into a large blue plastic container that was embossed with "Made in China"
on the brim.[9] Soon afterward, everyone began to sing magical songs that
purportedly had the ability to awaken the leaves' hidden powers. One by
one, the leaves were crushed in the water to release their natural oils and
spiritual essences. By the end of the ritual, the water had been stained a
bright—almost fluorescent—green. Our fádékwín were washed in this magical bath, refreshed and empowered by the leaves' power, and then placed
back into their terra-cotta dishes. Those present offered Fá kola nuts, gin,
and an orange Fanta. Auguste and I were given a small piece of the bitter
kola nut to consume in communion with Fá. When I bit into the kola nut my
mouth filled with the nut's distinctive dry, bitter taste that was only allevi-
ated when I took a sip of sweet Fanta and a mouthful of gin. Auguste, of
course, enjoyed the kola nut and drank the Fanta and gin, not as a reprieve
but just as a part of the process.

After everyone had a taste of the kola nut, Jean added salt and pepper to
Fá's terra-cotta dishes and filled them with just enough red palm oil so as to
barely miss submerging the tops of the palm nuts. In quick succession, two
hens—one white and one beige—were sacrificed (Figure 4). Their blood
poured from the gashes on their throats and into the dishes, where it mixed
with the bright orange color of the palm oil. The fádékwín were washed
clean of the palm oil and blood and then taken, alongside Auguste and me,
into the forest.

Following behind the fásέn, Jean and his diviners once again led Auguste
and me to fázùn. After sacrificing another rooster to Lĕgbá, we approached
the fásέn, which was now planted into the ground just outside the forest's

Figure 4. Romar sacrificing chickens to Fá. Fádékwín rest in two terra-cotta
bowls that have been filled with palm oil. Photograph by the author.

entrance. Each diviner present, along with Auguste and me, was marked by
having palm fronds tied to our left wrists and ankles. Just as the forest had
been demarcated by the azàn, now the palm fronds marked our bodies as
secret, powerful, and dangerous.

"Put your left hand on the fásén and put your foot at the base," Jean
instructed. Forming a symbolic community of diviners who are joined in
their ability to speak to Fá, each of the diviners who were present placed
their hands on top of ours and their feet at the base, with the fásén passing
between their big toe and second toe, one on top of the other (Figure 5).
Buried in the ground, at the fásén's base, were our fádékwín. For ten minutes
or more, we held on to the top of the fásén, while Fá, buried under the
ground, "grasped" the base, under the pressure of our feet. Connected by the
fásén, we all sang the names of the sixteen primary binary patterns (dù)
found in Fá divination, in order to bring them into being. At this moment, Fá
and diviner began to merge—linked together by the earth and held up by the
power of the fásén.

Figure 5. Diviners placing their marked hands on top of the new initiate's hand, which is placed on the top of the fásén. Photograph by the author.

"Find your fádékwín!" Jean shouted. "They are buried under the fásén."

Auguste and I quickly fell to our knees and began to dig with our hands at the fásén's base. One by one, the fádékwín emerged from the earth, and one by one they were collected in a small calabash and rinsed with Gbǎdù's powerful and secret medicine (Gbǎdùsìn). Enacting an important story in Yorùbá mythology, whereby Ọ̀rùnmìlà (Fon, Fá) sacrifices a crying rooster to chase away death, a rooster was sacrificed to the fásén, but only after its tail feathers were plucked to compel the rooster to cry out in pain, thereby diverting death's attention from everyone present (Drewal and Drewal 1983: 65–66).

With our fádékwín washed and fed, Lĕgbá placated, and death's dangerous gaze averted, Auguste and I were finally ready to enter the fázùn. We knelt at the forest's edge. In front of us, stopping just before the forest's entrance, were two columns of evenly spaced, grapefruit-sized mounds of dirt—eight to the left and eight to the right, with a much larger mound at the apex between the two columns. Each of the small mounds embodied one of the sixteen major dù found in the Fá corpus. Resting on each of the sixteen red-soil mounds was a single bright white cowrie shell. Before Auguste and I were able to thoroughly survey our surroundings, we were blindfolded.

"Can you see?" Jean asked.

Too afraid and too anxious to say anything else, we both responded by saying "no."

Because I was the oldest, Jean began with me and then moved to Auguste. Moving left to right, he pressed our foreheads into the small mounds, effectively pushing the cowrie shells into the earth, to pay the dù for passage into the forest. We ended by lying on our stomachs, between the two columns, our arms crossed under our chins, with the entrance to the fázùn just a few feet from our faces (Figure 6). We were now closer than we had ever been to Gbǎdù. Just as the diviners had just placed pressure on Fá a few moments before, at the fásén, using the foot, Jean now put pressure on our backs as we hugged the earth and prepared to enter the forest.

"Okay, stand up!" An unfamiliar voice shouted.

Upon rising to our feet, our blindfolds were removed.

"Tilt your head back," Romar commanded.

Romar held our eyes open and flushed them with the Gbǎdùsìn—the same shea butter and snail blood–fortified herbal mixture that had washed our fádékwín a few moments earlier. He used the red tail feather of an African grey parrot to channel the leaf water directly into our eyes. One by one,

Figure 6. Auguste preparing to enter the fázùn. Photograph by the author.

all the initiated diviners who would be entering the sacred forest washed their eyes with the same medicine, to prevent Gbǎdù's explosive and creative power from causing blindness or even death. The mixture, however necessary, stung my eyes. Auguste seemed unaffected. For him, this initiation was just as much about his masculinity as it was about learning his destiny. Auguste had more to prove socially than I did. Before walking past the palm-frond barrier and into the forest, I rubbed my eyes to find relief from the burning.

"Don't do that, Tim. It's supposed to hurt. It means the leaves are working," Jean reassured me.

Fighting back the pain, Auguste and I both smiled at Jean and waited for his instructions. With Gbǎdùsìn running from our swollen, bloodshot eyes and down our cheeks, we were finally ready to "receive Fá's forest" and walk into the space that had, up until now, been forbidden.[10]

After entering the forest on our knees, Jean led us into the forest's inner grove that was hidden behind a second palm-frond curtain.

"This is Gbǎdù's home," Jean announced.

For the first time, we had seen Fá's secret. Gbǎdù and *lɔkpò*, a large split iroko branch on which the secret signs of Fá are marked, sat in the center of the small grove. For the first time, Auguste and I knelt before Gbǎdù and watched as Jean and his other apprentices tended to the spirit who is believed to have given birth to the cosmos. I could not help but feel overcome by the symbolic potency and awe of the space. It was as if we sat at the center of the universe from which humanity and the spirits were born. Each of the rituals and conversations that Auguste and I had experienced up until now empowered this moment. I imagined a parallel ritual happening in Kútómè. In my mind's eye, I watched as Gbǎdù initiated Fá into *our* mysteries, and I thought about how Fá and the other vodún must have consumed the sacrificial blood in the same way that we would soon consume the initiatory meat that the ritual provided. Just as quickly as it started, the ritual was over and the secret revealed. Our bodies were changed forever. If we decided never to participate in Vodún again, we could not unsee Gbǎdù or unexperience our initiations—we were forever changed. With Gbǎdù placated, we left the inner grove of the forest and moved to the forest's larger meeting area.

"Sit there! Pick up your Fá and divine," Jean commanded, pointing to a small mound of dirt.

In front of the mound on which we were to sit was another dirt mound that was about eighteen inches wide and perfectly flat.

"This is the forest's *fátè*. You will draw the dù there," Jean explained.

Outside of the forest, the fátè is a wooden divining board upon which the diviner draws the dù that are revealed during divination. The edge of the board is usually intricately carved with images that reflect stories from mythology or important lessons that are revealed by the dù. Indexing a cross-section of the calabash in which the universe is believed to rest, the smooth, flat center of the board on which the diviner inscribes the dù is simultaneously the center of the universe and the mythical place of creation.[11]

In the forest, everything was simpler—or, as Jean described it, the way in which "God intended." Even as an outsider, I appreciated the cumulative and ephemeral power that came from inscribing the dù, which revealed my personal destiny, onto the forest floor where hundreds of diviners before me had done the same (Rush 2010). In this way, the forest's divine power accumulates spiritual potency and effectiveness over time. The power attributed to accumulation in Vodún has also been noted by Rush, who argues that accumulation and an object's forever unfinished nature—such as the never-finished forest floor on which dù are inscribed endlessly—are the roots of "Vodun's aesthetic power" (2013: 34).

We were about to perform divination for the first time to determine under which one of the 256 signs our priesthoods would be born. I clenched the sixteen fádékwín in my palm and began to ask Fá to disclose my dù. The dù would reveal insights into my personal destiny, which taboos I must respect, and which of the vodún were most important to me as a priest. As I removed the palm nuts from their calabash dish, I began to feel nervous. When Jean performed divination, he made the process seem effortless and elegant. There was a certain beauty to the way he manipulated the fádékwín. I knew from the way my hands were beginning to sweat that my attempt would be disastrous. I did not have Jean's forty years of experience or Auguste's cultural habitus that he cultivated as a child pretending to perform divination using small stones or nuts that he found on the forest floor. For me, divination was truly foreign.

To speak to Fá, the diviner holds sixteen of his or her fádékwín in the palm of the left hand while quickly lowering the right palm, cupped slightly, toward the fádékwín. In a quick, almost invisible gesture, a skilled diviner tosses the sixteen palm nuts into the air while almost simultaneously catching the fádékwín in the right hand, revealing that either one or two palm nuts remain resting in the diviner's left palm. When one palm nut remains, using his or her left middle and ring fingers, in a single upward stroke, the diviner marks two lines, each one to two inches long, onto the fátè. If two palm nuts remain, only one line is drawn. This process is then repeated eight times, in two columns, moving first from right to left and then from top to bottom, until all of the sign's eight segments are revealed.

My sweaty palms did not make this complex task easier. As my left palm met my right, four of the fádékwín fell to the ground. Jean picked them up, placed them back in my hand, and quietly said, "Again!"

After half a dozen clumsy attempts, I finally started to familiarize myself with the feel of the palm nuts in my hand. While my efforts were not as graceful as Jean's, I managed to reveal my sign.

"Call the name, Tim! It's not there until you call its name."

"*Wólì-Gbè*," I announced.

"You must trust Fá to live a peaceful life," Honoré proclaimed.

Fá had begun to reveal himself to me. Little by little, I would start to learn what it means to be a *bokɔ́nɔ̀* (diviner; Yr., *babaláwo*).

After Auguste and I learned our signs, Jean shaved our heads. The removal of one's hair, which also occurs to mourn the death of a family member, simultaneously marks the ritual death of one's uninitiated self and one's birth as a new diviner who, through a relationship with Fá, can now shed the past and overcome future struggles. This portion of the ritual marked the first time that initiation was inscribed physically onto our bodies. Our shaven heads, which would stay that way for at least a couple of weeks, would signal to the community that we were recently initiated.

"Hold the bundle with your hand," Jean instructed as he balanced a heavy, six-foot bundle of materials on our freshly shaven heads. "We are going to the lake to finish your initiation."

Balancing on our heads the bundles, which I estimated must have weighed a good fifteen pounds each, we followed Jean and the other diviners to the lake, where our bodies were ritually bathed and wrapped in new white cloth. Our heads, where our souls are believed to reside, were covered in kaolin and then marked with a single strand of Fá's ubiquitous alternating green and yellow glass beads. In the middle of our foreheads, tucked behind the beaded strand, Jean placed a single red tail feather of the African grey parrot.

"This will ward off jealousy. Don't lose it," Jean said, as he secured the feather.

Feeling refreshed from the ritual bath, Auguste and I followed Jean and the other diviners to Fátòmè. When we emerged from the forest, we found the entire village awaiting our return. We were greeted with cheers and with invitations to join the rest of the community in dance. Before dark, we washed our Fá one final time and offered him a she-goat. After the goat was sacrificed and butchered, the goat's head and portions of its meat were left to rest on our fádékwín so they could absorb Fá's divine power. The fádékwín were covered and then draped in palm fronds, thereby marking Fá's final transformation into a secret (Figure 7).

"Give me your left wrists," Jean said. "Take this. It will protect you from an early death. It will mark you as a child of Fá," Jean added as he tied a small bracelet of alternating yellow and green beads onto our wrists.

The following day, the goat's meat was cooked and consumed. In so doing, Auguste and I took Fá's secrets and divine power into our stomachs, thereby allowing us to complete our transformation and become diviners.

Over the previous two days, Auguste and I had successfully navigated our way through the sacred forest and into Gbădù's inner grove. We had seen

Figure 7. The fádékwín were draped in palm fronds.
Photograph by the author.

Gbădù and survived. We had learned of our destinies. We had offered sacrifices to Fá and Gbădù. We had consumed Gbădù's sacrificial meat that had previously been forbidden to us, thereby taking Fá's divine power into stomachs. We had shared meals of Fá's sacrificial meat with the community. Our heads had been shaved and marked in honor of Fá. Our bodies had been washed and draped in yards upon yards of bright white cloth. We had danced for the first time as bokónò. We were, for the first time, diviners.

When Acè Is Insufficient

After my initiation, I studied with Jean. During our sessions, he taught me how to consult with Fá and how to recognize each of the dù by sight. He gave me the power/right (acè) to construct shrines of spirits such as Lĕgbá, Gbădù, and even Fá himself—powers that are central to divination. As time

Figure 8. Egúngún. Photograph by the author.

continued, my studies deepened, and the residents of Fátòmè moved from being "informants" to friends who frequently invited me to ceremonies in neighboring villages. It did not take long for me to realize that my initiation into Fá had become socially inadequate. Because I was only initiated as a diviner and not as a member of any of the secret societies, I was often forced to sit on the sidelines and observe—a research strategy I had previously critiqued (Landry 2008). After expressing my frustration to Jean, he suggested that it was time to expand my knowledge of Vodún and become initiated into Egúngún and Orò, two of the major men's secret societies (Figure 8). He argued that this would allow me to participate more actively while also gaining a deeper understanding of the ways in which international spiritual seekers negotiate access to restricted—and often secret—spaces. With Jean's encouragement, I agreed.

My initiations into Egúngún and Orò (Fon Oló) unexpectedly bolstered my credibility in the eyes of many local practitioners. Jean insisted that my initiation into the major secret societies present at Fátòmè would expand my knowledge of Fá and make me both a more rounded and efficient diviner and a better anthropologist. Once I began to plan my initiations, I became increasingly anxious. If I had learned one thing in Bénin, it was that Egúngún and Orò societies especially demand respect through fear. Until this point, I had always kept these two societies at arm's length—observing their dynamism from afar. Frankly, the sight of an Egúngún or the blood-curdling night cry of Orò made me rightfully nervous. But I knew Jean was right, as I could not think of a single diviner who was not also initiated into Egúngún and Orò—two of the major ancestor societies in southern Bénin. Thus, with the support of Jean and my friends at Fátòmè, I agreed to prepare for initiation.

After spending a few weeks managing ceremonial logistics, the day came for my initiations into Egúngún and Orò. Bare-chested, wrapped at the waist in a white cloth, and blindfolded, I was led into the sacred forest of Orò (Yr., *Igborò*) by all the men of Fátòmè. After an hour of rituals, I emerged from the forest as an initiate of the Orò society. As is done with many young men who are initiated into these societies, I was quickly blindfolded once more and ushered into the Egúngún temple (*balɛ*) for my next initiation. Hidden from public space, I was taught the fundamental secrets of the society, which led to my emergence as a new initiate of a second secret society.

For a few days after my ceremonies, my initiators and friends continued to teach me the secret handshakes, passwords, gestures, and vocabularies of the two societies. My initiations led to me being included in Fátòmè's midnight Orò ceremonies and neighboring Egúngún dance performances. During these ceremonies, my knowledge was reinforced, sharpened, and broadened as my relationships with the villagers became more dynamic. Spending time with the other initiates in controlled ritual spaces fostered social experiences that seemed to create a sense of "delirium" among us (Durkheim 1965 [1912]: 218–26). Long ago, Durkheim argued that religiously induced "delirium" fostered what he called "social effervescence" when "men believe themselves transported into an entirely different world from the one they have before their eyes" (226). Like Durkheim, who recognized that religious "faith" and "belief" are often encouraged by "effervescent" experiences, it has been my experience that religious "delirium" perpetuates not only belief but also community. And it is the lasting effects of effervescent experiences that extend beyond ritual and into everyday life that provides practitioners of Vodún with a sense of value (Mossière 2007).

While initiation into secret societies helps to forge a strong community among local practitioners, as the Vodún community expands globally, shared effervescent experiences between local and international practitioners contribute to expanding everyone's concept of "community." This type of "communitas," as Victor Turner (1969) called it, helps to develop a strong sense of "solidarity" and "togetherness" that expands beyond Bénin's borders. The expansion of "community" has led to Vodún being more openly valued among some local Vodún practitioners. When I asked Alfred, a twenty-seven-year-old diviner, what he thought about international tourists who wanted to become initiated into Vodún, he said, "It's a good thing. Because now I know that the [Christian] missionaries are lying to us. Now I know that Vodún, and especially Fá, can help people all around the world, and that makes me happy."

This potential shift in Vodún's international capital as a result of a new basis for transnational communitas and shared effervescent ritual experiences has implications for the ways that both local and international people understand and participate in Vodún. For me, these group experiences helped to develop close relationships with my fellow initiates, based on a ritually created—and reinforced—sense of community that eventually led to me feeling (however incomplete) a part of the community.

As I participated in ceremonies more frequently, I became more comfortable with what I had learned. After a few months, I left Fátòmè to visit Michel, a friend who lived to the north in Abomey. Upon my arrival, I was met with a freshly killed hen stewed in a tomato sauce and poured over heaps of white rice. Over dinner and cold beers, Michel told me that we had been invited to attend a small Egúngún dance the following afternoon. He explained to me that the village chief would be honoring his ancestors in a remote village outside of Abomey. I was eager to participate and observe the ceremonies with which I had become intimately involved, but now in a different location. I thought that this would be a perfect opportunity for me to look at regional differences in ancestor veneration while also double-checking the information I had been taught in Fátòmè.

Once in the village, I was introduced to the village chief and Gérard, the head Egúngún priest. Michel explained that I had been already initiated into the Egúngún society and was eager to contribute to the day's festivities. Upon being summoned, greeted, and fed, the ancestors—draped in ornately sequined cloth—leave the safety of the temple to dance for the public, often providing festivalgoers with messages, warnings, or blessings. Locals maintain that the ancestors animate the elaborate costumes, and that each Egúngún is a manifestation of someone who once lived in the past and, through elaborate and expensive ceremonies, was transformed after death into an Egúngún. Community members can often recognize the precise ancestors who dance in specific costumes, thereby making each Egúngún the manifestation of a particular deceased member of the family, who is easily identified by the layers upon layers of cloth that beautifully spin and swirl as the Egúngún dances.

While entertaining, the ceremonies can be technically challenging for the audience, as onlookers are prohibited from touching all clothing worn by the Egúngún. In fact, touching the cloth can reportedly bring death to a person who breaks the taboo and is financially unable, or unwilling, to undergo elaborate cleansing and placation ceremonies. Aware of the dangers that come with Egúngún performances, those present typically remain alert and prepare to move quickly, should an Egúngún approach. The dance of the Egúngún plays out with Egúngún taunting onlookers by trying to touch them with their cloth through elaborate displays that involve chasing, charging, and beating onlookers with branches, paddles, and sticks. Meanwhile, spectators are running, dodging, and in turn even taunting the Egúngún, as initiates of the Egúngún society run along with the Egúngún, each armed with an intricately carved stick that they use to control the Egúngún and push the swishing cloth away from the public, thus keeping the audience safe from certain death (Figure 9). The taboos and performance mark the Egúngún as otherworldly, while the push-and-pull of the social drama that plays out during the performances seems to proclaim symbolically, and provide social evidence for, the power of the ancestors—who can, with a simple touch of cloth, take one's life. This display of power is then translated into everyday life as a verified belief—and has been "proven" countless times by the social drama that plays out each time an Egúngún dances.

As I watched the dance, I thought about the Egúngún's social power. I sat in awe as if it were the first time I had seen the ceremony. The symbolic chase that proved the Egúngún's power erupted before my eyes as one of the Egúngún approached me. I greeted him properly; he blessed my family and me. Just as I was beginning to enjoy the ceremony—just as the ceremony picked up in tempo, as the dances became more erratic, and the onlookers more brazen—Gérard leaned over to me and asked, "Would you like a tour?"

Unsure of the context he had in mind, I agreed—perhaps too flippantly. However, regardless of what he meant, I was there to learn, and the anthropologist in me could not turn down the opportunity. This jump-in-head-first approach to ethnography led to an event that turned into one of my most

Figure 9. Egúngún chasing onlookers. Photograph by the author.

frightening and complicated moments while in Bénin. Perhaps not surprisingly, what was to pass also proved to be one of my most compelling and
informative experiences.

We got up from our seats to take our mysterious "tour." From there, we
walked around the perimeter of the ceremonial area that had been demarcated by an ever-growing audience—all wanting to catch a glimpse of, and
sometimes taunt, the Egúngún. We then moved away from the group and
approached a small structure made of red mud and protected by a corrugated
tin door that had been haphazardly nailed into the hardened earthen walls.
Just past the entrance, carved into the mud wall was an image of an Egúngún.
It was then that I realized what Gérard meant. He was taking me into the
balε, the ceremonial, and highly restricted, center of the Egúngún cult, where
only initiates were allowed. I noticed the perfunctory Egúngún shrine resting
in the corner. The offerings of red palm oil, chicken blood, liquor, and kola
nuts were fresh. They glistened and coagulated on the shrine's surface in a
cacophony of colors and textures. Egúngún themselves walked among the
initiates as they waited for their turns to dance and perform for the "audience" that awaited their attention outside.

When I breached the inner doorway of the temple, everyone froze. Some twenty or thirty sets of eyes fixated on me. Finally, after what felt like ten minutes but must have been only a matter of seconds, one of the young men said what everyone else was thinking: "I have never seen a *yovó* [outsider] in a balε. Why are you here?"

Mumbling ensued as the initiates discussed among themselves the issue they had with my presence. My whiteness and foreignness stood before them in stark contrast to the realities in which they lived. My space was outside, among the public while their space was inside, separated by secrecy. Even though I was "legitimately" an initiate of the Egúngún cult, my foreignness both to Bénin in general and to this village in particular complicated the issue as my body and personhood seemingly polluted their social space. To these men, my presence in the balε was an anomaly to the "normal" experience of everyday life. Mary Douglas (1966) points out that anomalous events, if not controlled, can disrupt social order and fragment the ways we categorize our worlds. Although I was an initiated member of the society and therefore had the right and power to be there, my race and perceived nationality marked me as being at variance with everyday religious life in Bénin. Having acὲ was a fragile and insufficient state. Indeed, I was beginning to see that acὲ, especially when confronted with secrecy, had to be constantly verified, validated, and scrutinized. The acὲ that been given to me in Fátòmὲ was deficient in this new space, and I worried about what that would mean to these men, most of whom I had just met.

After a few brief moments, a visiting Egúngún chief emerged from the crowd.

"Are you an initiate?" he asked.

"Yes," I stumbled.

"Okay! Then prove it."

I approached him and began doing as I was taught in Fátòmὲ. Unfortunately, my memory failed me, making my efforts insufficient.[12] Under pressure and out of practice, I was unable to pass the chief's test.

For months, I had been hearing rumors of uninitiated people entering sacred spaces where they did not belong and being immediately murdered and buried inside the temple, "where government and police officials would not tread." Whenever I heard these claims, I always dismissed the accounts as anti-Vodún propaganda put forth by the Christian majority to subvert Vodún and devalue—and perhaps recriminalize—Vodún's "culture of secrecy." But at this moment, as fear, shame, and discomfort overcame me, I suddenly panicked that the claims might be true. But then I forced myself to brush aside the sensational anxieties of my own possible murder and regain my rationality. Just as I stopped thinking of my possible death, I heard people around me calling for me to be beaten for my misstep—and thus a new, more realistic fear arose. How would I get out of this? It was clear to me that many people felt that I was spoiling the sacred space. I was aware more than ever that my race and nationality created a palatable nervousness among the crowd. Later, it was revealed to me that many people were anxious because they believed that I might sell or publish what I learned, in order to become rich, while, according to them, Béninois people—the real custodians of the Egúngún's mysteries—remained subject to abject poverty.

As I managed my anxieties, I also tried to placate the people around me whose space I had unintentionally disrupted. Nevertheless, frustrations grew inside the temple. I sent for my friend Michel, hoping he would be able to mediate the problem. A young man left the temple in search of Michel and quickly returned, telling me that Michel could not come inside because he was not an initiated member of the Egúngún society. My mind raced as I tried to come up with solutions that were socially acceptable and respectful of the tradition into which I had thrown myself. After a few moments of discussion, Michel was escorted inside the temple—shirtless, bound, and blindfolded. His own initiation ceremonies had begun. After half an hour of singing, sacrifices, and prayers, Michel consumed the Egúngúns' power and became a full member of the Egúngún society. As a man interested in Vodún, it was something he had always wanted to do but had put off because of professional interests and obligations. However, at this moment, Michel's feelings of responsibility for my well-being motivated him to undergo the initiation. After Michel's initiation, the attention of the society shifted from me to two local young men in their early twenties who, like me, had illegitimately breached the temple's inner sanctum.

While these two men and I were guilty of the same infraction, the ways in which we were "punished" differed dramatically. The two young men were immediately scolded, stripped down, and made to lie on their stomachs. They were beaten until their skin began to whelp; care was taken not to break the skin. The beatings are just forceful enough to "annihilate any kind of resistance in order to impose on them a state of undeniable passivity" (Gabail 2012: 144). The raised patches of skin on their backs matched the thin shape of Egúngún staves that were used to punish the men. They were then made to stand up and beg forgiveness by submissively prostrating before the senior members of the society in the ways that ceremonial rules demanded. After their penance had been paid, they were made to sign an agreement that they would return with 5,000 CFA to cover the costs of their initiations. Because secret shrines and events cannot be unseen and secret passwords not unheard, after the papers were signed, the men were initiated, thereby giving them the right to see and know what they had just learned while inside the Egúngún temple.

By contrast, I was scolded and ceremoniously "beaten," but with only a small fraction of the force that my fellow violators endured. Like the others, I was also asked to pay 5,000 CFA to have my initiation ceremonies repeated—so the Egúngún priests present were sure I was correctly initiated. However, I was also required to pay an additional 10,000 CFA to the sacred Egúngún staff to avoid being severely beaten for my infraction. While I had previously heard that "paying the *baton*" was always an option for everyone, I noticed that my fellow rule breakers had not been offered this opportunity, while I was all but forced to pay instead of suffering a beating. I left that evening with a new understanding of secrecy and the ways that my foreignness, race, and perceived wealth shaped my access to the domains of secret knowledge. While I was relieved that I did not suffer a serious beating, I also felt ashamed of my own privileged difference that had "saved" me.

This experience convinced me that while one's being transforms as a result of the acè he or she consumes during initiation, this ontological transformation is insufficient for understanding the lasting effects of ritual meaning. Ritual is a layered and condensed social event that draws on the symbolic worlds in which the rituals and the actors are embedded. As this vignette shows, ritual initiation continues to influence one's social world long after the ritual has concluded. However, rituals do not exist apart from local politics. Béninois Vodúnisants are born into and live their lives embedded within complex social networks. Foreigners, despite their initiations, are only connected to Béninois by virtue of their initiation. The farther they move away from the center of their initiatory community—as I did when traveling from Fátòmè to Abomey—the less likely that the acè they received during their initiation will be sufficient in authenticating their initiation to those Béninois practitioners with whom foreign practitioners are not intimately connected. While ritual initiation may transform foreign spiritual seekers into ritual secrets themselves, foreigners must work to develop a sense of inclusion in a community, to affirm their ritually prescribed roles as devotees, priests, and diviners. Paradoxically, foreigners' peripheral connection to local communities restricts their widespread access to secrecy while also facilitating their ability to initiate. When I asked a diviner whom I met in Ouidah why he was comfortable revealing ritual secrets to foreigners, he echoed this ritual paradox when he said, "Well, they don't live here. I don't have to worry about them making [social] mistakes. I just hope they do something good with it once they are home."

The Transnational Power of Ritual

Béninois Vodúnisants describe Fá initiation as "receiving the forest" (Fázùnyí). Not only do initiates receive Fá's secrets that are hidden deep in fázùn, but the forest also becomes a permanent feature of a diviner's being. For Béninois such as Auguste, "receiving the forest" gives them access to important social spaces that reinforce their gender and their positions within their families. After his initiation, Auguste returned to school and lived his life relatively unchanged. The initiation allowed for him to train with his father to become a diviner; it gave him the social permission to enter the forest with the other men; and it made it safe for him to consume Gbǎdù's sacrificial meat. But, as Jean told all of his initiates, "this is just the beginning." Some of Jean's sons became serious students and had even begun to develop their own reputations as diviners, while others left Fátòmè to study at the university. Regardless of their practical proficiency, when they were home, they were all initiates. They retained their inalienable right to enter the forest and consume Gbǎdù's dangerous acè. With foreign spiritual seekers paying thousands of dollars for initiations, it is not uncommon for Béninois, drawn by the promise of wealth, to become initiated. Even so, for most Béninois I met, initiation was about their spiritual safety and their development into social adults who were in full control of their destinies. It was not about a social commitment to their becoming adept diviners so much as it was both a social commitment to their families and the fulfillment of the destinies that the initiation would reveal.

Foreign spiritual seekers tend to experience ritual initiation from a different reference point. While most of the foreigners I met asserted that they sought initiation to help them to "develop a relationship with divinity," most of them—if not all of them—were also influenced by capitalism. Coming from societies such as the United States that are deeply invested in global capitalism, foreign spiritual seekers often talk about initiation as a product.

One evening, Kevin, an American spiritual seeker in his forties who paid 2,500 USD to receive Gbădù, lamented to me, "I paid $2,500 for Gbădù and [my initiator] won't even teach me how to make [the shrine]. I feel like I am being scammed. How am I going to make my money back if I can't make Gbădù for other people? No one is going to take me seriously as a priest!" What Kevin did not realize was that most Béninois diviners do not know how to make Gbădù. In fact, of Jean's twenty or more apprentices, only Romar, his eldest son, had even begun to learn the difficult and purportedly dangerous process. While Kevin believes he paid for the right to know, most Béninois diviners go their entire lives not learning the rituals or the materials required to incarnate Gbădù into her shrine.[13] For initiates such as Kevin, the transformation that ritual provides them has nothing to do with their commitment to their families and more to do with their international success as priests and diviners. On another occasion, Kevin told me of his plans to build a website once he was back home in the United States so that he could attract students and bring them to Bénin to be initiated.[14] Kevin, like so many foreign diviners, embarked on initiation to validate his religious authority so that he could initiate others. By contrast, Béninois initiates tended to place religious authority in the hands of the local gerontocracy, who saw ritual proficiency not as a product of initiation, but as something that is garnered gradually, along with age and wisdom.

As ritual meaning reacts to an influx of new religious agents, so too do the social effects of ritual. The same ritual that legitimizes foreign spiritual seekers and allows them to perform initiations and spiritual services for economic benefit also makes them a part of a "family"—defined not by blood but by initiation. Their initiator becomes their "parent," and the foreign initiate is often expected to contribute financially to family funerals, weddings, and births. There is no doubt that these international networks encourage Béninois to initiate foreign spiritual seekers. Romar, Jean's eldest son, once confessed to me, "I know more [about Fá] than all my brothers. But Auguste is the smartest. I worry that he will be able to take over for our father one day because he speaks French. Even if he doesn't know Fá like I do." Romar often opined that he regretted forgoing a school-based education in favor of one that allowed him to focus solely on Fá. In fact, Romar has a lot going for him in a world where his deep knowledge attracts foreign spiritual seekers who are looking to learn. In contemporary Bénin, where spiritual tourism is on the rise and kinship remains socially important, ritual initiation seems to allow for adjustments in ritual horizons as new ritual meanings continue to thrive and to expand outward.

As rituals in Vodún take on new global horizons, secrecy becomes especially important to understanding the religion's global expansion. As Johnson points out, "It is through secretism, the circulation of a secret's inaccessibility, the words and actions that throw that absence into relief, that a secret's power grows, quite independently of whether or not it exists" (2002: 3). In this way, processes of secrecy add social power to ritual events and reinforce the value of initiation by increasing the ritual's desirability. In the case of Fá, secrecy is embodied multisensorially as the sacred forest and the human merge. The deliberate and steady movement into the forest; the smell of crushed leaves and livestock; the ever-present sounds of bells, prayers, and ritual songs; the consumption of divine power, sacrificial meat, drinks, and kola nuts; and Gbădù's visual unveiling in fázùn—all these work together to transform initiates and consecrate their authority as diviners. Likewise, the blindfolds; the flushing of an initiate's eyes with Gbădùsìn; the stark separation of the forest from the village; the restricted access to the forest; the performed resistance that is overcome every step of the way; and the palm-frond barrier that marks the entrance to the sacred forest and its secrets—all these reaffirm and intensify the power of those secrets that are embedded in the ritual experience. As initiates move closer and closer to the forest's secrets, they undergo ontological changes that prepare them to be a holder of secrets. Ritual and consumption become the processes through which embodied secrets are manufactured, and they become the way in which foreign spiritual seekers develop the community they need to have rendered as globally authentic. As we will see in Chapter 3, foreign spiritual seekers not only seek to consume ritual power but also secret-laden objects as a way to further validate their ritual experiences in a world they knew little about before traveling to Bénin.

CHAPTER 3

Secrecy, Objects, and Expanding Markets

Secrets play a vital role in Fon society and art, as much
through their revelation as through their concealment.

—Blier 1993: 193

It was about 1 a.m. I had been sleeping for hours when my phone rang. *Who is calling me at this hour?* I wondered.

"Tim? Are you awake?" a voice asked.

"Yeah, I'm up. Who's this?"

"It's Gilles. My brother's about to sell an Egúngún mask to a *yovó*. Do you want to come to the house?" he asked matter-of-factly.

"Um, yeah, sure. I'll be right over," I answered.

My mind was still groggy from sleep and I was a bit thrown off by what was happening. Egúngún are sacred and extremely secret, and older priests discourage the buying and selling of these masks, which embody the ancestors. Nevertheless, some of these masks command large sums of money from international buyers and spiritual tourists. Young Béninois initiates, and even some priests, frequently take advantage of these moments to make up to 4,000 USD for a single mask.

After a few minutes, I arrived at Gilles's compound, still dazed from sleep.

"*Kɔkɔkɔ!*" I said, announcing my arrival.

"*Mɛ́ wɛ?*" a faint voice asked from inside one of the houses.

"Gilles, it's Tim," I responded.

"Oh, good. Come in—hurry."

Gilles ushered me down an alleyway and then into a small moonlit room at the back of his house. Once my eyes adjusted to the darkness, I realized we were positioned to prevent everyone else in the compound from seeing us—even if they were awake. Strewn on the ground before us were three different Egúngún masks, each meticulously displayed for Pascal, a French man in his forties, who stood across from me, closely examining each of the masks without saying a word.

With his right arm folded across his chest and his left supporting his chin, Pascal finally spoke: "How much for this one?"

"One million, five hundred," Gilles responded.

"And this one?" Pascal asked.

"Two million," Gilles answered.

"How about both for three million?"

The negotiations continued, and eventually the two masks were sold for just over 6,000 USD.

"Are you here to buy costumes too?" Pascal asked me.

"Oh, no. I live here. I am an anthropologist studying Vodún."

"Oh, well, you really should buy one before you leave—they are magnificent," Pascal insisted.

"They really are beautiful," I agreed.

After the masks were neatly wrapped and covered in sheets to conceal their identities, they were thrown over an eight-foot brick wall where Pascal's rented truck was parked, down a narrow, dark alleyway. This performance was done to prevent people in the compound from seeing what Gilles and his brothers had done, as well as to protect their buyer. "We don't want a lot of people to know he just purchased two Egúngún—no telling what people would do," Gilles explained.

The masks that Gilles and his brothers sold that night had been made for the purpose of selling. They had never been danced in or consecrated—yet they were authentic in every other way. Many of the elders with whom I spoke abhorred the idea of selling Egúngún to European or American buyers—unless they were initiates themselves, several of them added. Youth, however, were faced with the pressures of modernity in ways that their fathers and grandfathers could not understand. Young men like Gilles need to present themselves outwardly as young, urban, internationally connected, and financially fluid—all components of their vision of the youthful modern man, an image that now speaks to many young men across urban Africa

(Scheld 2007; Newell 2012). Working with foreign buyers, making masquerades to sell, and having large sums of money at their disposal all help to
make this image possible. Dealing with similar modernity-driven desires to
become rich in rural South Africa, Jean and John Comaroff documented the
ways in which occult powers have been deployed "for material ends" or for
"the conjuring of wealth," which often "involve[s] the destruction of others
and their capacity to create value" (1999: 297n31). In this chapter I take a
similar, yet divergent approach. I examine the ways in which religiously
potent objects, such as the secrecy-laden Egúngún masks and spiritual practices such as sorcery and witchcraft, "conjure wealth" for those Béninois
participants who are eager to participate in global religious markets. Examining the vitality of these markets, I explore the challenges of materiality
and transportation, consider the limits of adaptation, and examine the
importance of materiality for foreign spiritual seekers. In this way, I am
able to highlight the consequences and rewards of the commodification of
secret religious objects and powers while also showing how some Béninois
use secrecy to consecrate—and therefore authenticate—the sale of ghosts,
charms, and spirits.

Spirits in My Suitcase

Because I was a diviner's apprentice, my participation in Vodún's burgeoning international consumption of secrecy was inescapable. Before Jean
would agree to take me on as his apprentice, he consulted with Fá, the spiritual force behind the power of divination, to determine if he himself would
permit my initiation. Jean always asked Fá before taking on a new student.
However, I worried about what would happen if Fá refused.

Seated on Fá's traditional straw mat, Jean sang the opening prayers
required to begin a divination session. He poured a small amount of water
onto the ground, and then delicately swung his divining chain in front of him
before abruptly tossing it to the ground. After the primary sign (dù) that
would govern the entire session opened on the mat before us, he reached into
his divination bag (fákpò) and searched for indicators (vode) that he would
use to ask yes-or-no questions. Finding what he was looking for, Jean handed
me a cowrie shell to represent "yes" and a small piece of a broken ceramic
dish to represent "no."

"Hold one in your left and one in your right hand—cover them so I can't see them," Jean instructed.

My palms began to sweat as I tightly clenched the shell and ceramic shard. It was hard not to think about what would happen if Fá asked me to reveal my right hand and uncover the broken ceramic—and therefore a refusal. My mind raced, and I became increasingly nervous.

"Open your right hand," Jean said.

My right hand? Fá had selected the ceramic shard and refused me as a student. My heart sank. I remember thinking, "*Well, it's all data.*" But, somehow, these data stung more than I expected. I wondered if I could convince Jean to work with me anyway. I opened my right hand.

"Drop it," Jean commanded.

He picked up the broken shard and placed it in his bag and, just as quickly, took the cowrie shell from my left hand and placed it on the straw mat in front of him. Later I learned that Jean had an unusual habit of removing the indicators that Fá refused before revealing the indicator that Fá actually selected. Relief swept over me as I let out an audible sigh. Fá had accepted me as a student and sanctioned my apprenticeship with Jean.

As the divination continued, I learned that before Fá would permit me to become a diviner, there was another ceremony I needed to undergo.

"Do you have twins in your family?" Jean asked.

"I have twin cousins," I answered.

"Are they alive?"

"Yes."

"It's not them, then."

"I have twin uncles who were stillborn. Does that count?"

After receiving confirmation from Fá, Jean explained, "You need to birth your uncles into dolls [*atínkpaví*] before you can begin your initiation ceremonies."

The number of religious tools and spirits I was beginning to accumulate was becoming overwhelming—and so were my spiritual responsibilities. Along with receiving Fá, I was also required to receive Lĕgbà, the spirit of the crossroads who is charged with opening the paths of communication to the spirit realm—and now my two, never-born uncles, along with my other spirits, would make the journey back to the United States safely packed away in my baggage. By the end of my stay, my bags were filled beyond capacity with spirits—and evidence—of my initiations. Xɛbyosò (the spirit of thunder), Lĕgbà, Fá, Gbădù: they all followed me home, bringing with them their secrets, some of which I knew and some I would never know (see Gottlieb 2006).

Initiation into Vodún brings many long-term spiritual obligations—including caring for one's new spirits. The spirits must be prayed to, fed, and given money and drink. Many informants described the process of adding a shrine to one's home; it was akin to having a family member move in with them. But caring for the spirits, providing them with food and drink, and honoring them with praise and respect came with rewards—promises of protection, abundance, long life, and a large family, just to name a few.

Some shrines, such as those of Xɛbyosò or Fá, are small and hence simple for spiritual tourists to transport back home, as they consist of specially prepared stones and palm nuts, respectively. The spirit is installed into these seemingly ordinary objects with complex rituals that involve countless sessions of divination, extensive and complex leaf baths (for the priests and the objects), numerous supplications, and many sacrifices and offerings—after which the stones and palm nuts are said to become physical incarnations of the spirits on earth. Other shrines, such as those for Lĕgbà and Gbădù, provide interesting problems for international visitors who wish to return home with these spirits in tow. Unlike Xɛbyosò and Fá, Lĕgbà and Gbădù are incarnated to earth by combining a number of botanical, zoological (e.g., Adeola 1992; Nikolaus 2011; Landry 2016), and environmental materials, some of which are challenging (and in some cases illegal) to pack in one's luggage, due to national and international customs regulations.[1] Leopard hides, bird eggs, parrot feathers, insects, and elephant ivory—to name a few—can all complicate the transportation of shrines from Bénin to a traveler's country of origin.[2] Even if my shrines did not contain any illegal materials, I was still anxious.

"How will I travel home with my shrines?" I asked Jean.

"[Airport personnel] couldn't open your bag if they wanted to!" Jean exclaimed.

Jean had confidence in the vodún—that they would protect themselves from being "violated" or "destroyed."

"If you don't believe me, just ask Fá and you'll know what I already know. You'll see—everything will be just fine."

He was right. As a diviner, I should ask Fá, even if I remained somewhat unconvinced that the divination would make me less anxious about my eventual return home.

After a few days, I finally built up the nerve to perform the divination with Jean to determine the outcome of traveling back to the United States with my new shrines. Just as Jean said, Fá indicated that my spirits would not cause a problem. During my initiations, I had the distinct advantage of helping Jean construct most of my shrines—something that most spiritual tourists do not get to experience on their first trip, because they usually are not in the country long enough. Because of Jean's openness, I knew that nothing hidden inside my shrines—under the layers of mud, shea butter, and dried palm oil—would cause a problem at customs. Grateful to Jean for letting me participate in the construction of most of my shrines, I marveled at the tourists' confidence—or naïveté—that they would be able to travel without incident. A few tourists told me about times that shrines were taken from them at the airport for being "too bloody" or for having visible zoological ingredients (such as horsetail fibers) that were restricted due to agricultural regulations. In all cases, the items were confiscated, and the spiritual travelers returned home without their shrines, while still bound to their new spiritual responsibilities.

With the transnational flow of ritual secrecy also comes the movement of secret-charged objects and religious artifacts. Although I never encountered any tourists traveling from Bénin or Nigeria who experienced significant legal setbacks as they tried to return home with their new spiritual treasures, I have known cases where problems arose for people traveling from Haiti or Cuba after being initiated into Vodou or Lucumí. In July 2007 two American spiritual tourists traveled to Haiti to become initiated priests of Haitian Vodou. According to online reports, the two American spiritual seekers traveled to Haiti to become initiated after meeting Mambo Laura, a Euro-American mambo (a Haitian Vodou priestess), in Las Vegas. During that time, Mambo Laura maintained a temple (Haitian Kreyol, *hounfort*) in Haiti and regularly accepted foreigners into her congregation.

During their stay in Haiti, the two Americans expressed a special interest in ancestor veneration, which led Mambo Laura to refer them to a local expert, and one of her Haitian initiates, Houngan David. During their interactions with Houngan David, the two U.S. citizens acquired two human skulls, one male and one female, that were to be used in ceremonies designed to honor, feed, and empower the dead. After their ceremonies were completed, they packed their bags and headed to the airport to return home as newly initiated priests of Haitian Vodou. At one of the security checkpoints at L'Aéroport International Toussaint Louverture (in Port-au-Prince, Haiti), airport officials discovered the skulls in the Americans' bags, and the two were immediately detained and placed in a Haitian prison for trafficking in human remains while their U.S. attorneys negotiated their release.

Several months prior to this case, in February 2006, a Haitian American woman and Vodou initiate was arrested in Ft. Lauderdale, Florida, by U.S. customs officials for entering the United States with a human skull in her bag (Haas and Jean-Francois 2006). In January 2012 two Cuban American women were detained at Miami International Airport by customs agents when two human fetuses were discovered in a small clay jar hidden in their bags; according to the two women, the jar was to be delivered to a diviner in the United States for a Lucumí ceremony ("Human Fetuses" 2012).

Cases such as these may be exaggerated—or at least sensationalized—by the media. Yet it is also clear that some people who have spiritual investments in two spaces—whether that be U.S./Bénin, U.S./Haiti, U.S./Cuba, or any number of other combinations—are met with legal and logistical challenges regarding the practice of their religion that binational practitioners of other more mainstream religions are not. Human skulls, or rare, and sometimes illegal, zoological or botanical religious ingredients, make the strict maintenance of some West African–derived religious traditions difficult, thereby inspiring practitioners of Vodún, Vodou, Lucumí, and others to do what they do best in the face of adversity and social challenges—adapt.

Although these religious systems are adaptable, especially in the face of pressure, out of fear of being delegitimized by their African initiators, foreign initiates are unlikely to encourage ritual change. Legally procuring (mostly Chinese) human skulls from online medical distributors,[3] or substituting botanical or zoological ceremonial ingredients with more easily (and legally) obtained alternatives, seems less authentic to many foreign spiritual seekers, who imbue a tremendous amount of symbolic and social capital in what many of them call "traditional" or "authentic" spiritual recipes. The question of ceremonial substitutions was always one that fascinated me. It was a question that often caused anxiety for foreign spiritual seekers, who felt a need to re-create what they learned exactly as they had experienced them in Africa. However, for Jean, these discussions were invariably less interesting.

"Walk in the forest by your home in the United States," Jean instructed me. "Look at the plants and animals around you and learn to determine which of them produce the same results as what you have found here."

For Jean, and for every other Béninois practitioner I encountered, the spirits were extensions of the natural world around them, and incarnating them to earth through shrines, or through performing acts of magic by combining certain ingredients together, was an ever-changing process that, when guided by divination, could be replicated anywhere in the world using local ingredients.

"We don't have termite mounds where I am from. How can I construct Lĕgbà without that soil?" I once asked Jean.

"Find something similar, and ask Fá if using the soil that you found will work."

"Can you ask Fá about all ceremonial substitutions?" I inquired.

"Yeah, of course."

"What about Fá himself? Can I substitute the palm nuts needed to make Fá with something else?"

"No!" Jean quickly answered.

Clearly there are components that are immutable and nonnegotiable. These dominant symbols, often tied to a specific spirit cult, embody the condensed power of the spirit. For Fá, sixteen palm nuts represent the major sixteen dù (Yr., *odù*), or signs, of Fá divination, chosen by Ọ̀rúnmìlà (another name for Fá, known primarily by Yorùbá speakers) to embody his spiritual self on earth so that his priests—the diviners—could speak to him and could, at any time, know the will of the spirits. In the case of Fá divination, palm nuts are more than representational. They are the earthly manifestation, or incarnation, of Fá. While Jean and others believe that many ingredients in ritual can be changed, some—like Fá's sacred palm nuts—are unchangeable. To move away from the palm nuts would be a move away from Fá himself.

Fá is not the only spirit whose meaning is condensed within earthly objects. Xɛbyosò, the spirit of thunder, manifests himself in "thunderstones" (*sò kpén*) that, according to local lore, are made when lightning strikes the earth;[4] and Lĕgbà, the spirit of the crossroads and esoteric communication who is typically installed in pathways, crossroads, or at village or house entrances, manifests on earth as mounds of soil. Lĕgbà shrines are typically fashioned by forming a small, conical pile of soil, typically no more than two feet tall, from the moistened soil of a termite mound,[5] because, according to Jean, "termite mounds look like Lĕgbà."[6] While the "power" of a Lĕgbà shrine rests buried under the mound itself, a Lĕgbà shrine without a mound would be unrecognizable and therefore unusable.[7] (See Figure 10.)

Figure 10. Lĕgbà. Photograph by the author.

Certain symbols used in Vodún, such as Fá's palm nuts or Xɛbyosò's thunderstones, are considered to be earthly presences of the spirit's life force, power, or *acè*. In some ways, identifying the crossroads as one of Lěgbà's "symbols" misrepresents the way in which Fon speakers understand their spirits. Instead, the crossroads (like Fá's palm nuts and Xɛbyosò's thunderstones) are extensions of the spirit's spiritual selves from the realm of the spirits (*kútòmè*) to that of the earth. Those symbols that are most clearly manifestations of the spirits on earth become somewhat nonnegotiable in praxis.[8] I say "somewhat" because some symbols, such as Xɛbyosò's thunderstones, can move from being meteorites to being axe-shaped stones while also maintaining their value, power, and mythos, as people still say these axe-shaped stones are formed from lightning. Although the type of stone may have changed, stones themselves are, in one form or another, still central to Xɛbyosò's cult.

However, spiritual tourists who travel to Bénin for only a short period of time often miss Vodún's subtle symbolic valence. When spiritual tourists become initiated into Vodún and then return home, armed with new spiritual secrets and powers, many of them do so without a clear understanding of a spirit's symbolic grammar. While some symbols, such as blood and leaves, carry social value among all the spirit groups, each spirit group also comes embedded in its own "symbolic universe" (Kriebel 2016: 43). Defining which symbols of a certain spirit are central to ritual practice is important in determining which symbols embody the spirit. For spiritual tourists, replacing local African symbols for more available symbols found back in the United States might be acceptable, but replacing a dominant or key symbol for something more available in the United States could be destructive to a ceremony's transnational value and perceived authenticity. This conundrum places foreign spiritual seekers in a precarious position. On the one hand, their practice must be recognizable by the larger West African and African diasporic community, or they risk being ostracized by those from which they seek to draw clients or new initiates, and therefore an income. On the other hand, their practice must also maintain the "authentic" structure taught to them in Africa, or they risk being labeled as a fraud.

Both foreign and Béninois *Vodúnisants* attempt to manage the ebb and flow of religious meaning in a world that is becoming increasingly global and interconnected. As I and others have already noted, Vodún has over the centuries been remarkably amenable to change and shifts in religious meaning. However, globalization has affected these processes. Foreign seekers come to Bénin for initiation after spending considerable time being exposed to Christianity and Western positivist science. As a result, they often place significant value in the written word and come with fixed notions of how ritual and ceremony should occur to be considered authentic or trustworthy (Shapin 1996). While Vodún has certainly been influenced by the textualization of knowledge, the religious system is, at its core, *meaningfully* flexible. As people, spirits, and religious objects move from location to location so too does meaning—even as it localizes to meet the needs of new spaces and adapts to changing perspectives and goals from a growing breadth of human agents. The feminist literary critic Toril Moi reminds us that "the attempt to *fix* meaning is always in part doomed to failure, for it is of the nature of meaning to be always already everywhere" (1985: 60), and Vodún proves her point perfectly.[9]

As foreign and Béninois initiates build Vodún into a growing number of urban, transnational, and global landscapes they use objects both to authenticate and "remind" themselves and others of their religious commitments to the spirits (cf. McDannell 1995) and to serve as "forums for the representation of a [diversifying] community situated in transnational spaces" (D'Alisera 2001: 93). Shrines, charms, and masks all become reference points that at once authenticate the initiates' time in West Africa and reinforce their authority as "legitimately" initiated priests. Because the display and use of religious objects is, as JoAnn D'Alisera has argued, "transformative," objects function as vehicles "for turning experience into space" where shrines, charms, and masks become the tools by which Vodúnisants mediate "social experience" (2001: 94). In this way, Vodún's rich material culture becomes part of what it means to be a Vodún priest and the marketing, selling, ownership, and display of shrines, ritual paraphernalia, and secret masks all become rich points of meaning making and negotiation.

"Now I Am Bulletproof": The Buying and Selling of Bŏ

For a few foreign spiritual seekers, acquiring ritual objects and learning the spirits' mysteries are not their only interests. These travelers also seek to learn magic's secrets. After working with Jean for six months, I began to realize that, while guarded, secret rituals and shrines were still quite accessible, especially if one has the time and desire to invest in the social relationships necessary to garner trust. However, magic's primary secrets—in effect, a magician's recipes—are so highly guarded that many Béninois told me that "the only real secret in Vodún, the only secret with real power, is magic." Magic among Fon speakers in southern Bénin is somewhat complicated, especially when considered alongside witchcraft and in a space where, at least in Fonland, E. E. Evans-Pritchard's (1976 [1937]) classic Azande-based divisions of witchcraft and sorcery are ethnographically problematic (e.g., Falen 2007).

Witchcraft: Azĕ

In Bénin, *azĕ*, most commonly translated as "witchcraft" (or *sorcellerie* by French-speaking Béninois), is, at its most basic level, a projection of psychic energy directed at people usually to harm or "eat" others. Witchcraft is seen as one of the most powerful spiritual forces among the Fon and Yorùbá peoples of southern Bénin. In a survey I conducted, 72 percent of 125 survey respondents (90 of 125) identified azĕ as being more powerful than other spiritual forces known to them, and 93 percent (116 of 125) described azĕ as being "the most dangerous."[10] Remarkably, 100 percent of my respondents noted that a person who has been afflicted by azĕ has two primary chances for survival—either Jesus Christ or the vodún Gbădù. Aside from that, 35 percent of respondents also listed Tron, a recent introduction into the Vodún pantheon by way of Ewe-speaking people from Ghana and Togo, as an additional spiritual solution to fighting witchcraft.[11]

As some of my Béninois friends have suggested, Tron's recent increase in popularity with Vodún practitioners might lie in his relative safety when compared to Gbădù. Gbădù, envisioned at once as the wife of Fá and as the cosmic womb of creation, is the spirit who gives Fá and all diviners their power. Controlled by male diviners,[12] Gbădù is reported to "burn the eyes" or "cause sudden death" to any woman or any uninitiated man who sees her shrine or wander too close to it. Even initiated men who view the shrine are required to wash their faces and flush their eyes with a specially prepared medicine (*Gbădùsìn*) that contains a secret collection of leaves, snail blood, and shea butter, or they too risk becoming blind.[13] Jean has suggested that the precautions that center around Gbădù's rituals are in place because of her immense power—which is precisely what gives her the ability to defeat azĕ. Ironically, Gbădù's marked power, when taken with her numerous ritual taboos and dangers, has led many people, especially the un- or underinitiated, to assert that Gbădù and azĕ are one and the same. Yet despite some diviners' claim that Tron is only effective against azĕ because, when incarnated to earth in shrines, Tron and Gbădù are composed of similar materials, Tron is said to fight azĕ without the dangers and precautions that come with Gbădù—making Tron, for some, a more reasonable choice when seeking protection against witchcraft.

The belief that azĕ must be fought with azĕ (see Geschiere 1997; Gottlieb 1989), however paradoxical to Western logic, has highlighted a curious bifurcation in local azĕ classification: *azĕ wiwi* (black witchcraft or *magie noire*) and *azĕ wèwé* (white witchcraft or *magie blanche*). Mirroring Western notions of "white" and "black" witchcraft, the Fon-speaking people of Bénin believe that azĕ wiwi represents azĕ's destructive and harmful side while azĕ wèwé, the "white" variety, embodies azĕ's potential for benevolence and protection. Douglas Falen has argued that "witchcraft in Benin may actually be seen as the source of productive power, and even pride" (2007: 22), something he attributes to an increase in azĕ's public presence. According to Falen, this has led to an "emerging trend in the Republic of Benin [that] positions witchcraft as a potentially positive force" (2007: 2). A similar parallel, but one that Falen does not consider as a possible influence on Fon speakers' understanding of azĕ, can be drawn from the interior of Yorùbáland. There, *àjẹ́ funfun* (white witchcraft) is "said to perform benevolent acts, such as imparting wealth, prosperity, good health, and protection" whereas *àjẹ́ dúdu* (black witchcraft) is used "to cause misfortune and bad luck and to induce people to commit criminal offenses and suicide" (Washington 2005: 25). These Yorùbá categories of witchcraft (Yr., àjẹ́) are further complicated by their irrevocable connection to the *Ìyàmi* (the mysterious mothers, known to Fon speakers as *Mĭnɔna*), who occupy an important, and sometimes positive, position in the creation of the cosmos, and whose powers are condensed, both symbolically and metaphysically, in the *òrìṣà Odù* (known to Fon speakers as Gbădù), the wife of Ifá/Fá. Given their proximity, and given the high degree of Fon-Yorùbá connectedness (Rush 2013: 65–67), it is also possible that Fon speakers have adopted these complex Yorùbá categories of àjẹ́ and mapped them onto azĕ where azĕ wiwi has, at least in public spheres, reigned supreme.[14]

Regardless of how, or from where, contemporary Fon speakers have categorized witchcraft, during my stay in Bénin, like Falen, I met several self-proclaimed "witches" (*azĕtɔ́*) who claimed to be *azĕtɔ́ wèwé* (white witches). Each of them purchased the medicine that irrevocably transformed them into azĕtɔ́ for the sole purpose of protecting their families from *azĕtɔ́ wiwi* (black witches)—who, according to local lore, had to kill someone successfully, usually a relative, by using azě in order to be initiated properly. Nevertheless, despite these good intentions, people also warned that azě wèwé is a slippery slope that eventually—regardless of the witch's true intentions—leads to one becoming an evil and murderous "black witch." Some people come to azě for the power and others are transformed into azětɔ wiwi unwillingly (and some say irreversibly) by consuming food or drink that has been contaminated with azě. Either way, it is understood that azě's power comes at a cost that may include a shortening of the azětɔ's life and an increased propensity for illness.

For many Fon-speaking Béninois, the costs of becoming an azětɔ are just too great. Initiation into azě, despite many offers, was something I always avoided. The social risks were too high, and, like many spiritual tourists, I lacked the interest. As it was, as public awareness of my apprenticeship with Jean grew and people began to know me as both an anthropologist and an initiate of Vodún, asking questions about azě was challenging.

"You're a diviner. Why are you asking about azě? You want to be a witch too?" a young woman asked.

"Tim, you need to be careful. People know you're interested in Vodún and willing to be initiated. If people hear you asking about azě, they may assume that you're asking because of a personal interest," Marie warned.

For the first time, my apprenticeship and my status as a diviner compromised my ability to ask questions, because I could no longer rely on my role as the curious anthropologist. Tourists faced similar issues, although not to the same degree. While I never met a tourist who wanted to become a witch, Béninois people often spoke of tourists who sought azě for the powers it promised. More than a few mentioned one American tourist by name who they claimed had come to Bénin for initiation into Mamíwátá and had apparently left as a powerful and dangerous witch.

Charms: Bǒ

Unlike azě, which few tourists seek out, bǒ—described to me as "the only real secret of Vodún"—is actively sought out by spiritual tourists. At its most basic level, bǒ is best translated into English as "charm" and called *gris-gris* by many French-speaking Béninois. Unlike azě, which is typically presented as a psychic force, bǒ are created by carefully combining zoological and botanical curios and then empowered by speaking closely guarded words of empowerment, or incantations.[15] Béninois feverishly protect their tried-and-true magical formulae for constructing bǒ. Recipes are passed down from generation to generation, and some recipes are so hidden that they end up dying with the magicians who once knew them.

Interested in the claim that bǒ is Vodún's last "real secret," I wanted to see how far my questions would take me and whether I would be able to learn recipes for some of the more infamous and tightly guarded bǒ—especially recipes for *zǐn bǒ* and *fífó bǒ*, the charms that grant the user an ability to become invisible and to translocate, respectively. Unlike my attempt to become an initiated diviner, my foray into the world of charms and magic was not met with tremendous success. I met people who claimed to have these powerful charms but refused to provide me with a demonstration of their power unless I paid for the charm up front—usually at a cost exceeding 1,000 USD. I met others who told me, "Those bǒ don't exist anymore. They've been lost for decades, and anyone who claims to have these powers is lying to take your money."

One magician told me, "I have these powers, but not as bǒ. If you want them, you will have to become a witch." The powers of invisibility, translation, transmutation, and flight are all linked to azě, as witches are believed to be able to transform into animals (especially owls) and to fly at will.[16] Most magicians I encountered agreed that the powers of invisibility and teleportation come in two varieties: azě, which is seen as more powerful but comes with consequences, such as the removal of years from one's life; and bǒ, which comes without negative side effects but is often seen as less reliable and "probably lost."[17] While I never gained either of these powers, I did meet some magicians who were willing to share other secrets with me—although less actively than Jean. And I met one young man who even wanted to sell me a photocopy of his family's recipes of countless bǒ, for 500 USD, which I declined. Nevertheless, I found the ways in which bǒ and magical formulae are marketed to be compelling, especially in the ways that local priests negotiated access to these secrets.

Many of my friends warned me, "Never buy a bǒ without first seeing it work with your own eyes." Heeding this advice, I asked for countless performances of an alleged bǒ's power and hardly found a single person who was willing to prove—through a controlled display of the bǒ's power—that he or she indeed had the particular bǒ that he or she claimed to have. Satisfied with what I had learned about bǒ and how knowledge, or even perceived knowledge, generates social friction that must be negotiated by both actors, I moved on from these questions and continued working with Jean.

As is the case with many of my fieldwork goals, as soon as I gave up on my quest to find these elusive powers, or the "real secrets of Vodún," something serendipitous happened. While in Abomey visiting Pierre, a close friend, we attended a local Vodún ceremony designed to honor the village chief's ancestors. While there, my friend and I met a man with dozens of bǒ tied around his neck and waist.

"You have a lot of bǒ," Pierre noted.

"Yes, I do have a lot," the old man responded.

"Did you make all of these yourself?"

"Most of them, yes."

"What's the best charm that you have?"

"I have one that no one else has. I have a charm that will make you bulletproof."

Intensely fascinated by bǒ, Pierre's interest was immediately piqued. For Pierre, bǒ were one of the few remaining sources of real power in Vodún.

"Bulletproof?" Pierre asked.

"Yes. I am one of the few people left who knows how to make this charm."

"Can you make them for me? Can I see it work? Can you teach me?" Pierre bombarded the old man with questions.

After coming to a financial agreement, the old man agreed to make the bǒ for Pierre and to provide us both with a demonstration of its power. Pierre and I went to the local market; purchased ingredients such as sacred leaves, magical powders, and a special bird feather; and gave them to the old man so he could begin making the bǒ. The following day we returned to experience the bǒ's occult power.

The old man held the walnut-sized cloth-wrapped bundle to his lips and whispered a secret incantation. He then tied the bǒ to the leg of a live chicken and strapped the chicken to a nearby tree while a friend of his, a local hunter, loaded his gun. Firing a test shot into the forest, he announced, "I am ready." I watched him carefully as he loaded the black powder rifle—black powder, cloth patch, buckshot, and another cloth patch. The black powder rifle was properly loaded and aimed at the chicken from about five yards away. The hunter pulled the trigger and the gun fired. The wide circular shotgun-like pattern of the buckshot caused leaves and tree bark all around the chicken to fly into the air; I was sure the chicken was dead. Pierre walked over to the chicken, untied it, and laughed.

"It's alive," he said looking at me. "Not a single drop of blood is on the chicken—it worked."

I was speechless. I had to admit that the bǒ quite possibly had worked. Pierre and I both left with one of the old man's bǒ—each amazed and each satisfied with the old man's power.

Deeply curious about how bǒ are marketed, bought, and sold, I searched for functioning bǒ over the next six months. During that time, I spoke with more than thirty people who claimed to have powerful bǒ that they would sell. One man even claimed proudly that he once sold a bǒ that granted invisibility to an American for 10,000 USD. However, he told me he could not make one himself because the man he bought it from years before had died without teaching him the composition. I searched for bǒ almost daily, yet the old man's bulletproofing bǒ was the first and last time I saw what I thought might be a bǒ's power with my own eyes.

While I set out to find bǒ that provided dramatic displays of power, tourists typically seek out bǒ that grant protection while traveling, or that attract wealth or love—bǒ that can help them to transform their current situations. The sales of bǒ such as these are so prevalent that some priests I encountered kept an inventory of prefabricated bǒ to sell to interested people, including to tourists for prices that often exceeded 100 USD each. Likewise, the local market for bǒ is expansive. Local radio shows market and sell bǒ that reportedly protect from witchcraft or grant luck in games of chance. Diviners make a good living selling bǒ to their local and, in some cases, foreign clients. With a thriving and well-established local market, extending that market transnationally to tourists makes economic sense to many diviners. However, when compared to the ease with which many initiates learn how to incarnate spirits to earth (shrine construction), those who knew bǒ were far less likely to provide spiritual seekers, whether foreign or local, with instructions for how to make bǒ themselves. Whereas many of the spirits were seen as public resources, bǒ and their formulae were most clearly seen as the private intellectual property of individuals or families. Although I learned at least some of the ingredients needed to make the bǒ that makes its wearer bulletproof, the old man who helped Pierre and me insisted on being alone when he constructed the charm. Pierre and I both knew that the old man was likely adding additional secret ingredients to the recipe and using privacy as a way of keeping the *bŏgbé* (Fon, literally the "bŏ's language" or incanta-tion), needed to activate the bŏ's power, a personal secret.

Azĕ, Bŏ, and an Emerging Tourist Market

Over the past twenty years, since Bénin began marketing its Vodún heritage in the early 1990s, Béninois have expanded the ways in which bŏ have been sold. Today, bŏ are traded in local markets, promoted during Béninois radio programs, and, more recently, advertised on Internet sites such as Facebook. The reasons people from all around the world seek the power of bŏ varies. A woman may purchase bŏ to keep her husband from straying; a university student may use bŏ to help him or her pass an especially difficult exam; a solider may use bŏ to protect him from harm; a man may turn to bŏ to help him to find stable work. In all of these cases, individuals may simply visit a *bòtɔ́* (sorcerer) or a diviner in Bénin in order to purchase the bŏ they need to help them solve their problems. However, as Vodún becomes increasingly global, new cyber-based networks that are not bound by the limitations of transnational travel and face-to-face interactions have begun to emerge. Today, one can easily log on to Facebook and, with the right collection of Facebook friends, find the particular bŏ that has the power to transform one's life.

Béninois and foreigners purchase bŏ from priests or over the Internet to transform their current—often desperate—circumstances into something more favorable. However, despite azĕ's immense power, witchcraft has mostly been ignored by foreign spiritual seekers. This then raises the question of why for-eigners are typically more interested in bŏ than they are in azĕ. A close look at the values that foreign initiates bring with them as they seek acceptance within global Vodún and, once home, with practitioners of other African and African diasporic religious traditions reveals a couple possibilities.

Foreign and Béninois Vodún devotees need the religion's inescapable connection to the material world. Vodún myth and cosmology teach its adherents that objects provide the spirits with bodies by the way of shrines, they allow for divinities and people to communicate by using divination tools, and they contribute to magic as natural objects are reimagined in ways that allow them to be used to create powerful charms (Landry 2016). Global trends in capitalism have shown that objects can take on new values as they become the products of economic markets, labor, and trade. From Karl Marx's assertion that individuals lose a part of themselves in the value they give to objects, to Daniel Miller's (2010, 2011) claim that consumption may bring people great comfort, social theorists have long shown that global capitalism changes one's relationship to those objects they seek.

I suggest that, in Vodún's case, capitalism's inseparable relationship to objects and also the religion's established history in which individuals pay their diviners, priests, and magicians for their services have coalesced to heighten the economic value that is placed on Vodún's vast repertoire of objects that initiates and devotees need in order to perform ritual or ceremony. This becomes especially important when one considers that objects allow for the buying, selling, and transnational movement of acè, Vodún's most important—yet intangible—commodity. As Béninois and foreign initiates alike have argued, "Shrines, bǒ, and ritual objects enable us to touch something [acè] that we could not normally touch." For Vodúnisants, the ethereal nature of divine power (acè) is entangled within Vodún's objects, such as bǒ, spirit shrines, and specialized ritual paraphernalia (Landry 2016).

Capitalism and Vodún converge to propel Vodún into global religious markets, thereby allowing acè to travel from place to place while embedded ritually in the initiates' physical bodies, in the spirits' material bodies (shrines), and in power objects such as bǒ. As both economic and ritual patterns expand to take on new transnational trends in African religion, acè has become global as Vodún's quintessential commodity from which can be derived both divine power and religious authority (or the right to act). With acè finding new homes all over the world in places such as New York City, foreign initiates use the objects they have acquired to legitimize their religious authority to potential clients and to the global Vodún community. To achieve this, foreign initiates often create websites and Facebook pages on which photographs and videos of themselves receiving shrines or bǒ are prominently displayed. These initiates then use their shrines and bǒ along with photographs of these objects (much like secular tourists use photographs of themselves at famous or exotic locales) as evidence of their successful journey into what one American initiate described to me as the "secret world of Vodún."

Michael, a New Yorker and American Vodún initiate in his thirties, illustrates this point perfectly. One evening while I was visiting him in his New York apartment, he gave me an impromptu tour of his shrines. One by one he pointed to each shrine and recounted the day he was initiated and given the authority to own the shrines that now rest on a series of shelves that transformed his former coat closet into a Vodún temple.

"That's Lĕgbà. He's the first spirit I received back in 2007," Michael said, while pointing to a grapefruit-sized dirt mound fashioned in the shape of a head who was crowned with a tuft of exotic feathers, two cowrie-shell eyes, and an iron-forged, forever-erect iron penis.

"But this one. You'll love this one," Michael said as he moved to grab a small plastic bottle of red palm oil from the shelf.

He began to pour the nearly coagulated oil into a large terra-cotta pot that was decorated with red, blue, and white dots, which were meant to represent smallpox scars.

"The oil soothes his skin lesions," Michael explained. "This is Sakpatá, the vodún of smallpox. I received him in 2009 to help me with a medical issue that I was having with my stomach."

On that day, Michael introduced me to more than ten of his spirits, including Gbădù, Fá, Xɛbyosò, and Yalódè. With each introduction, he recounted the fascinating circumstances that surrounded each of the initiations he received during several trips to Bénin. Once he introduced me to each of his spirits, he invited me to wait for him in his living room while he prepared a pot of tea for us.

"There's one more thing I want to show you," he shouted from the kitchen. "I need to show you the good stuff! Hang on, let me finish this tea." After a few minutes, he made his way back into the living room. He was holding a small, circular brass tray on which was balanced precariously a pot of tea, two cups, and a small, carved wooden box. He smiled and opened the box, revealing a series of small objects inside.

"This one lets you see the future," he explained, pulling out a two-inch mirror that had been backed with white leather.

Holding a small cowrie shell wrapped in red thread, Michael said, "This one brings wealth." As he retrieved a thin brass bracelet from the box, he said, "And this one. This one is my favorite. It took years before they agreed to teach me how to make this one. But it was worth it. I think I am the only foreigner that knows this recipe! I've sold tons of them to women. I know it looks like a simple bangle. But it's powerful. It requires lots of special leaves. Rare leaves. It helps women to become pregnant. And it works, fast."

Michael regularly sold bǒ and spirit shrines that he learned to construct while in Bénin. For Michael, and others like him, it is precisely the spirit's and bǒ's materiality—that is to say, the emphasis initiates place on the ritual construction of objects, evidence of effective recipes, and proof of the initiate's right and power to own, market, and sell bǒ and shrines—that authenticates their roles as priests, verifies their right to acè, and therefore contributes to the globalization of Vodún. However, by shifting one's focus to azě, a more intimate story in which foreigners have shown little interest can be told.

Similar to the ways in which bǒ may empower individuals, azě too may be empowered by objects. Objects, such as a carefully constructed witchcraft gourd (azěká), are made with azě to increase the power of the witch and initiate new witches into the cult. Animals such as owls, black cats, and vultures are often thought of as dangerous agents of azě or even witches who have used their powers to polymorph into these animals so as to move among people undetected. In fact, owls are so strongly connected to azě that the word for "owl" in Fɔngbè is azěxè, meaning "witchcraft bird." Finally, spirits such as Kɛnnɛsi, Mǐnɔna, and Gbǎdù are all widely believed to have azě—the universal force from which these divinities draw their powers to protect their devotees. Yet, unlike bǒ, which arguably depends on material objects in order to be made manifest in the world, azě, as a universal and invisible power, exists apart from its materiality. Instead, azětɔ́ use the occult potency of objects to empower azě. But azě's connection to objects is even more elusive than azě itself. In fact, I was in Bénin for more than ten months before I ever heard of an azěká or learned that some of the vodún are thought to be empowered by this force that almost everyone I met described to me as "dangerous."

Béninois worry that azětɔ́ may attack them from the inside—an "inside" that has admittedly been expanding for decades, reflecting a broadening in the ways one may experience their communities (Geschiere 2013). However, even as their notion of who is, or who is not, close to them expands, Béninois continue to worry that their success may attract the attention of powerful witches who are living secretly within their own families, villages, neighborhoods, towns, and cities. For many of the Béninois with whom I spoke, witchcraft was, as Peter Geschiere has described it, the "dark side of kinship" (1997: 11). For these individuals, azě is a reaction to the paradox and vulnerability of closeness where jealousy and aggression emerge from the intimacy that proximity creates.

If Geschiere is correct and witchcraft is indeed "anchored in intimacy" (2013: 35), then this might explain why foreign spiritual seekers find witchcraft to be "uninteresting" or "unnecessary" to the ways they practice Vodún in their own countries. In my own case, it was not until I had been in Bénin for nearly a year, been initiated into Vodún, and become deeply connected with my initiator and his family that my Béninois friends warned me of attacks from witches. As Geschiere points out, it was not until I had developed intimate relationships in Bénin that I became vulnerable to witchcraft. Even so, Geschiere himself reminds us that intimacy is a flexible concept that has expanded a great deal over the past few decades. Witchcraft fears have expanded from the family now to include nearby urban centers and even across oceans as more Africans move to places such as the United States. As one's intimate world expands, so do the salience and power of witchcraft.

In the case of Vodún, azě is still mainly a Béninois preoccupation. After foreigners become initiated into Vodún they often return to West Africa and develop intimate relationships with their initiators, and this, I believe, will transform the value of azě into a transnational interest. Over time, as ritual allows for Vodún's global and racial expansion, foreign spiritual seekers will become more profoundly intermeshed with Béninois families as well as their politics and struggles. When this happens, it will not take long for foreign Vodúnisants to discover that "intimacy can . . . evoke feelings of both safety and danger" (Geschiere 2013: 25). Once this occurs, I am convinced that the need for azě, along with a foregrounding of its now-hidden materiality, will arise. But for now, in a search for acceptance, foreign initiates seek out the power of bǒ, which promises its owner transformation and power without the entanglement of closeness.

As Vodún expands to include individuals from all over the globe, I predict that Béninois concepts of intimacy will change to include an ever-broadening global multinational and multiracial community. This then will result in azě becoming increasingly more available to people outside Bénin and West Africa, thereby encouraging azě's now-secret material culture to emerge, as bǒ has done, to adapt to trends in the religion's global development. I am certain that azě will one day be as successful if not more successful than bǒ has been in Vodún's developing global marketplace.

Ghosts as Contraband

Although the buying and selling of azě and bǒ are an important part of the local Vodún economy, tourists are just now beginning to participate as local priests marketing their powers. By contrast, the buying and selling of other religious artifacts began long ago. For example, as I highlighted in the opening vignette to this chapter, elaborately decorated ancestral masks known as Egúngún have caught the eyes of international African art dealers for decades—each often fetching more than 10,000 USD on the international retail art market. Contrary to the buying and selling of azě and bǒ, which are dominated by local agents, the exchange of important—and secret—religious artifacts such as Egúngún has been mostly controlled by international buyers.

When I asked Béninois about Egúngún masks, they often described them to me as being "created by the ancestors and for the ancestors," highlighting the belief that "after an Egúngún masquerade, the ancestors leave the earth for the spirit world, taking the masks with them." Others told me that Egúngún masks are created by ritual specialists who store the masks in secrecy until the ancestors are summoned into the masks in order to dance among the living. Either way, access to Egúngún masks is controlled tightly, and exact information surrounding Egúngún is always considered secret. Due to the culture of secrecy that surrounds the Egúngún cult, no sizable local market exists for the masks outside the special market that flourishes between members of the Egúngún society, the ritual specialists who make the masks, and the families who need the masks to remember and honor their dead. Nevertheless, a few savvy locals have begun targeting tourists who may be interested in buying masks for their art collections at home. Avoiding masks that are still important to the masquerade, these local agents often sell newly constructed masks or masks that have been retired due to their disrepair or age—although this is not always the case.

The few times I was able to observe the buying and selling of Egúngún masks, it consistently occurred at night, and the sellers were always young men, typically in their early twenties to late thirties. Older Egúngún society members were more likely to speak against this growing market, claiming that buying and selling their "culture" is not good for anyone. Nevertheless, Béninois also acknowledged that poverty motivated people to take actions they normally would not do otherwise. The selling of Egúngún is a small but lucrative market, as foreign buyers often pay as much as 4,000 USD—more than the average annual income for most Béninois—for a single mask.

Encounters between foreign buyers and local sellers always seemed unsettling, as these meetings were usually after midnight, down a dark alley, and behind locked doors. Secrecy was paramount—not just to keep noninitiates from seeing the masks on display, but also to keep other people in the community from knowing who was selling Egúngún and to whom. With subterfuge in the air, indexing the discomfort of the situation, one French buyer even commented one evening, "It's too heavy in here! We're buying art, not cocaine." While he underestimated the social potency of the "art" he was buying, he certainly intuited the social maneuvering that this particular market required—equating the buying and selling of Egúngún to contraband as serious as cocaine was not too far off the mark.

Even as the Egúngún art market grabs international attention—even if somewhat underground—there is another type of exchange that is more in line with local sensibilities regarding the processes surrounding Egúngún secrecy. Foreign spiritual seekers who become initiated into the Egúngún society often have a different experience from the French buyer I just described. For example, when I became initiated into the Egúngún Society at Fátòmè, Jean told me, "Before you leave, you'll need to have a mask made, and you'll need to dance." I had no idea that my initiation into the Egúngún society was going to be so complicated. These expectations are known by local candidates because they have lived in the culture their entire lives; because of my foreignness, I was unaware of many of these obligations before I became initiated.

Over time, I became friends with some of the local mask makers and eventually ended up with one of my own—freshly made and undanced, the only way my moral compass would allow me to make the purchase. My exchange was different from that of the French buyer. My mask was shown to me in broad daylight; I helped with its construction; and the Egúngún Society, including the Egúngún elders, was involved in the "transaction." Even though economic gain was a likely motivator, the Béninois Egúngún initiates saw our exchange as one sanctioned by my initiation, and as one that valued the symbolic and spiritual potency of what I was acquiring. "We know it's not art to you," "We know you won't sell this for profit," "We know you will respect the mask," "We know you will use this properly"—these were all sentiments that I heard from the people involved during the transaction.

There is a significant difference in these types of exchanges. The selling of Egúngún, and other types of restricted religious artifacts, to foreign art dealers or collectors has a different "feel" to local people than does selling the same items to foreign initiates. Indeed, after my initiation, when I expressed a disinterest in acquiring an Egúngún, several people asked me, "Didn't you take your initiation seriously?" While it is entirely possible that people insisted that I "need" an Egúngún mask for economic reasons, I believe that my friends, fellow initiates, and teachers were concerned that I would be unable to meet my obligations to the Egúngún without having a mask with me when I returned home. There was a difference in the way that foreign initiates, including myself, were treated in contrast to buyers who were clearly art dealers or collectors. While the economic component of the buying and selling of secret religious artifacts was always present, for some foreign initiates, the social capital given to them by virtue of their initiation seemed to remove the unsettling, forbidden, or even polluted feel of exchanges that, in other contexts, were deemed purely economic.

Technology and Transnational Occult Economies

As tourists and anthropologists add global layers to face-to-face religious exchanges, the Internet and other technologies, such as Western Union's money-transfer service, have also contributed to their economic expansion in profound ways. While I lived in Bénin, three Vodún priests separately asked me to help them set up a website for the explicit purpose of "attracting foreign clients," and three entrepreneurs asked me about how they might set up an e-store on the Internet so that they could sell Vodún paraphernalia— including Egúngún masks, bǒ, and spirit shrines—to foreign buyers. On one occasion, I even helped a local diviner receive electronic payment for a ceremony he was to perform for an American client he met on Facebook who wanted to take magical steps to win back her estranged boyfriend.

The emerging use of the Internet as a form of advertising, or e-commerce, for the Béninois Vodún community is compelling but not unexpected. In contemporary Bénin, radio, television, and billboard advertisements are used by many urban and semiurban Vodún who wish to attract a local clientele. While these strategies attract some foreign business,[18] many of my contacts believed the Internet to be integral to their international success in a growing market that is becoming increasingly competitive. Facebook now allows Béninois to develop an online persona, which is then maintained and enhanced through the site (see Gershon 2011: 867) by posting photographs of spirit shrines, information about initiations of local and foreign practitioners, frequent status updates, and religious "lessons." Béninois use Facebook as a way of participating in what some scholars have thought of as a quintessential element of neoliberalism (Martin 2000; Gershon 2011); that is, they use their online personas to develop a "collection of assets that must be continually invested in, nurtured, managed, and developed" (Martin 2000: 582), which in turn provides them with clients and capital. On Facebook, West Africans strive to maintain their online personas and bolster their creditability and authentic value in order to compete in an ever-growing market in which, as Erving Goffman (1959) might have predicted, the effective performance of one's identity becomes crucial.

Remarkably, the Internet, especially since the advent of Facebook, has for quite some time served as a powerful tool for English-speaking Nigerians who wish to attract international—especially American—clients for spiritual services, including initiation. Because most foreign spiritual seekers who travel to West Africa to become initiated come from the United States, those Béninois who are interested in high levels of technological success are hampered due to their lack of proficiency in English, combined with the average American's inability to speak French. Some local practitioners are working to overcome these language barriers either by insisting that their children learn English in school or by hiring English-speaking interpreters for their American clients.

Reaching out to an international audience and developing relationships with foreign buyers, whether through the Internet or as a result of face-to-face business, do not just involve marketing ceremonies and initiations. Selling an Egúngún mask, distributing bǒ to international buyers, and initiating foreigners help Béninois Vodúnisants develop both transnational communities and international capital.

"It's good to know we have family in America," Jean's son would always tell me.

"I am excited to work with you. Maybe you could help me set up an exhibit of my work in the United States," an Egúngún tailor once confided.

"If you ever find anyone in the United States who needs Vodún supplies, send them to me."

"When you're home and you find students of your own—and you will find students—do not forget about us here. Bring your clients here to us, and we will initiate them," Jean told me as we parted on my last day in Bénin.

All these moments express interest in developing a network—not only to garner potential economic capital but also to develop transnational networks that provide those Béninois who actively work with foreign spiritual seekers with the social capital necessary to draw upon these global networks. Conversely, being initiated comes with new responsibilities for the foreign initiate. In my case, the people of Fátòmè are a part of me forever. They shared their knowledge and experiences with me; they initiated me and brought me into their sacred—and secret—temples, groves, and rituals. In exchange, they gained an ally in the United States and extended their network beyond West Africa and into the Americas.

For some foreign travelers, these pseudo-familial networks that are formed as a result of initiation are profound. Many American initiates return home and establish a web presence to attract clients and future initiates as they begin living as diviners in their home country. While many foreign initiates perform ceremonies for clients in the United States, they also help their initiators in Africa develop international capital by praising the names of initiators on their websites, in newsgroup forums, or on Facebook. In turn, the repeated mentions of their West African initiators attract attention and, in some cases, have created them into Facebook celebrities whose reputations attract a great deal of international business.

Additionally, many foreigners who become initiated in West Africa return to undergo additional initiations into various spirit cults, and they occasionally bring clients with them to Africa who also became initiated. Even a cursory examination of the Facebook profiles of West African priests and American initiates reveals a steady photographic stream of these types of dynamic interactions. Although most of these photographic essays come from Nigeria, which has a longer history of foreign initiations than Bénin, tourists are traveling to Bénin for similar encounters in increasing numbers—especially as Nigeria suffers from internal political and religious strife and concomitant defamation from the international media. Increasingly, all these networks have become dependent on the Internet as a tool for advertising and as a way for people to develop and maintain international Vodún communities. The Internet has allowed foreign spiritual seekers both to pay for their initiations in advance of their trips to West Africa and to purchase ritual artifacts from a distance in creative ways. Fon and Yorùbá spiritual entrepreneurs have caught on quickly to the increasing importance of an Internet presence and have even begun accepting all major credit cards through Western Union's money-transfer service.

Upon returning to the United States, I set up a Facebook account for the primary purpose of keeping in touch with my friends in Bénin. Since July 2011, I have received an influx of friend requests from people living in Bénin, Nigeria, Haiti, Cuba, Brazil, Europe, and the United States—all of whom practice some variant of Vodún or òrìṣà worship. In many ways, Facebook has opened up an entire world of possibilities to me. I have been able to maintain contacts with my friends in Bénin while developing new contacts with important players in spiritual tourism who live in Nigeria, Brazil, and Haiti. Facebook has also highlighted new layers that are thriving in the international occult economy that originated in West Africa. Within less than three months of setting up my account, I was approached by four people who wanted to sell me Vodún supplies, five people who offered me initiation into various spirit cults, and three artisans who specialized in making and providing Vodún masks, wood carvings, and metalwork. An international occult market in Bénin and Nigeria is apparent not only on the ground but also on the Internet and on Facebook especially as it thrives and expands immeasurably.

Religious Markets Support Religious Expansion

In this chapter, I examined the ways in which objects such as Egúngún masks have entered a transnational market; how Vodún's globalization has contributed to the transnational marketability of witchcraft and sorcery in Bénin; and how these markets are supported, and in some ways, encouraged by new technological resources such as Facebook. Béninois and international Vodún practitioners see the spiritual economy in which they participate as transnational, secretive, and, in some cases, dangerous and legally challenging. However, for them the risks are worth the spiritual and economic rewards. As the Comaroffs have shown for South Africa, both Béninois and foreign practitioners of Vodún construct bǒ to mitigate the risk and enhance the rewards of this market. In fact, when I expressed my own anxieties about traveling back to the United States from Bénin with my spirit shrines, a Béninois friend removed a small leather bundle from his pants pocket, placed it in my hand, and told me that the bǒ would ensure that I had a "safe and uneventful" trip home.

The global market that bridges West Africa and the African Americas is growing; thanks to spiritual tourism and emerging Internet-supported transnational religious markets, there is no sign of this growth slowing down. Each week I receive new friend requests on Facebook from individuals who seek to be a part of West Africa's transnational community. On Facebook, I see hundreds of photographs of people from the United States, Brazil, and Europe being initiated into various West African religions; I see famous Nigerian religious woodcarvers and mask makers sell their art for hundreds and sometimes thousands of dollars; I see Béninois and Nigerian diviners use Skype to provide their international clients with a divination session while thousands of miles apart; and I see American, Brazilian, and European Vodún priests advertise "initiations in Africa." Each day, objects are sold, divination is performed, initiations are scheduled, and friends are made on Facebook as Vodún's global market continues to expand. In many of these exchanges, secrecy becomes the marker of authenticity, where the backroom of "real treasures" extends beyond an art dealer's "private office" (cf. Steiner 1994: 30) and onto a large multinational stage where spiritual tourism and an emerging transnational occult economy converge—sometimes in Africa, sometimes abroad, and sometimes in cyberspace. In all these cases, occult objects are consecrated and authenticated through the performance of secrecy. Whether it is the secret nature of an object or the secret manner in which the object is sold, each of these objects leaves Africa and enters the international market as an authentic and potent component of Vodún's emerging transnational market. In the next chapter, I will show how the involvement of foreign spiritual seekers and the development of a complex spiritual marketplace for Vodún have begun to transform the way in which Vodúnisants experience belief.

CHAPTER 4

Belief, Efficacy, and Transnationalism

> Obviously action can be guided by belief. What tends
> to be less recognized—and cuts against the common
> stereotype—is that belief can be guided by action.
> —Luhrmann 1989: 310

"Do you believe in Fá divination?" Marc asked.

"Yeah, I think so," I replied. "I've seen the words of Fá come true! I can't explain it—but, yeah, I believe."

"Do you believe in the *vodún*?"

"Yeah, if I believe in the power of Fá, then I must believe in the power of the spirits—don't you think?" I responded.

"Do you believe in witchcraft?" Marc continued.

To this question, I hesitated, unsure how to respond. Witchcraft was still too abstract for me. At this point I had been in Bénin for slightly over twelve months. I had studied as a diviner's apprentice with Jean and had seen Fá divination help people understand, cope with, and eventually overcome life's obstacles. It was not until a couple of months later, when I saw Jean take on a new client, that my relationship with Fá and witchcraft began to change.

One afternoon, a few months before my conversation with Marc, I sat with Jean as he performed divination for a few clients. As he divined, all his apprentices sat around him as he interpreted the signs. On occasion he would ask one of us to interpret the sign we saw so that he could correct our mistakes and reinforce our successes. Jean had just finished divining for a young man who wanted Fá to help him to pass an important college entrance exam. Just as the hopeful student began to leave with a list of rituals and sacrifices that he must perform, a haunting Béninois woman walked through the door and into Jean's consultation room. She was tall, with paper-thin skin that seemed to barely fit over her fragile frame. Her clothes, too big for her body, were falling off her severely emaciated shoulders. The woman, who I later learned was named Marianne, was visibly and deathly ill.

"I need help," Marianne whispered. "I am dying."

"Come in! Romar, get her some water," Jean said while gesturing for her to sit on a small wooden stool in front of him. "What's wrong? How can I help you?"

"My brother's wife is a witch. She's trying to kill me," Marianne explained.

Marianne was weak and heavy with the impression of death. One could not help but feel deep sorrow for her as she struggled to speak. Every word seemed to cost her a part of her already fading life. After a few minutes of prayers and libations, Jean was ready to reveal the sign from which Fá would speak.

"*Osa-Meji!*" Jean announced, bringing the sign into being. "It's witchcraft," Jean confirmed. "But I can help you. You will need to stay here for a couple of weeks. I will feed you while you're here. There are a lot of ceremonies we need to do. But Fá says you will live." Jean spoke with startling certainty. He was just as confident that she would live as I was that she would succumb to her mysterious illness.

Over the next two weeks, Jean consulted Fá daily and performed the sacrifices and prayers that Fá prescribed. Each day Marianne did as Fá suggested and offered Gbădù kola nuts, giant snails, and shea butter. She burned four white offertory candles in front of the locked door that led to Gbădù's forbidden room while begging the powerful, but dangerous, vodún for what seemed to be an unlikely cure.

"Fá says only Gbădù can save her," Jean said to me, careful that Marianne did not hear him.

"Do you think she will live? Will Gbădù help her?" I asked.

Jean simply replied, "Yes. Just wait. You'll see what Gbădù and Fá can do."

I envied Jean's certainty and respected his trust in the vodún. While I struggled to believe that Marianne would live, over time she slowly regained her strength and began to look more and more vibrant. I was stunned. Jean had succeeded. By the end of Marianne's two-week stay in Fátòmɛ, she had gained both weight and vitality. She was, as Jean said she would be, healed.

Marianne did not come to Jean for healing because she believed in Fá or in Jean's ability to help her. She came to Jean because she had experienced Fá's power in the past and had come to appreciate what Fá could accomplish. Healing is central to Vodún. Compelled by one's search for well-being, Vodún's amorphous boundaries provide the space for Béninois like Marianne to rely on Fá and any number of other beings, including Christ—often at the same time. It seems clear that postcolonial and capitalist struggles in Bénin, and in Africa more broadly, have fostered the mixing and blending of African religious systems so that individuals may draw on indigenous African religious cults, Christianity, and Islam simultaneously and with a focus on what works and what helps them to overcome struggles. For Marianne, and others like her, their beliefs in spiritual and occult powers ebb and flow creatively, strategically, and politically as their needs and desires react to everyday challenges. Simply put, healing is always Vodún's focus and goal, and it is central to understanding how and why Vodún fulfills its devotees today (Brown 2001 [1991]). Healing, whether from physical, spiritual, or social woes, gives purpose to ritual, divination, and the spirits themselves. Desjarlais (1992) observed in Nepal that "health not only implies well-being on an individual, bodily scale; it means that one's familial, social, and cosmic relations proceed as a harmonious whole" (161). This also holds true in Bénin. Marianne not only sought to be healed physically but also wished to have the social drama that surrounds all accusations of witchcraft redressed and made right again. While some may suggest that Marianne sought to be cured, what she truly desired was a holistic sense of well-being.

Yet, despite knowing that it was Marianne's desire for well-being that compelled her to seek out Fá's help, and regardless of the effects of witchcraft being visually obvious on Marianne's frail body, I could not bring myself to believe that a mystical force caused her near-death. Mirroring the experiences of many spiritual tourists, for me witchcraft was something different—something in which I could not bring myself to believe. I had a hard time believing that souls, who are said to leave their human bodies at night, could assemble in a tall tree—often in the form of birds, especially owls—to plot, and enact, the slow demise of community members by gradually eating the souls of their victims until the death of the target is achieved. I realized the contradiction in my belief. Despite my disbelief in witchcraft, this woman was, in some ways, evidence of witchcraft's social power. I could see witchcraft's influence on her life. It was obvious to me that she would have died had Jean, Fá, and Gbǎdù not stepped in. I seemed caught in a belief paradox in which witchcraft was beginning to seem real to me while fantastic stories from people who claimed to see women turning into birds kept my belief in witchcraft from forming fully.

My struggle with the occult principles of witchcraft was not something I concealed. In fact, I thought of my own conundrum of belief as a theme that both haunted and inspired me throughout my time in Bénin. My neighbors and friends were curious but patient with me as I struggled with my disbelief in witchcraft—despite my publicly perceived belief in Fá and Vodún. As I learned, I was not alone in my struggle: most other international spiritual seekers grappled with similar issues. In this chapter, at the broadest level, I explore the analytical salience of belief in the study of West African religion while focusing on how belief is maintained and creatively negotiated as Vodún and tourism intersect on the global stage. To achieve this, I will present ethnographic stories that help to explicate how both Béninois and foreign spiritual seekers come to believe in Vodún and how spiritual tourism has begun to change Vodún's beliefscape.

Witchcraft: Belief and Identity

American and European spiritual seekers may understand what it means to believe in the spirits' power. But, as other scholars have pointed out, in these cases, the experience of belief, or how one comes to a belief, tends to be defined in exclusively Christian terms and, moreover, often remains too abstract. Malcolm Ruel has argued that the very concept of "belief is too strongly connected to Western ideas of Christianity for scholars to apply the term to other [non-Western] religious traditions" (1982: 27). But then how do we talk about those experiences that approach what we may call belief in Vodún—if not with belief itself?

As I will show, for African religions, we can no longer take the easy route and simply say that belief is too Christian or too Western to be analytically valuable. We cannot, as Rodney Needham (1972) advocated four decades ago, avoid the study of belief altogether, just because accessing internalized truths is a task in futility. Béninois and foreign Vodún practitioners actively discuss belief in everyday contexts to talk about their embodied religious truths, even if these truths are performative or nascent. As with other topics of inquiry, scholars can gain a rich understanding of Vodún practices if we attempt to understand how the experience of belief plays out in social space. Without contextualization, terms such as *faith, belief,* and *knowledge* all fall short in allowing us to understand how belieflike experiences in Vodún play out. To mobilize belief in Vodún, I draw on the ways in which Béninois *Vodúnisants* conceptualize belief in concert with efficacy. For them, belief is always a consequence of their experience with effectiveness and not an initial requirement for religious identity. This point is further reflected linguistically, as in Fɔngbè the verb "to believe" and the verb "to be efficacious" are the same (*ɖì*). As I will show, among Fon speakers one's belief is often reinforced by evidentiary events that meaningfully prove the effectiveness of one's religion.

Witchcraft provides a compelling backdrop for this discussion. For many Béninois, like Marianne and Jean, the belief in witchcraft (*azĕ*) is a nonnegotiable component of their belief systems. Witchcraft was something everyone I spoke with in Bénin believed in—albeit with varying intensities. I quickly found that no one, including me, was immune to its social power. These experiences were highlighted when I became friends with a market woman whom everyone affectionately called Nafí.[1] She sold tomatoes and peppers in unimaginable quantities, moving bushels of tomatoes from Togo, Burkina Faso, and Nigeria to Bénin. Her economic success was predicated on her continuously developing new strategies to sell her vegetables to more people. We met because she is the mother-in-law of my research assistant's daughter. Each market day she helped me by breaking a larger CFA note into coins. I found the coins useful in managing the markets, taxis, and street vendors (who all seemed to operate consistently "without change"), while Nafí appreciated large bills in order to buy tomatoes in large quantities.

Over time, Nafí and I became close friends. I attended her mother's funeral and often visited her at her home. Sometimes I joined her at her tomato stand in Ouidah's market just to discuss local politics or the town's everyday goings-on. Our friendship was unusual. While my apprenticeship positioned me in the community as a diviner and practitioner of Vodún, Nafí was known to have rejected Vodún—despite being raised by a father who was a prominent Vodún priest—for what she considered to be the "calmer" and "simpler" life of an evangelical Christian. She took Bible study classes at the local evangelical church and proudly hung her graduation certificate in a gold plastic frame in her home. Her certificate symbolized Nafí's belief in Christ and her espoused expulsion of Vodún from her life. She literally carried her Bible with her everywhere and hosted weekly prayer sessions at her home under a covered meeting area that she constructed just for this purpose.

Some of Nafi's friends wondered how she and I could be friends—one a perceived Vodúnisant, the other an established evangelical Christian. Ethnographers have always had an interesting and sometimes paradoxical relationship with their major informants and research assistants. Some have had informants chosen for them by the local community (e.g., Turner 1967; Griaule 1975 [1948]); some find great comfort, regret, and hope in the people they meet in the field (Gottlieb and Graham 1994, 2012); some take on the role of student so that they may learn from local teachers (Stoller and Olkes 1987; Stoller 2004; Landry 2008); and others actively collaborate with the local community who opened their homes and their lives to them (Gujar and Gold 1992; Keller and Kuautonga 2007). Nafi and I were friends whose differences encouraged our friendship. While we never collaborated directly on any aspect of my project, she enthusiastically offered to be my next research assistant should I return to work on a project that was focused on Jesus. As much as it pains me to acknowledge, Nafi's offer was partly rooted in a certain proselytizing zeal, motivated by a sincere belief that if I were to research Christianity in Bénin, I would be "saved" from Vodún—an outcome she was quietly eager to facilitate. I was aware that our pairing would have not been possible in the United States: neither of us would have given the other a chance. But genuine interest and curiosity, combined with our distance from each other's national and social politics, softened our differences. I was curious how a woman who grew up deeply entrenched in Vodún could reject that belief system for Christianity, and I imagine she wondered the opposite of me. Her curiosity was expressed often as she questioned me about my involvement in Vodún.

"I don't understand how you came to be interested in Vodún. Why would you throw away your chance to get into Heaven?" she asked.

"I guess I don't see it like that," I said, trying to avoid confrontation.

"Tim, you're white. The gates of Heaven are open to you freely—don't ruin that for yourself. I am black. I have to work hard to get into Heaven," Nafi explained, switching between French and Fɔngbè.

My heart sank when I heard her say these words. Years of inequality, colonialism, missionary work, and the global oppression of African religious systems and knowledge on both global and local stages had created an ideology that propagated the devaluation and demonization of her Africanness and blackness. For Nafi, as with many others, her blackness positioned her as a likely pariah in her imagined afterlife—an imagined scenario that in turn forced her to work harder than someone such as myself, who she imagined could enter the "gates of Heaven" seemingly by the virtue of his race.

Whether by telling compelling stories of Vodún's dangers, by challenging my own involvement with Fá divination, or by criticizing her Vodún neighbors under her breath and in the safety of her own compound, for Nafí, our conversations and time together often gave her the chance to defend her belief in Christ. Yet, despite our numerous interactions, she never actively tried to save me—even if she did suggest that I would be more fulfilled by Christ than by Fá—and, for my part, I never challenged her choice to convert. My friendship with Nafí existed beyond our basic fondness for each other—it was a friendship that thrived on conversations that highlighted processes of religious conversion and belief, topics in which we were both deeply interested.

After several broad yet somewhat perfunctory conversations, I built up the nerve to ask Nafí to talk about her conversion experience. It was a story she was waiting to tell.

"I was very sick," she answered. "I couldn't stand. I couldn't eat. I was dying. Someone wanted to kill me with witchcraft because they were jealous of my success [in the market]."

"So, you believe in witchcraft?" I questioned.

"Of course I do! And Jesus healed me. Jesus saved me. And Jesus continues to protect me and my family from witchcraft," Nafí responded.

"Couldn't the spirits also protect you from witchcraft?"

"Yes, but for a price! Sometimes a big price! Tim, why would I choose to offer drinks, chickens, and goats to the spirits to protect me? Why would I spend all that money to make sure I am safe from witches—especially since witches are such a problem here in Ouidah—when I can pray to Jesus for free and achieve the same results?"

I did not have anything to add. I sat in amazement, sipping on a cold Coke that Nafí had just bought for us to share. I reminded myself that Nafí's fear of witchcraft was undoubtedly deepened by her fear of jealousy as a result of her financial success (LeMay-Boucher, Noret, and Somville 2011). Even so, I was struck by Nafí's admission that while economics and neoliberal markets certainly came into play, it was precisely her profound belief and not her disbelief in the efficacy of witchcraft—a belief that was proven to her by the illness materialized on her body, and, by extension, in the Vodún worldview—that made evangelical Christianity appealing.

Nafī's story of religious conversion was not unique. In fact, her reasons for converting followed common trends that Béninois often spoke about when they discussed their conversion from Vodún to Christianity. Time and time again, I heard from Christians that they had converted from Vodún because they felt that they needed to be protected from witchcraft—a force they all had seen "work" and therefore intensely believed was real, and to be feared (see Tall 1995). For individuals such as Nafi, Christianity provided her with an efficient way to protect her and her family from witchcraft that did not require the expense of sacrifice (Meyer 1999). For Nafī, prayer was both free and effective.

Even so, we should consider the possibility that, in cases such as Nafī's, perhaps current notions of conversion are inadequate tools of interpretation. Our need to examine religious conversion is necessary because colonial religious regimes have "named, translated, and systematized" African religious thought in order to produce analogous religious structures and categories in an attempt to create new African Christianities (Landau 1999: 27). If not for colonialism, globalization, transnationalism, and the Western labeling of religious practice, according to Paul Landau, the term "religion" might even be meaningless in many African contexts, and religious conversion would be impossible, as many West African religions commonly—and comfortably—absorb and mobilize esoteric knowledge and practices of power, regardless of their origin.

Nafī's own "conversion" is the product of a creative, and shifting, layering of transnational and local ideologies that presumes the efficacy of both witchcraft and Christ without disempowering Vodún. In southern Bénin, I never saw evidence of a "powerful clash resulting from the shift from one realm of thought and action, to another," as described by Bennetta Jules-Rosette for another African context of Christian conversion (1975: 135), nor did I observe the complete replacement of ideology or worldview that one might expect of a religious convert (e.g., Nock 1933). Exploring conversion both to and from Vodún, even where spiritual tourists are concerned, is challenging because defining what is and what is not Vodún requires us to place boundaries around a system that has historically defied categorization. The perceived indefinable nature of Vodún is a result of attempts by U.S. and European scholars and practitioners to treat Vodún as a single religion comparable to religions such as Christianity. Even though today the religion has been conceptually homogenized into a densely packed, multivocal category, it is still tremendously porous, flexible, and absorptive to the point that belief is frequently determined by proven efficacy. As Dana Rush has shown, in Vodún, "when something 'works' more will be added. When something doesn't work, a new solution . . . will be explored" (2013: 33)—and, for Nafĩ, Christ is proving to be effective at waylaying the dangers of azĕ.

While Christ provides Nafĩ with spiritual protection, Nafĩ is also clearly a product of a postcolonial and neoliberal world in which Christian missionaries mark, and market, certain practices as "right" and "wrong" (Orta 2004), relegating other social practices such as dress, language, and ancestor veneration as "elements of 'culture' with no intrinsic religious value" (Kaplan 2004: 376). Like so many other Béninois, Nafĩ maneuvers though a world caught between the flexible framework of her Africanness and the perceived rigidity of her imported religion. As a result, Nafĩ is outwardly a Christian who considers Vodún and witchcraft to be at once powerful and effective—yet diabolic and, paradoxically, necessary. Nafĩ neither denied the reality of the spirits nor doubted their influence on the social world in which she lived. Convinced by missionaries and missionary propaganda that the spirits are nothing more than demons sent to earth by Satan, Nafĩ embraced Christianity as the "right path to heaven and goodness"—regardless of the spirits' ability to heal, protect, and empower.[2] To Nafĩ, these positive attributes commonly associated with the spirits were nothing more than Satan's trickery to mislead people.

Nafi never gave up her belief in the vodún—their power remained indelibly present on her landscape just like the small oil stain that had set into her expensive Hollandaise cloth she wrapped around her waist. Like the spirits in Nafĩ's life, the oil stain had faded from years of washing yet was still visible. Nafĩ's experience, including her devotion to Christ and her sustained belief in the spirits, supports T. M. Luhrmann's point that "there does not seem to be any experience comparable to a sudden . . . different way of thinking" (1989: 312) when it comes to religious conversion. For Luhrmann, conversion is a slow, gradual process that she calls "interpretive drift"—a process that occurs as one becomes more "involved with a particular activity" (312). Nafĩ's case, like so many others, spotlights these processes at work. Conversion, as Nafĩ has shown, is not always a clear case of replacing one set of beliefs with another. Instead, new and old beliefs may be negotiated and filtered through one's personal experiences and politics while also considering the maintenance or harnessing of old or new types of social, religious, or symbolic forms of capital. This model is especially relevant in West Africa, where religious beliefs have long moved, layered, melded, and expanded as a result of transnationalism, wars, marriages, and multiple modes of cultural "borrowing."

While some Béninois Christians such as Nafi embrace Christ to protect them from others' jealousy—often additionally citing the economic cost of Vodún ceremonies and sacrifice—others incorporate Christian practices, such as going to church and praying to Christ, into their lives without eschewing Vodún entirely.[3] Still others keep themselves protected from witchcraft by embracing Vodún and maintaining intense devotion to the spirits. No matter which strategy local people employ, the fear of witchcraft and the acknowledgment of its veracity are common in Bénin, regardless of whether they consider themselves to be Vodúnisant, Christian, or something between the two.

Although the belief in and fear of witchcraft motivate and even inspire some Béninois religious practice in profound ways, international spiritual seekers approach Vodún and Fá divination as practices that are distinct—or at least separable—from a belief in witchcraft. Witchcraft, at least the Béninois variety, is quite foreign to most Westerners, while spirits—and even divination—seem less removed from Western worldviews. While the spirits themselves are not a part of mainstream U.S. and European society, most of the foreign spiritual seekers I encountered came to Bénin after first exploring Cuban Santería, Haitian Vodou, Brazilian Candomblé, or Western Occult traditions such as Wicca. For them, a world animated by spirits seemed plausible and inspirational. These Western-inspired ways of knowing were made clear to me one evening while sitting in a small bar in Ouidah, sharing a drink and conversing with Angela, an African American woman who had traveled to Bénin to learn about practicing Vodún. In our conversation, Angela expressed a profound interest in the spirits. She marveled at the ways in which spirits expressed themselves through "possession-performance" (Brown 2001), and she understood Fá divination as "the most powerful system of knowing in the world." However, when we began talking about witchcraft, her tone changed—she made it clear that she did not believe in the power of witchcraft. As though she were reading from an old anthropological text about witchcraft in Africa,[4] she argued that "witchcraft is just a way of controlling older women! It's designed to create scapegoats and punish innocent people for not bowing to the whims of society. Witchcraft in the magical sense is not real." While I was certain that witchcraft was not always about scapegoating or marginalization, I also knew that Angela's interpretation was not completely unfounded.

One evening, while walking home from the market with my friend Paulette, I greeted an elderly woman who seemed very interested in saying "hello." We chatted briefly, then I respectfully gave her my hand as a way of saying goodbye. She took my hand in hers, smiled, and continued her walk down the street, away from town. Once the woman was out of earshot, Paulette slapped me on my shoulder and protested, "Why did you greet her? Why did you touch her? She is a witch! Look at her! Can't you see that? Tim, everyone in town knows you're a *bokɔ́nɔ̀* [diviner], you can't go around greeting witches! It's not good for you!"

In this case, Paulette used a visual grammar to marginalize the nameless woman and identify her as a witch.[5] It was then that I realized that a belief in witchcraft—and, perhaps more importantly, a belief-driven fear of witchcraft—is much more important to the social lives of Fon and Yorùbá people living in southern Bénin than is the act of witchcraft. For many southern Béninois, a belief in witchcraft seemed to be inherently tied to beliefs in other occult forces such as the spirits, and even in Christ. By contrast, spiritual tourists' beliefs in local religious ideologies were encouraged by their connection to the spirits—but not by witchcraft. Yet as foreign spiritual tourists converge with Béninois practitioners of Vodún, their differing perspectives have begun to exist alongside each other, thereby expanding the definition of a "Vodún worldview."

The average tourist in Bénin does not believe in the power of witchcraft, and international spiritual seekers tend to deemphasize the abilities of reputed witches to kill or harm them or their families using mystical means. By contrast, in a survey I conducted of 125 Béninois of varying ethnicities, age groups, genders, and religious affiliations, 76 percent (95 of 125) indicated witchcraft as being the "most powerful," and 71 percent (89 of 125) thought it was the "most dangerous" spiritual force they knew. Additionally, pointing to the pervasive power of witchcraft across religious lines, 92 percent of Béninois respondents (115 of 125) positioned witchcraft as either being the "most powerful" or the "second most powerful" spiritual force they knew; of those who listed witchcraft as being the "second most powerful," 77 percent (20 of 26) positioned "Christ" as the "most powerful." As Christ and witchcraft struggle metaphorically for social power, their interdependence on each other's symbolic capital works to reinforce—instead of diminish—the salience of Béninois' collective belief in Vodún. Remarkably, it is a strong belief in witchcraft—and the Vodún worldview more broadly—that often encourages religious conversion from Vodún to Christianity; hence an unshakable belief in witchcraft is one of the factors that reinforces Vodún's position in a "modern" Bénin.

Despite believing in the spirits' power and understanding the pervasive presence of witchcraft in Bénin, I was unsure what I thought about witchcraft being a successful form of metaphysical warfare. The spirits and divination were familiar to many foreign spiritual seekers who traveled to West Africa. For many of them, myself included, azĕ was more like a foreign country that one must take time to understand and become acquainted with before visiting it. Like many foreign spiritual seekers, I came to Bénin having experienced African diasporic religion first. Before my first trip to Bénin I was initiated as a *houngan asogwe* in Haitian Vodou and I had developed close friendships with men and women who practiced Vodou and Lucumí in Haiti and the United States.

The spirits had become normal to me. Over a decade I watched two women who were thought to be infertile become pregnant with the help of a diviner. I saw a man overcome crippling unemployment with the help of the spirits. I looked on as a woman sought out a diviner to help her to manage and eventually overcome cancer. Simply put, the spirits had proven themselves empirically to those men and women who sought their help, and over time I had become convinced of their social efficacy. As my trust in divination grew, my interest in azĕ laid dormant. When I confided in Jean, my teacher and mentor, that I did not believe in the ability of witchcraft to kill or harm people, he said to me, "That's okay. You will one day. You just need to change the way you're thinking about it and see the effects of witchcraft for yourself. Then you won't be able to say that you don't believe." To Jean, I did not believe in azĕ because azĕ had yet to show me its power.

Over the course of my fifteen-month apprenticeship with Jean, I met sickly people like Marianne whose illness proved to them that they were the victims of witchcraft. Some of them Jean was able to help, but others unfortunately died. The symptoms were certainly real. While local people— including some devout Christians—could not see any other explanation for their sudden illnesses besides witchcraft, Western spiritual seekers had a hard time believing that witchcraft was the reason that these people were dying: their Western-trained eyes saw disease and accidents, not witchcraft and occult power. While Marianne's story certainly pushed me closer to believing in witchcraft, I, like many foreign spiritual seekers, struggled with the disconnect that emerged between the medical severity of her illness and her seemingly miraculous recovery. My experience with Marianne made me wonder, what was it about the ways in which tourists' beliefs were structured that made believing in witchcraft impossible while believing in divination and spirits remained possible? These questions haunted them daily. Many of them expressed uneasiness for not being unable to believe in witchcraft—an aspect of the Vodún worldview that flourished in Bénin's plural socioreligious landscape.

In trying to understand witchcraft, and simultaneously explore the reasons why many Western spiritual seekers refused to believe in its power, I began talking to people—especially Jean—about what witchcraft means to the local population. Interview after interview had the same results. Regardless of their professed religious affiliation, people insisted on the absolute power of witchcraft. Some insisted that only a type of witchcraft called azĕ wèwé (white witchcraft) could defeat the "evils" of azĕ wiwi (black witchcraft)—but they warned me that becoming a witch, even with "good intentions," is dangerous because it leads to one's inevitable fall into darkness and early death. The power of witchcraft was pervasive among locals but often denied among foreign spiritual seekers. I wondered how something so central to a belief system as witchcraft was to Vodún could be ignored and even rejected by international spiritual seekers, myself included.

With these questions swirling in my mind, one afternoon I met Marc at a small buvette (refreshment bar).

"Tim, I need to have some ceremonies performed," Marc proclaimed. "I'm worried people are going to start attacking me with witchcraft."

"Witchcraft? Really?" I questioned. "Don't you maintain your Fá?"

"Yes, I give food to my Fá," Marc retorted. "However, people are jealous—very jealous."

"Jealous of what?" I asked.

"Jealous of our friendship. People believe that I'm getting rich from you. People think that because you're white, you must be supporting me," Marc explained.

With this comment, I began to internalize the belief in witchcraft. For many Fon and Yorùbá people living in southern Bénin, the processes of witchcraft—that is to say, accusations, manifestations, anxieties, and prevention—are all performed in reaction to the suspicion that intimacy creates (Geschiere 2013).

Experiencing this in a personal way enabled me to believe in witchcraft—perhaps not in the metaphysical sense, but certainly as a meaningful cultural system that I, even as a foreigner, could experience. Through my close friendship with Marc, I began to feel witchcraft's pressure in my life as its social reach became tangible. I worried that his family no longer trusted me. I felt anxiety as I considered the possibility that Jean, Marc's uncle and my initiator, may no longer want to continue my apprenticeship. I felt azĕ's hold on me as despair overcame my thoughts. I was worried for Marc and I was worried for my ability to finish my project. In this moment, this experience began to merge with Marianne's story and witchcraft started to become real. Within a matter of days, Marc was able to perform the rituals that made him feel like less of a target and my relationship with everyone remained unscathed. However, from that day onward I forever worried about the challenges that closeness brought.

Peter Geschiere brilliantly explained the cross-cultural salience of witchcraft in his 2013 monograph, *Witchcraft, Intimacy, and Trust*. For Geschiere, "witchcraft has been seen as particularly frightening since it conjures up the danger of treacherous attacks from close by—from inside a social core where peace and harmony should reign" (2013: xv). The friendship that Marc and I shared became dangerous as we both became targets for azĕ. A belief in witchcraft not only curtails outward expressions of jealousy, but also provides people with the social tools necessary to cope with and defeat, or at least deflect, the challenges of intimacy while at the same time giving closeness— and the reaction against it—symbolic meaning.

Tourism and the Creation of Belief

"In just a few short weeks, I'll complete my ceremonies and become a priestess, Tim!" Marie exclaimed.

"Wow, Marie! When did this happen?" I asked her. "And how did you decide?"

"I don't know. I guess it was the tourists. Their questions made me think, and over time I began to see Vodún as beautiful and powerful. Yes. I can say that. It's because of the tourists that I became a Vodún priestess. Yes, it was tourists," Marie grinned.

Marie and her family were always gracious to me and eager to help me with my research in any way they could. But up until this point I had known Marie to be Catholic. Over the next few weeks, Marie built a small shrine to Tron to prepare for future clients and initiates of her own. After Marie was installed as the primary priestess of her new temple, she began waking up early each day to pray to Tron. Nearly each morning at sunrise, I would hear the indicative staccato clanking of Tron's sacred prayer stone as she slammed the golf ball–sized rock against the surface of her shrine; the sound of her prayer stone, which was unique to Tron, was muffled only by her soft singing and praying. Each morning she asked Tron to bless her and her family, to protect everyone in her home against witchcraft, and to continue to bring abundance to the family. The distinctive, and melodic, sound of her praying began to bring people to Marie's home who also wished to pray to Tron—mostly to protect themselves and their families from witchcraft, a specialty for which Tron is quite famous.[6]

In the three years that I knew Marie, she had effectively converted, although never fully, from Catholicism to Vodún. She still spoke of the power of Christ but has also begun believing in Tron, in the efficacy of divination, and in the power of the other spirits. Inspired by tourists, and motivated by a hunger to learn the answers to the many questions that foreigners had asked her over the years, Marie had become a *Vodúnɔ*. Marie was also a smart businesswoman—she was a successful tour guide, artist, and research assistant. She knew how to make money. Her focus on money made some people wonder whether her new belief in Vodún was just a "performance" to attract clients and give her the symbolic capital she needed to market herself not just to tourists and researchers but also to her own community as an expert of Vodún.

One could argue that Marie's personal participation—and belief—in Vodún increased as she became progressively involved so that Marie could conform to community expectations (e.g., Goody 1977; Humphrey and Laidlaw 1994) and actively tip the unpredictable scales of chance in her favor (e.g., Bourdieu 1980; Noret 2010). As Philippe LeMay-Boucher, Joël Noret, and Vincent Somville have pointed out, "Social involvement . . . does not necessarily imply personal and intimate belief in such phenomena" (2011: 4). Determining whether Marie's adherence to Vodún was an effort to conform or a reflection of "real" personal "beliefs" is most likely an exercise in futility: perhaps both are true. What is important to Marie is how her performance of belief (regardless of how "real" her beliefs may or may not be) imbued her with the symbolic capital she needed to attract new networks, clients, and funds—something a single mother of three children needed to do in order to take care of her family. Even so, Marie's beliefs always appeared "genuine."

Marie once told me, "The longer I do this [Vodún], the less skeptical I become." Even as Marie's involvement in Vodún surges, some local and foreign Vodún practitioners have suggested to me that she is just "playing" or is only "in [Vodún] for the money"—asserting that she does not "really believe." Marie, a member of a long-standing Catholic family, began her journey as many Western spiritual seekers do: curious, interested, but unaware of Vodún's secrets. Like spiritual tourists, Marie may have begun by "pretending" and mimicking observed Vodún practice and ritual action. Tourists may have inspired her conversion, but the change in worldview that allowed her to accept the spirits, divination, and Tron was her own, and it was complex and gradual.[7]

As with all systems of belief, Marie's belief in Vodún is no doubt part performance, part strategy, and part truth. I do not mean to suggest that Marie's case is any different from any case of believing. I take all cases of belief in Vodún to be creative processes pieced together and inspired by politics, goals, and the ways one performs his or her life (Kirsch 2004). Marie's case is a striking example of these processes at play. After all, given that an individual's beliefs are probably at some basic ontological level inaccessible (Needham 1972), who is to say which of Marie's outwardly performed beliefs are "true" expressions of her internal self? Reflecting on my own beliefs, especially as I navigate through the world of Vodún, I find it safe to say that few of us know where our beliefs fall on the truth-performance continuum. All one can say is that the construction and long-term maintenance of beliefs are creative processes that are inspired by a rich mix of symbolic capital, personal politics, and social strategy.

"Why Believe When You Can Know?"

Vodún's inherent flexibility is part of the reason Marie was able to easily—albeit gradually—convert.

"Vodún is more than a religion. It's a way of thinking, it's a philosophy," Marie explained.

This worldview, or "philosophy," permeates the sociocultural landscape in southern Bénin. Vodún has helped create a world of infinite flexibility in which beliefs and spirits are negotiated and accepted—around which new spirits such as Tron can enter the religion with relative ease, while old spirits such as Gǔ (Yr., Ògún) can change and adapt to modernity as his realm expands to include not just blacksmithing but also planes, trains, and automobiles that are constructed from metal (Barnes 1997). Vodún's pantheon is vast and ever-growing, and because each spirit cult comes with its own set of beliefs and practices, Vodún's flexibility has also allowed for some adherents to understand Christ as a cult of his own—as a vodún with his own particular rituals and customs. This type of acceptable, and even expected, mutability allows for great individual expression and varying beliefs within the religion.

While understanding what makes a religious practice or event "Vodún" or not can be challenging, there seems to be a socioreligious foundation that unifies the many contrasting belief systems within Vodún. A belief in divination and an awareness that divination provides a road map to well-being are part of that foundation. The centrality of divination to Vodún practice is reflected in the diverse practices of divination among the Fon and Yorùbá peoples of southern Bénin. Among the people with whom I worked, the supremacy of Fá divination was apparent. Many Fá diviners balked at the accuracy of some divination practices, such as mirror gazing, as practiced by priestesses of Mamíwátá, or kola-nut divination, as practiced by priests of Tron, claiming that, while potentially insightful, all divination systems outside of Fá lacked the acè necessary to be completely accurate. Whether Fá or other forms of seeing are used, divination is always centrally located in the lives of Vodúnisants, and Marie, despite her status as a new initiate in the religion, was no different.

Shortly after Marie's initiation, I began to notice that her reliance on divination became quite visible. She used kola nuts to speak with Tron on a near daily basis, and for exceptionally difficult times she visited Jean—the same diviner who had initiated me. Shortly after beginning the process to become a priestess, she underwent a small initiation ceremony into Fá along with her boyfriend at the time. During this introductory initiation she received Fá's sacred palm nuts and learned which of Fá's 256 sacred signs would reveal her destiny.[8] From then on, she took regular care of her Fá, often offering him prayer, gin, palm oil, and occasionally the blood of a small hen. Fá, speaking through the palm nuts, and Tron, speaking through kola nuts, became guiding forces in Marie's life that often provided her with advice or direction that she almost always took to heart. I can recall several times when Marie used divination to guide her as she faced serious personal problems that ranged from interpersonal relationships to legal issues. Having known Marie first as a Catholic and then as a Vodún priestess, I was able to observe Marie's outward beliefs in divination and Vodún expand. As Marie became more deeply involved in the local Vodún community, she began following Fá's advice more frequently.

When I first learned of Marie's new reliance on divination, I asked her, "Why are you following the advice of Fá now, when you hadn't before?"

She looked at me, smiled, and explained, "I've grown. Now I realize that Fá enables me to know, when before all I could do was guess."

Over time, Marie came to trust Fá. He predicted the birth of her grandchild, provided her with the necessary advice to win a court case, and helped her to overcome an escalating health issue.

Marie's "conversion" process was gradual and layered. Her trust in the vodún came slowly. She did not wake up one morning deciding to be a Vodún priestess. Instead, she was encouraged by her encounters with tourists and Western spiritual seekers who inadvertently piqued her interest. Indexing similar observations, Luhrmann points out that "action," such as a desire to initiate or offer sacrifice to the spirits, can be guided by belief. But she also provides us with an alternative to understanding the complex construction of belief within our own psyches—that is, that belief can also be guided by action (1989: 310).

It may be difficult to consider that our beliefs are constructed, at least in part, by the actions we take rather than vice versa, but Marie's case, whose actions were guided by tourist encounters, highlights the complex relationship between belief and action. Reflecting on my time in both Haiti and Bénin, I can now see how my own beliefs in and about Vodou/Vodún were nurtured as a result of my intimate involvement in both religions. As my beliefs grew, Jean, aware of the complicated nature of belief, always told me, "If you don't yet believe, just keep doing, you'll see." Thanks to Jean's urging and Marie's lived experiences, I came to see the development of those "new" beliefs that emerge during religious conversion as a psychosocial phenomenon that is at once individual and social, internal and external, instant and prolonged—that is to say that the maintenance of standing beliefs, the formation of new beliefs, and the negotiation between the two compose a creative process often driven by a combination of personal politics and the social capital that our beliefs may provide.

Secret Beliefs and Outward Identities

In Bénin, people such as Nafí often "convert" from Vodún to Christianity in the search for a "modern" identity or a "modern" way of dealing with the real threat of witchcraft. Others, such as Marie, "convert" from Christianity to Vodún hoping to be more intimately associated with their cultural or eth-nic identities. However, following a well-worn path long established by Vodún ideologies, most Fon and Yorùbá Béninois, whether they would say so or not, straddle multiple worlds of belief, often creatively incorporating both Vodún and Christian ideologies into their lives.

While working as a diviner's apprentice in Fátòmɛ, I saw residents, non-residents, and foreigners all become initiated Fá diviners. Most of the time the ceremonies were performed with exacting precision. Of the more than twenty initiation rituals I witnessed, two stuck out as special. During one of these rituals, Jean told me I should try to record the songs because learn-ing them would be important to my training, and he was uncomfortable singing them "out of context" because the songs' words could "make things happen." Following his advice, I planned to participate in the rituals as all his initiates did, but during important songs I turned on my digital voice recorder to capture the songs as they occurred. The first time I tried to do this, Jean's client, who had traveled from Cotonou, Bénin's economic capi-tal, to be initiated, told me to turn off my "camera." I assured him that I would not be taking pictures and explained to him that my device was just a sound recorder and I was only recording the songs. He then ordered the two people who had traveled with him to stand in front of me to block what he was sure was a camera. Instead of trying to continue to explain my technol-ogy, and disrupt the ritual, I turned off my voice recorder and slipped it into my shirt pocket. After about half an hour, and once the tension had settled, I began to talk with the man's friends.

"Why is he so against having pictures taken?" I asked.

"If voters knew he was becoming initiated, it would be the end of his career," one of the men explained.

"Really? What does he do?" I pressed.

"He's a politician. If his constituents knew that he believed in Vodún, they would not take him seriously! We have to be very careful."

"Why do you think people would care that he's being initiated into Fá?"

"Look at him. He came to this village in a Mercedes. Does he look like someone who could practice Vodún?"

In this case, the politician concealed his belief in Fá in order to "protect" his career. He feared that his status as an initiate of Fá made him overly "superstitious" and "traditional." Yet, contrary to what one might expect from a government official, he believed in Fá's power and felt he needed Fá to ensure his success in the upcoming election. After talking to the politician,

I learned that he did not have much interest in becoming an initiate to work as a diviner—he only wanted to have quick access to divination to ensure professional success, and he wanted the protection from witchcraft that Fá promised to provide. By the third day of his initiation rituals, he had become a fledgling diviner. He had learned some of the secrets of Fá divination and ate Fá's sacred food, thereby bringing Fá's power into his body. He had seen Gbădù's face, a sight that only initiates are allowed to see, and he had secured his space among the other diviners living in Fátòmè. However, when the time came for him to leave, he left dressed in a gray suit, riding in the back seat of his chauffeured black Mercedes-Benz. He carried with him a small leather briefcase that concealed the sacred palm nuts of his personal Fá that he had wrapped in white cloth and packed tightly in a small, unassuming white ceramic vessel that had been made in China. As he rode off down the reddish dirt road, I looked down and noticed that he had left behind his small clay Lĕgbà (a spirit other than Fá that is received by all Fá diviners). I looked intriguingly at the politician's Lĕgbà and then at Jean.

Jean shrugged. "He was not comfortable bringing it home with him. So we will take care of it here." The politician's Lĕgbà was then placed in a room among a few dozen other Lĕgbàs that, for similar reasons, never made it home.

Concealing Belief: An Evangelical Minister Becomes a Fá Diviner

Politicians are not the only ones who conceal their involvement in Vodún. Unlike other spirits, Fá is closely linked to individual people, guiding them with his reputed infinite knowledge, so that they may achieve their personal destinies. Because of Fá's pervasiveness among Fon and Yorùbá Béninois, even those who self-identify as nonpractitioners often believe that receiving their Fá, even at the most basic level, is a good practice for anyone, as Fá provides a detailed road map to one's life, telling the new initiate what he or she needs to do to be successful and reap life's rewards. Initiations, even simple ones such as receiving one's personal Fá, provide the practitioners with vital, and personal, information such as dietary and/or behavioral taboos that repeatedly reconfirm their destinies and places in the world. These taboos often inform the new initiate which foods they should avoid, which colors they should resist wearing, and which actions (e.g., drinking alcohol, smoking, walking alone at night) they should not perform. For example, upon becoming a diviner, I was told I could no longer eat papaya, guinea hen, or pork, and I was to resist wearing the color red or marrying a woman with "red skin." Many foreign initiates spoke of a "necessity" to keep their taboos or risk being killed or hurt by the spirits. However, Jean taught me that respecting one's taboos protects one's personal acè from being depleted or weakened while also ensuring that one is always working at his or her highest spiritual potential. He went on to explain, "Everyone is different and so acè is unique to each person. What depletes my potential may not deplete yours. That's why taboos vary from person to person—we're all different."

In addition to Fá's focus on the individual, Fá also has a wide appeal because of the way that initiations are performed. Unlike other spirit initiations, where a new initiate may be sequestered for several weeks to several months as he or she learns the dances, songs, and secrets of a particular Vodún, Fá initiations typically last less than a week, and often just a few days. Devotees of other vodún will often also be initiated into Fá (although they may not be full-fledged diviners), in hopes of taking advantage of the information they learn about their destinies as a result of the initiation. For these reasons, people often categorize Fá differently than other vodún, and they see having Fá as part of being well positioned in the world—despite the religious umbrella under which one may live and with which one may identify.

While I became aware of Fá's wide appeal early on, it took me nearly eight months to understand the breadth of Fá's social influence. Fá's widespread social value became clear one day when I arrived at Fátòmè to assist with an initiation that Jean was performing for a Béninois man who did not live in the village. When I arrived, I prostrated myself before Jean, who was sitting on a straw mat holding the sacred palm nuts of Fá in his hands, preparing to begin the divination that opened the ceremonies for Giles, the initiation candidate who had traveled some twenty kilometers to become a diviner. Everything proceeded normally until the time came for Jean to shave Giles's head—thereby preparing his head, the seat of the human soul, to receive Fá (as described in Chapter 2). Having seen Jean perform the initiation a dozen times before, I quickly noted that he skipped Giles's head shaving and moved onto the next step of the ritual—his ritual bath.

I peered at Jean with what must have been a look of confusion in my eyes, and Jean explained to me, "We can't. He's a priest."

"A priest?" I asked.

"Yes. A Christian priest."

"Catholic?" I questioned.

"No. Evangelical," Jean responded.

"Why is he doing this?"

"He wants Fá's blessing. But I guess, more than that, he wants his congregation's money too! So, we can't shave his head. Otherwise his followers would know what he did, and he'd lose everything."

"How can you do that?" I asked.

"We have to wash his head with special plants, and then, when his ceremonies are all over, he will have to make additional sacrifices to placate the spirits," Jean explained.

"So you don't ask Fá in advance?" I wondered aloud.

"No, if you did, Fá would refuse. We just continue [with the initiation] and apologize for the misstep at the end. It's easier," Jean laughed.

The above two narratives illustrate not only Vodún's flexibility but also its widespread cultural reach, value, and influence—regardless of a devotee's primary, or public, religious identity. Southern Bénin is clearly a multicultural space in which Christianity, Islam, and indigenous religions collide and at times coalesce—where Christianity's grip on the social world becomes increasingly evident while indigenous religions such as Vodún are also encouraged to flourish in a globalizing world.

Foreign Spiritual Seekers Who Are Changing Belief and Practice

Historically, Nigeria has attracted the majority of Western spiritual tourists who seek initiation. This is due to several factors. First, having performed their first reported foreign initiation in 1975, the Yorùbá of Nigeria have a longer tradition of working with Western spiritual tourists, often providing foreign initiates with "certificates of authenticity" that have been signed not only by the officiating priest but also by informal regulating agencies and royal households in Nigeria. To my knowledge, no such program exists in Bénin. Second, because most people interested in initiations from the African Americas are middle-class white or African American English speakers, Nigeria, which is officially Anglophone, is the more logical choice for them than Bénin, which is Francophone. Lastly, because of long-established Yorùbá practices in the African Americas with religions such as Lucumí and Haitian Vodou (especially *nago nasyon*), Yorùbáland has long been romanticized by practitioners in the Americas as the imagined "home" of worship and all things Yorùbá—despite Yorùbáland and Yorùbá practices such as Ifá (Fon, Fá) divination and ancestor veneration thriving across the border in the Republic of Bénin.

Whether initiated in Nigeria or Bénin, foreign initiates have creative strategies for dealing with gaps in their education and for making Fá divination, Vodún, and òrìṣà worship more palatable to Western sensibilities; these strategies have begun to reshape belief on both sides of the Atlantic. For example, the Ifa Foundation of North and Latin America, founded in the early 1980s by Philip and Vassa Neimark of Chicago, Illinois (now of Ormond Beach, Florida), began to offer "bloodless" initiations. The Neimarks argue that their ability to move beyond the "tool" of animal sacrifice and embrace (and market) "bloodless initiations" is a result of their spiritually "elevated status." However, it is worth noting that "bloodless initiations" also provide them with a way to attract American clients, many of whom may be involved in the New Age movement and may also be interested in initiation but are either morally opposed to, or physically squeamish around, animal sacrifice. Other lesser-known practitioners I have met have strategically filled in their gaps in knowledge from their time in Africa with some of the more established modalities long practiced in Lucumí and Haitian Vodou. When I asked one white American diviner in his sixties, who was initiated in Nigeria after years of practicing Lucumí, why he used ceremonies that he learned from Lucumí when he no longer considered himself to be a practitioner, he responded, "There are things we just can't do in the United States . . . so we have to change the way we do things or come to the realization that we can't practice in the United States. There are ingredients for certain ceremonies that we just can't find here, so we have to adapt. I see no problem in changing small things here and there to accommodate our practice here in America."

This American diviner, like so many people I met in Africa, spoke about Fá's inherent flexibility. For him, and for many other practitioners I encountered both in Africa and in the United States, the fact that the effective practice of Fá divination includes spirit worship in the so-called New World is evidence enough of the spirits' flexibility. I found that both African and foreign initiates were inclined at least to honor discursively the innovation of others, if not to innovate themselves. However, foreign initiates were more likely to innovate radically. Indeed, when I asked Fon and Yorùbá practitioners of Fá divination living in Bénin what they thought of the Ifa Foundation's claim that its "priests" could perform "authentic" and "powerful" initiations without the use of blood sacrifice, each of them rejected that as a possibility, often calling the practice a "fraud," "inauthentic," or "a sad waste of money."

Nevertheless, the priests at the Ifa Foundation are not the first people to question a belief in animal sacrifice as a ritual necessity. In her memoir, *Mark of Voodoo: Awakening to My African Spiritual Heritage* (2002), Sharon Caulder documented her time in Bénin when she was initiated into several spirit cults, including Xεbyosò (the spirit of thunder) and Mamíwátá, the mermaid spirit. In her memoir, Caulder expresses her concern about animal sacrifice to her initiator, claiming (rather ethnocentrically, and obviously inspired by Western occultism and the modern New Age movement) that animal sacrifice inhibits spiritual "transformation" (401–2).[9] While attempts to remove animal sacrifice from the practice of Fá divination and Vodún are met with great resistance by African practitioners, other adaptations, such as substituting one ingredient for another in the construction of spirit shrines or initiations, are far less problematic. In fact, these substitutions are expected. When I was learning from Jean, he once told me, "When you get home [in the United States], you need to walk in your woods and talk to your leaves. Ask them to reveal their powers to you so you can unlock their secrets. You won't find the same leaves there as you can find here, but I guarantee you, the same powers and secrets live in your forest too."

Jean's willingness to substitute leaves, ritual songs, and even the language used in prayer indicates Vodún's flexibility. However, as I have shown, there seem to be some beliefs and experiences (or practices) of belief, especially those that draw on dominant symbolic events (e.g., animal sacrifice), that are unchangeable among Béninois and Nigerian practitioners—at least for now.

Expanding Belief and Efficacy

Many, if not most, Béninois initiates, like Marie, undergo initiation once they already believe, even if creatively or strategically, in its effectiveness. Conversely, foreign spiritual seekers typically come to Bénin for initiation early in their desire to be initiated and while they are still struggling to know what they can, and cannot, believe. When I asked Jean if it bothered him that some foreigners struggle to believe in the spirits' power while also seeking initiation, Jean said, "Why would it? Once they see what the spirits can do, they will believe."

Simply put, applying Western notions of belief to Vodún is problematic. Ruel has argued that belief is too strongly connected to Western ideas of Christianity for scholars to apply the term to other (especially non-Western) religious traditions (1984: 27). Whether we are accounting for the Béninois politician who worried about the effect that Vodún would have on his career as his modern image was challenged, or the Vodún priestess who was ultimately initiated because of tourists, or the Vodún devotee who converted to evangelical Christianity in search of a cheaper form of protection from witchcraft, global perceptions of Christianity, modernity, and Vodún have profoundly changed the Béninois religious landscape. Given this, as an increasing number of Western spiritual seekers become involved in Vodún, and as transnationalism and globalization become important factors to consider, a critical analysis of belief becomes overdue. Still inspired by early thinkers such as Emile Durkheim who, in some ways, defined religion by the presence of a "sacred" belief system (1965 [1912]), scholars of religious traditions from around the world still strive to understand the meaning of religious belief. Even after decades of cross-cultural research focusing on belief from multiple disciplines, I have to concede that Needham (1972) was correct, and I may never know to what degree Marie believes in Vodún or how much Nafi believes in Christ. I am not even sure I can know how much I do or do not believe in witchcraft or Fá. Beliefs, those social acts that reflect our internal subjective objectivities, are fluid and often situational, strategic, and deeply embodied, social phenomena whose meanings extend beyond cognitive science. Along with scholars such as Talal Asad (1986, 1993), Durkheim (1965 [1912]), and Daniel Sperber (1985), instead of understanding belief as mental content, I think of beliefs as meaningful—and, I might add, creative—social actions. Our inability to access beliefs as mental contents is indexical of their fluidity, expressiveness, and always unfinished state (cf. Kirsch 2004). Frustrated by beliefs' cognitive inaccessibility, some scholars (e.g., Needham 1972; Lindquist and Coleman 2008) have even suggested that we should disregard beliefs as being inaccessible and too vague for study. However, as Charles Lindholm (2012) points out, the ambiguity and inaccessibility of belief should not detract from our attempts to understand them as social processes any more than the abstraction of culture should make the study of culture theoretically and intellectually meaningless.

Focusing on the meaning of belief-in-action, I have come to see beliefs not as objective truths that can be accessed by close observation, in-depth interviews, or even rich ethnography, but rather as creative and meaningful experiences of bricolage that are flexible, symbolic, and at times political.

Like Needham, I acknowledge that at a basic level, a person's individual beliefs are largely inaccessible. However, unlike Needham, my time in Bénin has revealed the study of the experience of belief to be important (see Landry 2015). I understand belief as a creative process that ebbs and flows with the changing tides of the belief holder. At times, our beliefs are slow to form, especially as one "converts" to a new religion, when beliefs are most strikingly renegotiated, layered, and complicated. Indeed, there is reason to suggest that conversion never truly results in an entire replacement of belief. Instead, what occurs is more of a belief layering, whereby old beliefs are overshadowed—but not completely replaced—by new ones, thereby leaving old and new beliefs in the individual's repertoire that can be called forth as one's social situation and needs change. In this way, Ludwig Wittgenstein was correct when he said that "a religious belief could only be something like a passionate commitment to a system of reference. Hence, although it's belief, it's really a way of living, or a way of assessing life" (1980 [1977]: 64e). Indeed, it is not our beliefs that change; controlled by our social needs, they simply layer, overshadow, and at times become subordinate to each other. What changes, in the words of Wittgenstein, is our "system of reference" and our ways of "living" or "assessing life." As these social structures ebb and flow meaningfully and strategically with culture change, so then do our beliefs.

Pointing to this formless, somewhat politicized understanding of belief expression, Luhrmann asserts that even under the pressure of gradual conversion, beliefs are not internalized and embodied on a linear continuum. Instead, beliefs are best understood as amorphous yet embodied experiences, highlighted as individuals negotiate their places within a particular community. As these processes play out, new beliefs may instigate new actions; but, as Luhrmann points out, and as was the case with Marie, new actions may also eventually foster new beliefs.

Other driving forces behind belief formation, especially in a globalizing world, are symbolic capital and capitalism. For Marie, the belief in Vodún, which led to her eventual initiation, provided her with increased social capital among the Vodún priests in her community. As her "conversion" progressed, she was eventually able to approach other Vodún priests as a colleague instead of as a Catholic outsider. Eventually, Marie's own status as a priest gave her increased symbolic capital with her tour groups, allowing her to speak with increased authority. By her admission, this new authority helped her to attract more tourists, hence more economic capital. Determining whether or not international tourism was the sole reason for Marie's initiation is both impossible and uninteresting—especially because it is clear that international tourism played an important role in the process. While it is uncertain whether Marie would have ever been initiated into Vodún had it not been for international tourism, it is quite clear that Marie now lives as a Vodún priest both around and away from tourists. For Marie, Vodún's emerging occult economy supports, inspires, and perhaps even encourages her belief in Vodún. In this way, spiritual tourism has helped Marie to find the social tools she needed to overthrow those Catholic shackles of power that she now finds oppressive, in favor of the economic freedom and spiritual liberation that Vodún seemingly provides.

As in the cases of Marie and Nafí, the global shrinking of the world through tourism and missionary work has presented new opportunities for believing. Although both women were Béninoise, for Nafí those new opportunities included a belief in Christ and for Marie a belief in Vodún. As compelling as the information would be, the ways that people such as Marie and Nafí have internalized, layered, and negotiated their beliefs will never be entirely clear. Asking Marie questions about her beliefs directly, for example, may have caused her to verbalize sentiments that she may have only embodied previously, which often makes it difficult to express exactly what one believes. Additionally, the layering of beliefs, especially in dynamic religious environments such as Bénin, makes pinpointing one's beliefs especially difficult. How does one negotiate simultaneous belief in Christ and witchcraft? How are these seemingly opposing worldviews reconciled on the ground? How does an evangelical minister rationalize his need/desire to become initiated into Fá?

All of these questions are nearly impossible to address while using traditional ethnographic methods such as interviews and intense observation. Using apprenticeship methods allowed me to interrogate my own belief systems, which eventually led me to understand belief—along with the embodiment and performance of belief—as a creative process that allows for beliefs to be accepted or rejected, even during brief social moments. Beliefs are both social and internalized fragments of one's truths that are embodied and eventually performed in socially driven ways.

In many ways, the creative nature of belief mirrors that of memory. Pointing to the creative processes of memory, Kathleen Stewart (1996) has discussed memory as a fragmented social reality that is creatively pieced together (or re-membered) by social actors. Beliefs work in a similar way. In Bénin and Nigeria, spiritual tourists, supported by transnationalism, add additional layers to these creative processes. Beliefs, rituals, social relationships, spiritual phenomena, economic or political aspirations, and cultural expectations all have a way of causing one's fragments of belief to coalesce in a believable reality that may shift creatively, depending on the social circumstances. While thinking of belief as a creative and never-ending process of negotiation that is simultaneously dependent on capital can be compelling, this formulation risks making our beliefs sound fickle, ill-formed, and entirely strategic. Although these critiques may be relevant in some instances, it is equally important to remember that these processes of capital, strategy, and absolute mutability are real and creative expressions of internal truths that are influenced by globalizing forces and transnational flows that are forever in a state of fluctuation, movement, and negotiation.

CHAPTER 5

Global Vodún, Diversity, and Looking Ahead

> While [ethnicity] is increasingly the stuff of existential
> passion, of the self-conscious fashioning of meaningful,
> morally anchored selfhood, ethnicity is also becoming
> more corporate, more commodified, more implicated
> than ever before in the economics of everyday life.
> —Comaroff and Comaroff 2009: 1

It was June 1, 2011, and my eighteen-month stay in Bénin had come to an end. I sat on the edge of my bed contemplating the last year and a half. I would miss my daily divination and ritual lessons with Jean. I would miss Marie, my research assistant, and her dear family, who had adopted me and treated me like their brother. As I surveyed my belongings I tried to mentally map how I would pack the last 18 months of my life into a few small bags. Nestled among my clothes and tattered field notebooks were my spirits, whom I had come to respect. In the corner, by the entrance to my bedroom, sat Lĕgbà, my consistent and reliable guardian. Locked in one of my larger bags was my most powerful spirit, Gbădù, the womb of creation. I contemplated each of my spirits and their roles in the cosmos as I had come to know them. Soon they and their secrets—some I may not have yet learned—would be leaving Bénin. Jean had told each of my spirits that they would be coming home with me to the United States, and each of them, Jean said, "was eager to make the trip." Was the United States really their home? Would they be happy? Would they long for Africa as I have longed for home?

As I packed each spirit into my bags, I worried that I was participating in cultural appropriation. Did my status as an anthropologist and a critical

participant add anxieties and different layers of ethical complexities to my
return home to which the average spiritual tourist was immune? Or was it, as
Jean assured me, simply the "next step" for Vodún—its next move, its next
flow, on the transnational stage? In the final pages of this book, I will (re)
examine the postcolonial and racial politics of Vodún's transnational journey
to show how secrecy, economic markets, and material culture have all contributed to the religion's migration, and I consider where I think Vodún is
headed in the future. Here, I speculate that as so-called indigenous religions
take hold in increasingly diverse, urban, and global nexuses, they will begin
to subsume progressively diverse practitioners from around the world who—
like the spaces these religions inhabit—will become what may best be described as "super-diverse" (see Vertovec 2007).

Vodún: An International Commodity

I have shown how ritual creates occult ontologies, that is, the hidden changes
to one's being, slowly and deliberately by using divine power to inoculate
participants to the social and spiritual dangers of secrecy. These changes, I
argue, transform initiates' bodies into contained secrets and religious commodities that are then bought and sold in emerging religious markets. Vodún
can travel, contained in initiates' bodies and in empowered forms of religious
material culture, across oceans and into new spaces around the world. Today,
Vodún finds itself thriving at the crossroads where Fon and Yorùbá, local and
global, urban and rural, tradition and modernity, Bénin and Nigeria, Africa
and the West, the "global North" and the "global South" all collide—with
each of these dualities showing how the categories of "us/them" and "here/
there" overlap.

   As my own involvement in Vodún's globalization became visible, tourists, especially Christian tourists, categorized me as "someone who practices
Voodoo," and Béninois friends grouped me as an "insider" or as an "initiate"
of Vodún. At other times, my difference was held in stark contrast and used
as evidence for why I should not have access to certain spiritual secrets. Like
many spiritual tourists, my apprenticeship allowed me to be categorized as
an "insider," but my race and nationality were ever-present social reminders
of the impossibility of total incorporation—regardless of how adept I became
at performing divination or speaking the language. My experiences as a
diviner in Bénin were in no way like those of local Fon- and Yorùbá-speaking

Béninois, and they were not like those of the average spiritual tourist, from whom my language skills, time in the field, and close proximity to Jean set my experiences apart. I occupied what Paul Stoller has called the "between," a place where anthropologists can "draw strength from both sides of the between and breathe in the creative air of indeterminacy . . . a space of enormous growth, a space of power and creativity" (2009: 4). Along with other spiritual tourists, my position on these borders always depended on many social variables, and my position was always in flux. Indeed, my racial and national identities seemingly connected me to the global North, while an invisible social elastic band—a band with just enough give to allow me to cross cultural borders, but with just enough spring to snap me back to the United States if I stretched the elasticity of my position too harshly—connected me to Vodún.

Many foreign spiritual tourists had similar experiences as they contemplated their families or jobs waiting for them back at home. Some of them spoke of the challenges of being in West Africa; often, their anxieties over the lack of hot showers, "good food," and "dependable technology" dominated our late-night conversations. But many of them also spoke of their real desire to traverse these borders easily—even if never completely. They wanted nothing more than to be considered "valid"—not just by their peers at home but also by the Africans who initiated them. The psychological need for "validity" was also something I experienced from time to time. I remember how I felt the first time a Béninoise showed up at my door wanting *me* to perform divination for *her*; or when, months later, while attending an Egúngún ceremony in a village outside of Ouidah, one of the Egúngún addressed me as *babaláwo*—my initiatory title in Yorùbá. In these moments, when the local community recognized my initiations, I felt "real" and "valid"—an authentication, a border crossing, that many spiritual tourists longed for but that, due to their short time in Bénin and/or Nigeria, few actually received.

West African people are not strangers to this kind of global pull from foreigners. Indeed, Ouidah has been located at an international border since the sixteenth century, when Europeans began purchasing slaves for export to the Americas. For almost two centuries, European slave traders docked in Ouidah to negotiate with the kings of Dahomey to purchase slaves. With some one million slaves leaving the shores of Ouidah bound for the Americas, Ouidah became the second most important slave port in all of Africa (Law 2004).[1] And before the transatlantic slave trade, Fon and Yorùbá kingdoms fought each

other consistently for resources and religious power, making southeast Bénin
a Fon-Yorùbá "contact zone"—and a point of cultural negotiation—that still
endures.

Today national and ethnic contact zones, especially those at the Bénin-
Nigeria border, add additional layers of complexity to understanding southern Bénin as both a domestic and international Vodún-inspired "contact
zone." Despite the fact that Yorùbá peoples live in both Nigeria (21 percent
of the population) and Bénin (13 percent of the population), a quick glance
of Vodún or òrìṣà Facebook groups and websites, Internet listservs, and
print publications will reveal that many, if not most, Western spiritual seekers connect "Yorùbáness" inevitably to Nigeria. In 2008, the United Nations
Educational, Scientific and Cultural Organization (UNESCO) strengthened
the Yorùbá-Nigeria connection when it listed Nigeria as the home of Ifá
divination—a new addition to UNESCO's list of "Intangible Cultural Heritage of Humanity." The symbolic marriage between Yorùbáland and Nigeria
that exists in the imaginations of Western spiritual seekers has profound
implications for the politics of religious validity, symbolic capital, and
power—three themes I have explored throughout the book.

These borders, which affect the experience of power and authenticity, are
not just felt by foreign spiritual seekers. Local Vodún practitioners also suffer and profit from the inequities that emerge. In a space such as Ouidah,
where multiple ethnic groups (e.g., Fon, Yorùbá, Ewe, and Xwẹ́dá, among
others) converge, questions of authenticity are always a concern. In Ouidah
for example, Yorùbá peoples—the progenitors of Fá/Ifá divination—are consistently thought of as having "the most powerful form of Fá."[2] This is felt so
strongly that some people who received the Fon variety of a Fá initiation
ceremony occasionally "convert" their initiation from the Fon to the Yorùbá
system of Fá by completing the "missing" ceremonies, performing additional
sacrifices, and learning "the Yorùbá way" of performing the act of divination. People who receive their initiations in the Fon system are often told,
"Your Fá wasn't done correctly," or "Your Fá is not as powerful as it could
be." While questions of authenticity and originality have a long history in
the region that predates spiritual tourism, spiritual tourism has exacerbated
these politics. As Béninois pay to have their ceremonies repeated and foreign
spiritual seekers emphasize their preference for Yorùbá rituals, discourses of
authenticity work to enhance the economic value of the Yorùbá system,
which then has a ripple effect on the international initiation market—where
Yorùbáness already enjoys a great deal of symbolic and social capital. Local

and foreign practitioners alike often cite the reality that Fá divination, Gbǎdù, Egúngún, and Orò all came from Yorùbáland—and therefore the Yorùbá system of practice must be the most authentic and powerful—so the politics of these border zones, which highlights the Yorùbá hegemony in the imaginations of Western spiritual seekers, continues.

The Politics of Globalization, Urbanization, and Religious Exchange

More and more international spiritual tourists are seeking initiation into Vodún (e.g., Forte 2010). This trend requires Béninois Vodún practitioners to negotiate actively with foreign spiritual seekers who wish to gain access to Fon and Yorùbá religious secrets and knowledge. Practitioners, both West African and foreign, are converging in cities around the world. Lagos, Cotonou, Lomé, Brooklyn, Miami, Chicago, Houston, São Paulo, Paris, London, Amsterdam, and Berlin have all become urban centers where cosmopolitan and "super-diverse" versions of Vodún and Yorùbá òrìṣà worship have begun to transcend ethnic and racial boundaries (Vertovec 2007). The religion's international reach and urban salience now suggest that scholars must reexamine those religions that may have been previously described as "ethnic," "traditional," or "indigenous" in ways that now attend to their many layers of experience and provide the social spaces necessary to bridge national, ethnic, racial, and class modalities. As a cacophony of identities—and all the global and postcolonial politics attached to them—collide, we are left wondering, Are foreign participants in Vodún appropriating cultural practices? If so, how do these cultural appropriations fit into anthropological discussions that surround postcolonial racist ideologies and politics? These questions become especially important in the shadow of existing paradigms of racial and national abuses and inequities of power throughout Africa. But attacking Vodún's increasing racial and ethnic diversity by making the claim that foreign practitioners are nothing more than "cultural appropriators" and therefore part of these regimes of power is not as simple as it may seem.

A great deal of political and racial gravitas exists behind the term "cultural appropriation," which is defined broadly by Richard Rogers as "the use of a culture's symbols, artifacts, genres, rituals, or technologies by members of another culture" (2006: 474).

Among indigenous populations—especially in Native America—a growing number of scholars and critics align Western involvement in indigenous

religions as a form of "cultural exploitation" whereby "aspects of marginal-
ized/colonized cultures are taken and used by a dominant/colonizing culture
in such a way as to serve the interests of the dominant" (Rogers 2006: 486).
While colonial structures of power are important considerations in understanding how and why local populations may or may not engage with foreign
spiritual seekers, in many situations this focus is an insufficient analysis.
Rogers (2006) aptly points out that "the production and sale of elements of
subordinated/colonized cultures with their active participation occurs under
economic conditions in which few other opportunities may be available to
earn a living in the economic system they have entered without, in many
cases, their consent" (490).

We cannot ignore, or devalue, the agency of native peoples in these
exchanges. While Africans are clearly affected by postcolonial structures
of power, to say that they are powerless in these exchanges is inaccurate.
There is no doubt that many Béninois practitioners of Vodún are pushed to
initiate foreign spiritual seekers for financial reasons, and some, especially
the poor, more so than others. However, local practitioners often perform
their power by participating actively in the emerging spiritual markets that
bridge West Africa and the African Americas while also restricting the
flow of information and religious secrecy to tourists (Comaroff and Comaroff 2009).

Local reactions against asymmetrical expressions of power manifest in
several ways. At times, spirit shrines or magical charms are given to tourists,
but tourists are usually not taught how to construct or formulate the shrines
or charms themselves. Such was the case when Luiz failed at learning how
to incarnate Gbădù. As Luiz's experience indicates, local pockets of resistance may prevent international spiritual seekers from embodying the same
postinitiation rights and privileges as a Béninois initiate might enjoy. Béninois may also use their power to limit a Western spiritual seeker's ability to
freely move in and out of religiously restricted spaces, such as was the case
when I inadvertently walked into an Egúngún temple in the middle of a secret
ritual. Still other times, Béninois may outright refuse to initiate or fully teach
foreign spiritual seekers, or recognize them as legitimate. While I found this
latter method of resistance to be quite rare, there is an undercurrent of belief
that worries Béninois about what foreign spiritual seekers may do with Vodún:
some feel Western tourists may "improve upon and profit from Vodún," while
others believe that, without the proper ancestry, service to Vodún is ineffective.
Whether these threads of resistance remain rare or become prominent, either

way there exists a local discourse that undermines—and perhaps rejects—
the transculturation of Vodún. The existence of such local acts of resistance
is enough to make both Western spiritual seekers and scholars stop and pause
to think about how we may actively participate in—and support—neocolonial politics.

Is foreign involvement in Vodún, whether academic or personal, necessarily a form of imperialism and neocolonialism (Nash 1989 [1978]) in West
Africa, where the needs and wants of the foreign spiritual seekers overshadow those of African agents? To appropriate another's spiritual belief
implies participation in cultural distortion, theft, and, to some, "profound
offense" (Young and Brunk 2009). Anthropologists, with our classic bottom-
up approach to ethnography, often come with a political bias that favors the
disempowered (in this case, local Vodún practitioners) and therefore criti-
cizes those who enjoy privilege (in this case, foreign spiritual seekers). In
this work, I attempted to understand the argument from both perspectives.

Many scholars have criticized "New Age" involvement in the "appropriation" of cultural and spiritual beliefs and practices from Native America
(e.g., Rose 1992; Churchill 1994; Jocks 1996; Smith 2005). However, I was
unable to find a single academic source that addressed specifically the racial
and postcolonial politics of religious or spiritual appropriation as it plays out
in West Africa.[3] In some ways, as victims of colonial agendas, Native America and West Africa share a geopolitical history. Because of West Africa's
and Native America's parallel statuses as postcolonial "states," one could
argue that spiritual tourism in both zones then places indigenous populations
at risk for exploitation (Churchill 1994), structural violence (Smith 2005),
and misrepresentation. Indeed, both Andrea Smith (2005) and Christopher
Jocks (1996) have implicated non-Native scholars who are commonly presented as experts (and, in their eyes, appropriators) of cultures of which they
are not a part, often at the expense of the "real" local experts.

Even so, despite the similarities, there is a great deal of difference in the
ways that spiritual tourism plays out in Native America and in West Africa.
Unlike foreign spiritual seekers interested in Native America, international
spiritual tourists who come to West Africa for initiation into Vodún are typically adamant that they are not the same as those who are involved in the
New Age movement. Indeed, pointing to the way that so-called "New Agers"
typically pick and choose from various spiritual traditions and promote a
"passive worldview," many of the spiritual tourists whom I met in Bénin
categorized New Agers as being "fluff heads," "white-lighters," "wannabes,"

and/or "spiritually lost." To them, New Agers *are* "cultural appropriators" precisely because, as Ward Churchill argued, New Agers "deform [Native American spirituality] beyond all recognition" (1994: 139). For those Western spiritual seekers whom I met in Bénin, their goal is not to "pick and choose" what they like, but to replicate Fon and Yorùbá religious practice as precisely as environmentally and ritually possible. This drive to replicate rituals has led to some rituals, such as animal sacrifice, to be reimagined or to take on new roles as ritual of authentication instead of as important symbolic expressions of familial nourishment.

Yet, despite their strong desire to replicate the rituals they learned in West Africa, many North American Vodún and òrìṣà priests find themselves paradoxically devoted to two diasporic "homelands"—the Afro-Caribbean and West Africa. Once back in the United States, religious travelers to West Africa tend to engage in a great deal of practical innovation and so-called blending and sharing among practitioners of Haitian Vodou, West African Vodún, and Cuban Santería. Many American practitioners of one or another of these religions see this type of bricolage as acceptable because of the religions' shared geopolitical space. Yet, regardless of the relationship among these West African derived religions, several American practitioners of Haitian Vodou, West African Vodún, and Yorùbá Ifá have argued that, despite the system's inherent flexibility, as an outsider it is not their right to innovate. Indeed, many of them contend that they strive to leave ritual innovation to the owners (that is, the local practitioners) of the tradition.

I do not mean to suggest that all Western spiritual seekers feel this way. While Vodún's beliefs in aggressive forms of magic, witchcraft, and blood sacrifice are usually enough to keep New Agers disinterested, there are unfortunately some who come to West Africa intent on changing specific cultural and religious practices, especially animal sacrifice, that they see as "inappropriate" or signs of "spiritual devolution" (e.g., Caulder 2002). And some, like Philip and Vassa Neimark of the Ifá Foundation International, have made a career of "whitening" Yorùbá religious practice, to make it more palatable—and marketable—to Western spiritual seekers by removing important, but uncomfortable, ritual practices such as animal sacrifice, the shaving of one's head, and the use of complicated praise poetry from their version of Ifá divination.

While replicating religious belief and practice is a primary goal of many of the spiritual tourists I have met, the vast majority (although not all) do so in deference to, and with the blessing, support, and guidance of, those communities whose members initiated them, thereby firmly placing the authority for these religious traditions on Africans themselves. Of course, even these exchanges are wrought with the problems of power—all of which are deeply entwined with postcolonial and racial politics. In West Africa, where religious knowledge seems to be more freely shared as compared to Native America, one can find some Béninois who believe that Vodún is a "weapon" that should not be shared in totality with everyone who seeks Vodún's mysteries. However, for every individual who told me about his or her wish to restrict access to Vodún to only Africans, many more expressed their belief that opening Vodún up to everyone could only help the world heal and move away from war and hate (Abimbọla 1997). Bron Taylor has observed a similar phenomenon in Native America, where some Native peoples openly claim that widespread adherence to "Native American religious practices are crucial if the world is to be preserved" (1997: 187).

Regardless of the possible global benefits that some indigenous people (whether from Native America, Africa, or elsewhere) see in Western involvement in once-local religions such as Vodún, it is important that Western spiritual tourists and scholars (especially those who use intimate research methods such as myself) remain aware of the politics of our positions. Scholars and international spiritual seekers alike must be careful that our own racialized position, nationality, economic position, and level of education do not set us up as false experts who have the potential to usurp power (and possible economic and political capital) from local populations (e.g., Taylor 1997: 197). In a world in which positivist science rules over knowledge production, and the West (and whiteness, by extension) rules over the world, the dangers are real. For this reason, the philosophers James Young and Conrad Brunk urge that "individuals who appropriate religious beliefs ought to be suitably deferential toward the culture from which they appropriate. Outsiders owe to the other culture every reasonable effort to understand precisely [regardless of how impossible that may actually be] what the culture believes" (2009: 111). And I might add that foreign spiritual seekers ought to remain critically aware of their/our status as a forever-outsider.

Whether one is an outsider or a native practitioner, the second primary difference between spiritual tourism in Native America and West Africa affects everyone. As I have shown, in Bénin and Nigeria (as well as places in the African Americas such as Haiti, Cuba, and Brazil), parallel to foreign tourism, there exists a vibrant local economy that focuses on the buying and selling of religious material culture and services. Vodún is a religious system that, regardless of foreign involvement, includes payment for initiations, shrines, ritual objects, consultations, magic, and even prayer. In Vodún, both priests and spirits require money for services rendered. While a sliding scale exists whereby family members pay the least and professional clients pay the most, everyone pays the priest and the spirits for their knowledge, blessings, power, and required ritual supplies. Given the recent influx of spiritual tourism, international travelers now enter an established occult market—one that to my knowledge exists only marginally in Native America—where they often pay the highest for religious goods and services.

This is not to say that postcolonial, economic, and racial politics do not change the exchanges. Indeed, international tourist involvement in Vodún creates new dynamics of power, and power abuses, that build on and depart from localized models. Vodún is a religious system that empowers its secret holders. Religious secrecy gives its owners power over spiritual forces and religious structures and practices, which in turn allows these owners to market their skills to their communities and support their families. As I have shown, foreign tourists—who enjoy economic, racialized, national, and political privileges—disrupt these structures of power by mobilizing their privileges in ways that shift the power from the local secret holders to the international secret seekers.

The third difference that I found between typical New Age tourists and those who travel to West Africa for initiation is one of historical pertinence. Unlike the spiritualities of Native America, derivatives of West African religions such as Cuban Santería, Brazilian Candomblé, and Haitian Vodou already have, at least in the imaginations of Béninois practitioners, significant numbers of adherents who are not of African descent. When I first arrived in Bénin, I spoke often about my experiences in Haiti—including my prior initiation as a *houngan asogwe* into Haitian Vodou (see Landry 2008). Just saying the words "houngan asogwe" bridged our two worlds instantly. A houngan in Haitian Vodou is a male priest (or *manbo*; *manbo* is the female equivalent in Haiti); in Fonland, the word *hùngán* carries the same meaning (literally, "spirit chief"; *hùn* = *vodún*/spirit/divinity and *gán* = chief).[4] In Haiti, a houngan (or manbo asogwe) is given the *asson*, the sacred, beaded gourd rattle of Haitian Vodou priesthood, by Papa Loko, the spiritual head of Vodou clergy. In Fonland, an *azɔgwé* is a gourd rattle that has been modified similarly to the Haitian asson, with a macramé net of beads that, when shaken, creates a staccato rustling sound as the net of beads collides with the side of the hollowed gourd.[5] While the azɔgwé of Fonland does not hold the

same ritual potency as the asson of Haiti, its linguistic and functional relationship is undeniable.

With a partially shared vocabulary at their disposal, many Western spiritual seekers come to Bénin using a recognizable lexicon, and they have an
awareness of certain rituals and ceremonies that further facilitates their ability
and solidifies their right to initiation. By contrast, Native America, due to a
different (albeit overlapping) political history of subjugation and colonialism
than that of Africa, has become more insular and therefore places a stronger
and more consistent emphasis on kinship as a prerequisite for religious participation (Timothy McCleary, personal communication, 2012), such that
non-Native practitioners of Native spirituality are almost exclusively seen as
"outsiders," "appropriators," and "post-colonial subjugators."[6]

Despite the differences that exist between the experiences of Native
American and West African cultural borrowing from outsiders, there remains
a great deal that scholars of West African religion can learn from the Native
American experience. Depoliticizing the anthropological gaze, as Jane Mulcock (2001) suggests, may allow the researcher to understand the perspective of the borrower and the borrowee without the anthropological angst that
comes along with our critical-of-power perspective. We need to remain
aware of structures and politics of power that exist in both tourist-local and
anthropologist-local encounters that are especially necessary when anthropologists incorporate intimate research methods such as religious apprenticeship into their research strategies, as I have done (Landry 2008)—where
the unethical dangers of cultural appropriation are at their height.

The Occult Economy of Secrecy

The social process and performance of secrecy seem to define Vodún. There
are three primary words in *fɔngbè* to talk about secrecy. *Xódoxomè* ("speech
inside the stomach"), *kpánú* ("thing fenced off"), and *kpáxó* ("speech fenced
off") all index something, most often words, being fenced in and separated
from the rest (Blier 1993: 185–86). As Suzanne Preston Blier notes, fences
and barriers, such as the palm fronds in the sacred forest, often serve as
"visual metaphors" in the Vodún landscape to demarcate a secret shrine,
place, or power object. However, in my experience the word most commonly
used to talk about religious secrecy is *awò*—a term borrowed from Yorùbá
meaning "secret." When used by Fon speakers, awò almost always denotes a
secret that confers or protects divine and spiritual power (*acè*). For global

practitioners of Vodún, acè, embedded in material culture, conferred by initiation, and protected by secrecy, is the divine power and right they seek. Bestowed upon devotees in ritual and sold in objects, shrines, and powers, acè, protected by secrecy, has become Vodún's commodity.

No matter where Vodún is found on the globe, secrecy is always a present and dominant force. When I began this project, secrecy was not one of my primary considerations. However, once in Bénin, secrecy was quickly foregrounded as I found it to be the primary contentious factor in local-tourist interactions. Who gets access to religious secrets? How do they gain access? Why do they gain access? These questions and more were always implicit in nearly every Vodún-focused tourist encounter I observed. Initiation promises access to secret knowledge and secret places, and divination guarantees the ability to know strategically what is not yet known. Where Vodún is concerned, the performance of secrecy is ubiquitous and essential to discourses of authenticity. Secrecy's value and power within Vodún have made it simultaneously important to the local practice of Vodún and to the religion's international flow and global efficacy.

Western spiritual seekers come to West Africa wanting access to secret religious knowledge, and, like local practitioners who are apprenticing to be Vodún priests, diviners, and devotees, many religious tourists receive secret information in small doses. Little by little, and sometimes only after multiple visits to the area, do they begin learning some of the more important Vodún secrets—such as how to ritually and materially incarnate a spirit to the earth. In fact, many tourists come to Bénin with a great deal of angst about receiving "correct" or "authentic" initiations, shrines, and charms. More than once, I was placed uncomfortably between spiritual tourists and their Béninois initiators or guides negotiating access to secret knowledge. In one instance, Luiz, a Brazilian tourist, asked to speak to me about the cost of his initiations "just to be sure he was not being scammed." With the underlying implication being that Africans are deceitful while white anthropologists are trustworthy, the racism in his request was palpable even if he did not consciously see it that way. When I responded to his request by saying, "You need to talk to Jacques [his Béninois initiator]. I don't really know how much these things cost," he only looked down and shook his head.

In this instance, Jacques was in a position of power, as he was the secret holder. He was the one who embodied the acè to know the occult secrets to which Luiz wanted to gain access. Questions of "authenticity" have been shown to be important to tourism studies (e.g., MacCannell 1973), especially when tourists talk about and highlight "authenticity" (Bruner 2005)—and locals know this. Despite Ouidah being one of Bénin's tourist centers, I was told at least a dozen times, "If you want real Vodún—Vodún that hasn't been destroyed by tourism—you need to go further north. Go to Abomey or, even better, Savalou."

Behind such recommendations is a sense that Ouidah has lost its authenticity and secret powers to tourism. Dean MacCannell might have argued that the entire city of Ouidah was a "frontstage" experience, one that lacks the realism of a city like Savalou that has, for now, guarded its religious secrecy from tourist consumption. Marie, my research assistant and a Vodún priestess in Ouidah, told me, "Daágbó has been spoiled by tourism. He is not even real anymore." Likewise, during an ancestral Egúngún dance for National Vodún Day on January 10, 2010, Michel, a close friend, confided in me that "Egúngún in Ouidah are powerless. Because they've made themselves available to tourists, they've lost their power. If you want to see real Egúngún you need to leave Ouidah." Although Michel never told me where I would need to go to see "real" Egúngún, his sentiment that much of Ouidah had been spoiled was a widespread belief. Ouidah had, to many locals, become what MacCannell would have called "staged authenticity" (1973)—a performance of realism that, for the average tourist, was sufficient.[7]

But spiritual tourists want to experience life "behind the scenes" to see what lies beyond MacCannell's frontstage. They want what Clifford Geertz might have called the "really real"—to experience Vodún in its "real" form—not as most tourists experience the religion, but just as local practitioners do. They want the unaltered experience, and secrecy becomes the way these experiences are measured. Secrecy, society's "backstage," has become the ultimate tourist experience, and the consumption of secrecy has come to stand for decisive "evidence" of tourists' "authentic" experience and of someone's validity as a Vodún priest, diviner, or devotee. In many ways, for these tourists, religious secrets become the final authenticator whereby resistance to access is critical to the secret's authenticity.

Spiritual Tourism, Authenticity, and the Value of Friction

When I began this project, it became clear, almost from the onset, that social friction—defined by Anna Tsing as "the awkward, unequal, unstable, and creative qualities of interconnection across difference" (2005: 4)—is central to understanding how local and foreign Vodún practitioners negotiate access to secrecy and how then the experience of secrecy, in the hands of initiates, is authenticated. International tourists experience and come to expect moderate amounts of social friction during encounters with Béninois Vodún practitioners. As was the case with Christine and Michelle, when friction was removed from tourist-local encounters, the experience's authenticity was challenged feverishly. Tourists, especially spiritual tourists who are actively seeking access to religious secrecy, need friction and resistance to validate an experience or a sacred object, space, or person and being. In these moments, friction and resistance become necessary experiences that allow spiritual tourists to navigate effectively Vodún's "really real" (e.g., Geertz 1973).

As spiritual tourists struggle with understanding, and in some cases believing in, Vodún's worldview, they also struggle with the assurance of authenticity. In some cases, friction serves as a social experience of authentication. Paradoxically, the resistance and sense of unease that outsiders often experience while entering a sacred forest, or a spiritual seeker's inability to access certain spirit cults, magical recipes, or even sacred spaces, all lend to the authentic experience of these unusual tourist encounters in which Western spiritual tourists seek to learn of religious powers that lie beyond the veil of secrecy.

Where Is Vodún Headed? Transnationalism and the City

Foreign participation in Vodún has undoubtedly highlighted colonially created power inequities between African initiators and foreign spiritual seekers. However, Béninois have used the power that ritual secrecy's commodification has given them to exert their own agency during tourist encounters. This marketplace has enriched Vodún, expanded its borders, and, in some ways, helped to revitalize the religion in the aftermath of colonialism, Christian missionaries, and the politics of modernity (Comaroff and Comaroff 1993, 2009; Meyer 1999; Bruner 2005). As one of Jean's nephews once told me, "[Foreign interest] in Vodún has convinced me that my family's religion is good. Now I don't feel like I need Jesus to live in today's world."

Tourism is often understood as a form of globalization (Lash and Urry 1994; Appadurai 1995; Ekholm-Friedman and Friedman 1995), even as the "epitome of global flows" (MacLeod 1999: 446). While the presence of for-

eign spiritual seekers reflect and in some ways support—as we have seen—
the emergence of transnational West African spiritual economies, these
expansions are not new to Fon or Yorùbá peoples. The Fon and Yorùbá have
long had a dialogue with each other (Bay 1998; Law 2004), and the contemporary transculturation of Yorùbá religion has long caught the attention of
scholars (e.g., Clarke 2004; Matory 2005; Olupona and Rey 2008).

More than a hundred years ago, Franz Boas broadly noted that cultural
"change" or "development" often depends on how and why societies have
interacted with their neighbors (1940 [1896]). In the case of Vodún and òrìṣà
worship, Fon and Yorùbá speakers living in Bénin and Nigeria have facili-
tated the transnational expansion of their religions via interactions with
American, European, and Caribbean agents through spiritual tourism and the
expansion of transnational religious markets. As processes of transnationalism continue, previously distant neighbors become ever closer, which then
allows for what David Held has called a "stretching of social relations"
(2004). As foreign spiritual tourists become Bénin's and Nigeria's global
"neighbors," Vodún and òrìṣà worship are propelled onto a global stage
where these West African religions redefine what Béninois and international
practitioners mean by here and there or local and global, and where the
boundaries that differentiate these categories begin to blur. As religions such
as Vodún become ever more globalized and diverse, they do what they have
done for centuries—they adapt and change, as they retain their local vibrancy
while also developing a new and increasingly diverse membership. International spiritual tourism may change the ways that Fon-speaking Béninois
conceptualize Vodún (Forte 2010), but it does not alter Vodún's efficacy, as
change and adaptability are just as much a part of what defines Vodún and (in
local conceptions) the spirits themselves (Augé 1988; Elwert-Kretschmer
1995; Tall 1995; Forte 2010).

International spiritual tourists travel to Bénin and Nigeria to become initiated into Vodún and òrìṣà worship. While in West Africa, they partake in local
religious practice, become initiated, and learn some of the religions' ritual
secrets. Upon returning home, their concept of the local shifts from Africa to
the United States, where foreign Vodún practitioners then "adopt a variety of
localizing strategies in order to succeed commercially" (Jackson 2004) and
spiritually. In order to make Western-driven spiritual markets in the global
South successful, American spiritual tourists, for example, are encouraged to
relocalize African spiritualties within the United States. At once, Africans are

changing to accept corporate capitalism, while some Americans are changing to accept African spiritual and economic realities (Comaroff and Comaroff 2012).

As the Africanization of the global North continues, foreign spiritual
tourist networks have become intensely focused on the city. Foreign spiritual
seekers now come to West Africa from cities around the world and, when
seeking initiation there, tend to congregate in urban centers. These cities,
each with their own Vodún-oriented cartography (Orsi 1999), become part of
a larger transnational map whereby cities have become important religious
hubs. Almost every spiritual tourist I encountered highlighted the importance
of U.S., European, Brazilian, or African cities as important centers of African religion. Each of these cities connects to the others in a series of historical, ethnographic, and embodied maps carried in the bodies, imaginations,
and expectations of practitioners. Despite the commonly held belief that
"traditional religions aren't practiced in the city," the city has become increasingly important, as these religions become more and more global. In fact,
much of my research has shown that, globally speaking, Vodún has become
an urban religion. Vodún has added to the religious diversity of urban centers
around the world by placing once-indigenous religions in conversation with
global religions such as Christianity and Islam. But those cities have also
added to the diversity of Vodún. As these religions contribute to a city's
diversity, the cities also contribute to the diversity of the religion. Like the
cities that house religions such as Vodún, the religions themselves are beginning to expand beyond racial and ethnic boundaries. And while a religion's
diversity may cause racial and ethnic tensions, the religions' practitioners are
beginning to diversify in ways that have made Vodún a religion of many
races, ethnicities, classes, and nationalities.

If the West, and especially the Western city, is diversifying to include
African religion, even if only in select spaces, Vodún practitioners have
announced loudly that they are ready to be included. In her 1997 doctoral
dissertation, Dana Rush wrote, "Vodun is on the move. A whirling vortex, an
absorbing sponge. . . . Vodun is in constant flux; where outside influences
become part of its organic existence; where provisional boundaries are indefi-
nite, forever permeable; where the external and the internal become indiffer-
entiable, synergetic, and coactive" (1).

In this moment, Rush characterized Vodún perfectly. Despite Vodún's
culture of secrecy, the religion is perfectly suited for an ever-changing world
in which Vodún's ability to react meaningfully to transnationalism is reflected

in its adaptability. As such, the search for *divine power*, as mentioned in the subtitle of this book, takes on a double meaning. It explicates foreign initiates' desires to maneuver successfully through ritual secrecy, become initiated, acquire power-laden objects, and eventually find divine power (acè) for themselves. But, more importantly, it indexes the ways in which Béninois initiators use their acè and religious right that initiates so desperately seek in order to turn the tables of power creatively in their favor, thereby at once combating hundreds of years of colonial and economic oppression while also propelling Vodún firmly onto the global stage.

By examining both interpretations of divine power, I have shown that, in the case of Vodún, religious secrecy paradoxically encourages, rather than restricts, the religion's transnational flow and presence. All around the world, secret religious knowledge, access to secret spirit cults and initiations, and knowledge of secret charms and religious recipes make Americo- and Euro-Vodún locally and globally "real." What is seen as local is in constant flux, as a person's practice strategically shifts to include—often simultaneously—West Africa, the United States, and the Afro-Caribbean. As an increasingly diverse set of agents seek divine power from Vodún, not only do West African religious secrets move about the globe, but the performance of secrecy also serves to ceremoniously authenticate, consecrate, and confirm Vodún's grip not just on a modern West Africa but also, increasingly, on the world.

Epilogue: Reflections on Belief
and Apprenticeship

> Anthropologists are always "between" things—between
> "being there," as the late Clifford Geertz put it, and
> "being-here," between two or more languages, between
> two or more cultural traditions, between two or more
> apprehensions of reality. Anthropologists are the
> sojourners of "the between." We go there and absorb a
> different language, culture, and way of being and return
> here, where we can never fully resume the lives we had
> previously led.
>
> —Stoller 2009: 4

Jean taught me to perform divination for myself once a week. He told me that doing so would allow me to fix my problems preemptively and give me the ability to reinforce my life's rewards. Determined to follow Jean's advice, when I returned home from Bénin, I was eager, but nervous, to divine for the first time in the United States and without Jean's help. I unfurled a straw mat onto my apartment floor and sat, just as Jean had always done, with my back against the wall. I prayed and poured libations of cool water and gin. Then, at the right moment, I tossed my *akplɛkàn* while asking Fá to reveal the *dù* that would speak to his new life in the United States.

"*Gbè-Méjì*," I spoke the sign's name aloud to bring it into being, just as Jean had taught me. Gbè-Méjì indicates paths being opened and a space in which all things are possible. I was reminded of Jean's claim that the *vodún* wanted to make the journey to the United States, and I was comforted by Fá's declaration that obstacles would be removed for me as a result of having the vodún in my life. Over the years, following my return to the United States, Fá predicted a medical issue with my stomach, a personal conflict with a friend, and even my current academic appointment at Trinity College. Fá had become a guiding fixture in my life. Yet questions concerning my belief in Vodún still seemed to be out of place and even inappropriate.

I often wonder how best to describe my relationship with the spirits if in Vodún beliefs are built on efficacy and not on the Christian concept of faith. When people ask me whether I believe in Vodún, they really want to know whether I became initiated because I *believe* in the spirits or whether I "received the forest" for the sake of something that they might call *science*. In this regard, apprenticeship, when applied to the anthropological study of religion, is a challenge. I did not enter the sacred forest believing or trusting in Fá's power from the onset. Jean knew that I was respectfully skeptical and even encouraged me to question everything. However, he also knew that I did not choose to become initiated for the sake of anthropology or to gain access to ritual secrets that would have been otherwise kept from me. There is no doubt that my apprenticeship with Jean helped me to approximate the ways in which foreign spiritual seekers study Vodún while they are in Bénin. The embodied nature of apprenticeship allowed me to understand Fá through initiation. I was able to experience camaraderie and excitement as I became caught up in the momentum of my initiation. I was able to experience what it was like to negotiate access to ritual secrecy and to know the sinking feeling when that access was denied.

I made a promise to Jean early in our relationship that I would never reveal the secrets that he entrusted to me. I knew I wanted to take steps to make sure that my work would not become a ritual manual or a magical cookbook for foreign spiritual seekers. To that end, when analytically possible, throughout the book I changed the order in which ritual events occur, left out ritual moments, and at times even changed the names of ritual ingredients. While I will never reveal the secrets Jean and others have taught me, my intimate relationship with Vodún's ritual and symbolic structure has greatly informed my overall analysis. As an apprentice, I experienced subtle, but symbolically potent, connections between the forest, the spirits, and the community; I learned that Vodún is, before all else, a religion focused on healing one's family; and I came to understand that secrecy is just as much about power as it is about inclusion, well-being, and belonging.

I do not mean to suggest that my experiences in Vodún's sacred forests were anything like that of Béninois initiates. To the contrary, I lacked the family, the ancestors, and the centuries of postcolonial racial oppression to understand truly what it means for a Béninois to serve the spirits and honor their dead in today's world. However, my language skills, coupled with my long-term stay in Bénin, made my experience vastly different from what most other foreign spiritual seekers undergo. I was caught in the middle of multiple worlds, betwixt-and-between the experiences of a local and a foreign initiate. Throughout my time as Jean's apprentice, I made every effort to draw creatively from my liminality. As Paul Stoller once said, "If . . . we find a way to draw strength from both sides of the between and breathe in the creative air of indeterminacy, we can find ourselves in a space of enormous growth, a space of power and creativity" (2009: 4).

Caught between being an anthropologist and a diviner, a believer and a nonbeliever, an insider and an outsider, I tried my best to grow from my indeterminacy as I moved between multiple worlds. My life in the between helped to sustain my complicated relationship with Jean. My time with Jean was defined by emotional highs and defeating lows. On occasion he refused, without explanation, to teach me how to perform certain rituals or how to create certain shrines. My education was always on his terms and in his time. He controlled the flow of information and I accepted that there were things about Fá that I may never learn. Then, one afternoon, shortly before I left Bénin, Jean came to me and said, "Let's go! Come with me. I am going to teach you how to make Gbǎdù."

Gbǎdù's construction was Jean's most coveted and guarded secret. A few months prior, he told me that his ability to make Gbǎdù "correctly" brought him both local and foreign clients, and he worried that if the composition became common knowledge he would lose an important source of income. The social and economic value that Jean ascribed to Gbǎdù made Jean's proposition all the more uncomfortable for me. I knew that Jean commonly refused to share this knowledge with most of his other apprentices, and I felt uneasy about learning something that so many Béninois had been barred from.

"Are you sure, Jean? Why today?" I asked.

"Because it's time."

"But why me? Why not the others?" I pushed.

"Don't argue with me. You're leaving and you need to know how to do this," Jean insisted.

There was no getting out of it. My initiation gave me the power to make Gbǎdù, while my foreignness distanced me from the local economy just enough to convince Jean that I could not sell Gbǎdù behind his back to other Béninois or steal prospective local or foreign initiates. Jean felt safe teaching me, but I also realized that, for Jean, teaching me how to construct Gbǎdù had a more important purpose. After he explained the final part of the process, he and I began to walk back to his house. Jean grabbed my hand and said to me, "Don't forget us, Tim. We're family."

How could I forget Jean? He and his family opened their homes to me and invited me into their secret worlds. For Jean, teaching me how to construct Gbădù was about the future. It was a gift, perfectly imbued with social obligation and meaning, that sealed our relationship and ensured a long-term promise to each other (Mauss 1990 [1950]).

Today, evidence of my time with Jean, including my initiations, fills my home. Shrines, divination tools, and Vodún-inspired art all remind me daily of the commitment that I made deep inside the sacred forest to the spirits and to Jean. During one of my weekly divination sessions, Fá told me that I should offer palm oil to Lĕgbá to overcome obstacles that would be placed in front of me over the coming days. I did as Fá instructed and poured the bright red-orange oil onto Lĕgbá while asking him to remove anything from my path that would inhibit my ability to move forward in life. Using a fresh kola nut that I had purchased at a West African food store in town, I confirmed that Lĕgbá accepted my offering. As I put the oil away, I began to wonder if I really believed in the spirits' power. One might assume that my commitment to divination would be evidence of my belief. But, like all things in Vodún, it was not that simple.

While I trusted that Lĕgbá would do as Fá said he would, I had also come to accept that, despite my trust in the vodún, I did not believe in them as a literal pantheon of spirits. Yet I recognized that the spirits inspired me and held sway over my life. Divination and sacrifice encouraged me to think through issues and find solutions. I found myself simultaneously believing and disbelieving in their existence. I struggled to come to grips with these contradictions that had become a part of my own belief system. Within a few days of making the offering, Lĕgbá had begun to remove obstacles from my life. Indeed, I was already beginning to understand the vodún differently. Toward the end of the week, I simply let go and remembered the lesson that I learned from the *agbègbé* vine. I was once again foolishly looking for agbègbé's elusive roots. I was trying too hard to rationalize something that defied rationality. Lĕgbá helped me to become comfortable with paradox. It was not my belief or disbelief that was a problem—it was the pressure that I felt to define my beliefs that became counterproductive.

Not too long after, I began to reflect on the academic value of my apprenticeship. I wondered whether my belief in the spirits is defined by paradox; if so, in the end, how useful could my apprenticeship have really been? I came away from this experience simultaneously believing and disbelieving in the vodún. As I began to realize that my beliefs' strengths were tethered to their indeterminacy, I started to consider that the same might also be true for my apprenticeship. Anthropologists benefit greatly from apprenticeship as a research method, because it forces the researcher into a state of between-ness, being caught between two indeterminate worlds and between two ways of being. Like Vodún, one must embrace apprenticeship's ability to blur our professional and personal boundaries. Religious apprenticeship is ethical and works only when the anthropologist lets go of the expectations of science, thereby giving in to the possibility of believing. In this way, religious apprenticeship is not about believing in new epistemologies as much as it is about anthropologists allowing for the way they exist in the world to be changed forever as they take on new realities and new possibilities in their quest to understand the social power of the divine.

NOTES

Introduction

1. The title of "supreme chief of Vodún in Bénin" is a contested one. Despite the fact that Daágbó has the words *le pontife du Vodún* (the pope of Vodún) inscribed on the back of his hunter-green Toyota RAV4, his power wanes dramatically outside of Ouidah and its surrounding areas. Within Ouidah, his influence fares better but is still disputed. At the time of this writing, the current Daágbó Xùnɔ is one of two claimants to the throne of the "supreme chief." Although Daágbó Xùnɔ is the chief recognized by the Béninois government and enthroned in the palace, the son of Tomadijekoukpon's predecessor has also made a claim to the throne. To complicate matters, both enjoy substantial community support.

2. Because Fá is one of Vodún's few possession-free cults, this may be one of the reasons foreign spiritual seekers predominantly seek initiation into Fá.

3. Countering Dean MacCannell's stance that tourists seek an "authentic" experience in all tourist encounters, Edward Bruner (2005) argues that "authenticity" should only be examined by scholars of tourism when our subjects spotlight its importance. The vast majority of those tourists I interviewed spoke of the importance of "authenticity" as a marker of "validity." So-called authentic initiations, shrines, power objects, and secret knowledge all give foreign spiritual tourists validity as new priests or spiritual seekers. While it is important to note that I see "authenticity" as a creative, subjective, and often political process (see Landry 2011), a detailed theoretical discussion of "authenticity" is beyond the scope of this book. I used the terms "authentic" and "authenticity" throughout only to index discursively the ways in which my informants, Béninois and foreign alike, spoke of the buying and selling of Vodún's secrets and how these exchanges highlighted an individual's need to be accepted by their communities as "valid."

4. As Robin Law has noted, the word "Nàgó," which is also used in Brazil and Haiti, has historically indicated those Yorùbá speakers who lived in western Yorùbáland. Despite the term's geographic beginnings, it became a popular gloss used by the Fon of Dahomey for all Yorùbá speakers during the transatlantic slave trade and the rise of the Dahomean empire in the region. As such, today, among Fon speakers, the word "Nàgó" is often used as a generic term for Yorùbá speakers (Law 1997).

5. "Ouidah was by far the most important point of embarkation for slaves. . . . Ouidah was a leading slaving port for almost two centuries from the 1670s to the 1860s. During this period, the Bight of Benin is thought to have accounted for around 22 per cent of all slaves exported to the Americas, and Ouidah for around 51 per cent of exports from the Bight. Given the current consensual estimate of between 10 and 11 million slaves exported from Africa in this period, this suggests that Ouidah supplied well over a million slaves" (Law 2004: 2).

6. While I am noting that Agajá was the "fourth ruler of Dahomey," many Béninois consider him to be Dahomey's third ruler. This is because the brief reign of Ahangbè (r. 1716–18), the older sister of Agajá, is often omitted, as she worked politically as regent to promote Agajá to the throne (Bay 1998: 53–54).

7. The term *malê* comes from the Yorùbá word *ìmàle*, meaning "Muslim." This term came to be used to describe the Great Revolt of 1835 in Bahia because the revolt was thought to have been inspired by Muslim teachers.

8. Throughout the book I use the concept of "the West" as a shorthand way of indexing the collective geopolitical, neoliberal, postcolonial, and racial similarities that exist between nation-states such as Australia, Canada, Europe, and the United States. While I wish to avoid the Orientalizing affects that "the West" may invoke in my readers, I have opted for its use for stylistic reasons so as to avoid long, clunky, undesirable descriptive phrases.

9. Despite its having occurred in 1993, the festival is known as "Ouidah '92." This is largely due to a delay that occurred after the event's posters, naming it "Ouidah '92," had already been printed. To escape a financial loss from having to reprint the festival's publicity materials, the original name was retained.

10. While I have translated the term "yovó" into English as "white person," "yovó" is actually quite complex and challenging to translate directly. In Bénin, "yovó" is commonly translated into French as *le blanc/la blanche* or into English as "white person" or "European." Contrarily, I observed Béninois address almost every African American tourist I encountered (regardless of their complexion) as "yovó" (cf. Clarke 2004: 14, 111; Bruner 2005: 109–10) while other Africans, from Ghana, for example, were simply called *gbèjí* (person from the outside). To complicate the matter further, Béninois who are born with a light complexion are often nicknamed "yovó" (and less commonly *wèwé*, the word for the color "white"), clearly linking yovó to phenotypical racial whiteness. I would argue that the Fon term "yovó" has clear, albeit fluid, simultaneous connections to both phenotypical and foreign "whiteness" with subtle (but important) connections to local perceptions of meta-European (read: white) privilege.

11. While my fifteen-month apprenticeship was effective, thought-provoking, and certainly useful in many ways, I want to be clear that it is in no way equivalent to the experiences of Béninois students.

12. When an initiate learns which of the 256 signs of Fá governs his or her individualized destiny, he or she receives a small, lightly beaded, palm-sized bundle (a *kpɔlí*) that contains secret ingredients that correspond with their personal *dù/odù*, along with a small glass or ceramic vessel that houses sixteen to eighteen palm nuts (*fádékwín*) and a small stone (*ken*) that is said to protect the new initiate from witchcraft. These objects together make up one's personal Fá.

Chapter 1

1. The spirit (vodún) known as Dangbé falls under the umbrella of Dàn spirits, who are all serpents. Dangbé in particular is the vodún associated with the "royal python," also known in English as the "ball python" (*Python regius*), and was originally worshiped by the Xwedá people of southern Bénin but became an important part of the Fon pantheon in the early 1700s, when King Agaja conquered the Xwedá kingdom and took control of the city known today as Ouidah and surrounding areas (Law 2004).

2. The vodún known locally as Lǒkò is associated with the iroko tree (*Chlorophora excelsa*).

3. The actual number of slaves who forcibly left Ouidah for the Americas is difficult to calculate precisely because of problematic and sometimes conflicting historical records. Robin Law, a historian of Dahomey, Bénin, and especially Ouidah, estimates that "given the current consensual estimate of between 10 and 11 million slaves exported from African in this period [1650–1870], this suggests that Ouidah supplied well over a million slaves" (2004: 2).

4. At the time of my research, the exchange rate was approximately 1 USD for 457 CFA. However, by the time of this writing the exchange rate had risen to 1 USD for 590 CFA.

5. For a detailed description of Gbǎdù, see Chapter 2.

6. The forehead is symbolically important because both Fon and Yorùbá peoples see the head as the seat of one's personal soul (Herskovits 1938: 236). During initiation ceremonies, a great deal of care is taken to prepare one's head for initiation and eventually to install the target spirit into the head of the devotee. This practice is so important that Daágbó Xùnɔ Houna (the predecessor of the current enthroned supreme chief of Vodún) made great strides in Ouidah to prevent teachers in school from slapping a child's head when disciplining them, because many of these children were already initiated, and to strike the head would be considered disrespectful not only to the child but also to the spirits inhabiting them. Given the symbolic importance of the head in Vodún, placing money on one's forehead is an important gesture both to the dancer/singer/drummer and to that person's personal vodún who may accompany them.

7. While "vĭgán" translates as "chief of the children," a more accurate translation might be "chief of the people" or "chief of the family members," as opposed to the "chief of the village."

8. The role of a vĭgán is a lifelong position decided through divination upon the death of the current holder of that position. While Jean served as vĭgán and his father as togán, this is not necessarily always the case. The holders of these positions are selected by Fá from a specific pool of people who are usually of the same lineage.

9. Indexing the connection to smallpox, initiates of Sakpatá often scar their bodies and decorate Sakpatá temples by using dots so as to mimic smallpox scars. However, Sakpatá, once the master of incurable smallpox, is now transforming as he begins to do battle with other incurable diseases such as HIV/AIDS.

10. Vode are small indicators that a diviner may collect over his lifetime. For example, a cowrie shell might represent "yes" or "wealth," and a piece of broken pottery might represent a "no" or "bad fortune." Diviners can collect hundreds of different indicators throughout his career. When using vode, a diviner will have his client clench two or more indicators in her or his hands so that they are not visible to the diviner. The diviner will then ask Fá to reveal the hand that holds the answer.

11. Over a period of fifteen months, I watched as Jean, my initiator, charged his nephew 50,000 CFA, a distantly related villager 100,000 CFA, an upwardly mobile family friend 350,000 CFA, and a French spiritual seeker 500,000 CFA—all for the same ceremony. In the case of his nephew, after Jean provided the sacrificial animals, fed the participants, and purchased other miscellaneous materials, it was clear that Jean had lost money performing the ceremony. However, for Jean the importance of his nephew's initiation outweighed the financial cost.

12. At the time of this writing, a round-trip, economy-fare ticket traveling on Delta Airlines from New York's John F. Kennedy International Airport to Bénin's Cadjehoun International Airport costs $1,955.25.

13. In 2003, while conducting research in Haiti, I became initiated into Haitian Vodou at the highest rank (houngan asogwe). For a theoretically oriented discussion of this experience, see Landry (2008).

Chapter 2

1. Robin Law has noted that "in pre-colonial West Africa . . . people were [sacrificed] not so much as offerings to a deity, but in order to carry messages to the deity on behalf of the sacrificing community" (1985: 57). In present-day Bénin, I observed individuals whispering messages to their ancestors into the ears of sacrificial animals on countless occasions. It is conceivable that this practice is ritual memory of a time when human sacrifice was used for this purpose.

2. For a sophisticated attempt at understanding the ritual power of leaves in Ifá divination, see Verger (1995a).

3. Agbègbé is a Fon word for the parasitic vine plant known in English as "seaside dodder" and scientifically as *Cassytha filiformis L.*

4. While Èjì-Ogbè (also known as *Ogbè-Méjì* or *Gbè-Méjì*) is commonly understood to be the "first" and "most senior" of the 256 signs, *Òfún-Méjì* (also known as *Fú-Méjì*), the sixteenth sign, is said to be the real chief of the signs and as such is given the same honor and respect as Ogbè-Méjì in ceremonies.

5. The typical age of initiation varies from spirit cult to spirit cult. There has been some controversy in Bénin surrounding the initiation of young boys and girls into Vodún. While some priests see initiating children as an important part of their Vodún-based educations and as a critical step for their preparation to be lifelong devotees, others prefer to hold off initiation in favor of sending their children to public school "to prepare them better for today's world." Jean typically initiates his sons by the time they are in their mid-teens. He waits until then because he values a school-based education for all his children and by then, he says, "I can be sure they will be able to keep a secret from their mothers."

6. The ritual I present here is not meant to be complete. I have left out stages and details that did not add to the overall value of my analysis, and I have refrained from revealing anything that might be construed as secret. I have done this to keep a dual ethical mandate: I avoid revealing any of the secrets that I learned while serving as Jean's apprentice, and I aim to prevent this ethnographic account from being used as a ritual manual by foreign spiritual seekers, as has been done with William Bascom's work (see Gottlieb 2000).

7. Drewal and Drewal have indicated this bird to be a hawk. According to Ositola, one of their informants, the hawk is present because "history told us that if we want something to act quickly, we should do it in the name of the hawk" (1993: 66). Jean always taught me that the bird was a rooster, because, according to Jean, "God dropped a rooster to the earth to kick up dirt and form the world." For Jean, the rooster indexed the creation of the world and the power of the diviner to also create.

8. A new fásén must be washed with special leaves and the blood of sixteen giant snails. Only women may do this job, and they must do it in seclusion, away from the eyes of boys and men. All roosters given to the fásén are eaten by women only. Jean told me, "The fásén keeps the diviner up, just as women keep the family up. How women do that is their secret. The fásén is their secret, even though it's our tool."

9. For a look at China's current involvement in African economics and development, see Brautigam 2009.

10. This ritual, and others like it, caused cases of eosinophilic meningitis among practitioners of West African and Afro-Caribbean religions within the United States. Practitioners can contract this rare form of meningitis from the parasites found in the giant land snails.

11. The fátὲ is often an indicator of a diviner's economic position. For those diviners who have a large clientele and are therefore financially stable, their fátὲ are typically elaborately carved. Foreign spiritual seekers and important Béninois diviners often pay woodcarvers to carve fátὲ for them that can cost upward of 400 USD. By contrast, those diviners who do not enjoy a significant local or international client base may have fátὲ made from inexpensive materials such as plastic or cardboard.

12. I am being intentionally vague here in order to protect the secrets of the Egúngún society.

13. The reason most Béninois never learn how to incarnate Gbǎdù into her shrine is that Gbǎdù is largely a communal shrine. In Bénin, families, not individuals, have Gbǎdù as the cornerstone of their lineage, in order to protect them from witchcraft. Lacking these kinship structures, foreign spiritual seekers have come to see Gbǎdù as a personal shrine, the ultimate symbol of their authenticity as a priest. Because of the difficulty in making this shrine, it is also one of the most expensive shrines a foreign spiritual seeker can obtain. I met an American man who admitted to paying 10,000 USD for Gbǎdù and the know-how to construct the shrine himself. The high cost of this shrine has generated some serious legal issues for Béninois. One evening, late at night, a young man whom I did not know came to my door saying that he was looking for someone who wanted to buy Gbǎdù from him for 5,000 USD. The following day, I learned that a local family had their Gbǎdù stolen—perhaps by this young man who knew of the shrine's high international value. I approached the family to tell them of the young man who was trying to sell what I believed was their stolen Gbǎdù but I never heard from the young man again.

14. Many foreign initiates had financial arrangements with their initiators that allowed for both the foreign and the Béninois initiator to make money. One such arrangement that I knew of required a 30/70 split in profits in favor of the Béninois initiator, calculated only after ritual supplies and sacrificial animals were purchased.

Chapter 3

1. I use the phrase "incarnated to earth" here and elsewhere to index the problems with using English words like "shrines" or "symbols" in this context. While there are shrines and altars in Vodún that are known as *vodúnkpὲ* (literally, spirit mound), where devotees can leave offerings and make sacrifices, in this context I am speaking about the making of the spirits themselves. In this way, for practitioners of Vodún, this type of shrine is neither representational nor symbolic as they are the presence of the actual spirit (*vodún*) incarnated onto earth from joining ritually a complex array of prayers and sacrifices with zoological, botanical, and artisanal objects. See Landry (2016) for more information.

2. Neither Lὲgbà nor Fá, for example, contains items taken from endangered or protected African wildlife, but other such items do require many of these and are purchased by Western spiritual seekers from local Vodún priests, who then, sometimes unknowingly, carry them home illegally in their luggage.

3. Although the sale of real human skulls is intended to be for "medical research" or for use by "health professionals," I have observed U.S.-based practitioners of West African–derived religions (Haitian Vodou, Lucumí, Vodún) purchasing legally procured human skulls from Internet distributors.

4. While these stones represent an unchangeable quality of Xɛbyosò, this particular example also demonstrates some changeability within the seemingly immutable symbolic structure of

this spirit cult in particular. The so-called thunderstones (Fon, *sò kpén*) were once probably meteorites that had fallen to the earth in a fiery crash, creating a similar visual effect to lightning and therefore seen as a manifestation of Xɛbyosò. While I was unable to verify this hypothesis for certain, old Xɛbyosò shrines are made of rough-edged stones that resemble meteorites, and J. Rassinoux (2000) in his French-Fon dictionary defines *sò kpén* as both *pierre à tonnerre* (thunderstone) and *météorite* (meteorite), echoing my suspicion that older stones were possibly meteorites. Today, *sò kpén* are typically stones that have been carved into the shape of an axe head, thereby blending two of Xɛbyosò's primary symbols—the axe and the thunderstone—while also maintaining the importance of the thunderstone to Xɛbyosò's cult.

5. For more on termites and termite mounds and symbols throughout West Africa, see Dilley (2005), Fairhead and Leach (2003), and Iroko (1982).

6. According to David Doris, a Yorùbá proverb says "the thing that resembles a thing is the thing we use to compare to that thing" (*Ohun tó bá jọ ohun la fi n wé ohun*) (2011: 231). Doris goes on to say that "visual resemblance plays a fundamental role in the manufacture and efficacy of Yoruba traditional medicine . . . 'sympathy' is activated in the visual likeness of disparate bodies" (231). This point made by Doris is also reflected in Jean's comment that a Lěgbà shrine is made from the soil from a termite mound because they resemble each other—a metaphysical trend that permeates Yorùbá and Fon ritual, ceremony, and magic.

7. While the interred contents of a Lěgbà shrine are secret and probably vary from priest to priest, the mound symbolism is repeated underground as well.

8. I place "symbols" in quotes to engage with the anthropological literature on symbols while also showing that local people do not see some of these objects as "representational" or "symbolic." In fact, many of these objects are considered to embody the spirits and therefore transcend contemporary approaches to symbolic analysis.

9. Quoted from McDannell 1995.

10. I conducted a survey of 125 respondents in the final month of my eighteen-month stay in Bénin. Although skeptical of survey methods, I decided to perform this survey at the end of my stay in order to test some general hunches I had about the nature of Vodún and the religion's relationship to international tourism and transnationalism.

11. Tron is the spirit of the kola nut. A recent addition to the Vodún pantheon, he is known for his ability to fight against and protect from azě. Although many Fá diviners—the men who keep the secrets of the vodún Gbǎdù—maintain that nothing is more powerful than Gbǎdù in curing an affliction or protecting a person, house, or village from azě, community fears of witchcraft have increased the local devotion to Tron, an otherwise "safe" and "cool" spirit.

12. Women are kept from Gbǎdù because, like Gbǎdù, women have the power to create (i.e., give life). Gbǎdù is the cosmic womb and the condensation of creation, and she contains the infinite possibilities of the universe as expressed in the 256 sacred odù/dù of Fá. As Jean told me, "Bringing women and Gbǎdù [who both embody creative forces] into the same room could be catastrophic." Even so, many female Western spiritual seekers see their exclusion as an affront to their femininity and as a way of men controlling so-called women's mysteries. These concerns, which may be rooted in Western feminism and Western occult traditions such as Wicca that praise female spiritual power, have led several American women to search for initiation into Gbǎdù despite the local taboo against doing so.

13. These fears are further expressed in a Fon-French dictionary (Segurola and Rassinoux 2009) whose authors, seemingly unaware that Gbǎdù is a spirit herself, key into the social anxiety generated by Gbǎdù and her cult and define Gbǎdù as "a sign of Fá of which the owner is

very fearful that Gbădù may cause problems around him" (*signe du Fá dont le possesseur est très craint: il peut entraîner des malheurs autour de lui*) (220).

14. While working in the Abomey area of Bénin, Falen (personal communication) has also found evidence for *azĕ vɔvɔ* (red witchcraft, or *sorcellerie rouge*), a third division of azĕ that I never encountered in Ouidah. Falen's finding of azĕ vɔvɔ also seems to confirm my hypothesis that Fon and Yorùbá speakers share a great deal of overlap in the ways in which they each understand witchcraft. Like Falen, who found red witchcraft in Abomey, Teresa Washington has also found red witchcraft (*àjẹ́ pupa*) in Yorùbáland, which, according to her, is "said to specialize in bloodletting, car wrecks, cuts—any incident that will result in blood-flow" (2007: 25).

15. While categorizing azĕ as a psychic force and bŏ as a materially generated force is the simplest way to differentiate the two systems of magic, the lines between them are blurrier than they seem. Azĕtɔ́ are believed to enhance their powers with an object called an *azĕká* (a cala-bash of witchcraft) that, because of its materiality and its secret contents, could be categorized as a bŏ. This seems to suggest that azĕ—even if perceived as a psychic force—can be strength-ened by bŏ. Conversely, some bŏ, especially those that are believed to grant quick travel, invis-ibility, transmutation, and flight, are often said to be azĕ in and of themselves, thereby blurring the boundaries even more.

16. For more on owls and other animals associated with witchcraft throughout sub-Saharan Africa, see Jackson (1975) and Offiong (1983).

17. One informant claimed that where translocation or teleportation was concerned, azĕ, the more powerful form, would allow one to pinpoint the exact destination of one's teleporta-tion, while bŏ's reach was random.

18. I met several French expats who purchased "protection charms" from a local Vodún priest after hearing an advertisement on the radio, and I have spoken to one French woman (married to a Béninois man) who sought out the services of a local diviner after seeing his roadside billboard.

Chapter 4

1. In Fɔngbè, "Nafi" is a kinship title given to the younger sisters of one's mother. This woman was widely called Nafi by close friends and family, perhaps because of her youthful appearance and her legitimate position as a Nafi to her sisters' large number of children. Her position as Nafi is so great that even her son and daughter-in-law both call her by this name.

2. Missionaries' linguistic legacy is evident in the ways children are taught to "translate" some Vodún terms from Fɔngbè into French. For example, Lĕgbà, the spirit of the crossroads, is often translated into French as *diable* (devil); and bokɔ́nɔ̀, the Fon title for a diviner (or priest of Fá), is often translated as *charlatan* (fraud or imposter).

3. Islam has also been incorporated into some aspects of Vodún, albeit at a lesser rate than Christianity. For example, in some cases, Béninois use Islamic script in magic and in the con-struction of charms (cf. Ferme 1994; Launay 2004).

4. For classic approaches to witchcraft and its relationship to marginality, scapegoating, and Othering, see Evans-Pritchard (1976 [1937]), Kluckhohn (1944), and Marwick (1965).

5. Typically, witches are not identifiable by their appearance or in the way they carry them-selves. According to local Fon and Yorùbá peoples, only divination—and some of my informants assert only divination from a Fá diviner—can truly identify a witch. Nevertheless, I observed several individuals, such as Paulette, point to someone they did not know and call them a "witch"

based on that person's comportment. Each time this happened, the person was an elderly woman, clearly disheveled, unkempt, and socially marginal or otherwise "odd." Although accusations of witchcraft in these instances (based on visual cues) worked to further marginalize the target, more serious social sanctions would not usually be invoked without confirmation from a reputable diviner.

6. Because of witchcraft's omnipotence in the community, some people have remarked that because Tron has the ability to fight, and sometimes win against, witchcraft, then Tron and his followers too must all be witches. This is a claim that most priests and priestesses of Tron deny. Instead, they argue that Tron, while not a witch, discovered the tools necessary to fight witchcraft. Indeed, some even argue that Tron's ability to fight witchcraft is so strong that witches cannot even step foot in a Tron temple or they risk defeat and possible death. As a result, people have been known to drag suspected witches to Tron temples as a way of verifying an accusation of witchcraft.

7. For a compelling discussion of the ways in which tourism can incite "cultural revival," see Bruner (2005: 119–21).

8. Most people who want to learn their destiny and have the occult protection that Fá affords do not undergo the complex initiation into the priesthood that is described in Chapter 2. Unlike the priestly initiation where one is said to "receive Fá's forest" (*Fázúnyí*), the initiation that Marie experienced was what is commonly called *la première initiation au culte de Fá* (the first initiation in the cult of Fá), or *yĭ Fá*, meaning simply "to receive Fá." Unlike the priestly initiation where an initiate would receive the forest, and all that the forest holds and hides, in the case of this initiation the initiate only receives Fá.

9. Caulder's work should not be read as an accurate ethnography of Vodún practice in Bénin. Rather, it is best read as one woman's account of her "Voodoo" initiations as she understood them through a Western-centric lens. Throughout the text, Caulder berates Béninois people for cultural practices such as animal sacrifice and polygyny while defying conventional ritual practice and simultaneously presenting herself as more spiritually "evolved" than her Béninois counterparts. Caulder's understanding of the metaphysical principles of "Voodoo" is greatly influenced by the contemporary New Age movement in the United States that focuses on a type of "individualism" that extols "noble savages," their interconnectedness to nature, and spiritual transcendence, among other factors (e.g., Prince and Riches 1999). Caulder's work was published by Llewellyn Publications, the largest New Age book publisher in the United States.

Chapter 5

1. Ouidah was only behind Luanda, Angola (Law 2004).

2. This is a theme I found common in Ouidah (a zone of ethnic and international convergence) but much less common in Abomey (a zone that is unequivocally situated in Fonland). Indeed, questions of authenticity seem to be highlighted in these border zones where the economic and political stakes are higher.

3. While Jung Ran Forte (2007) has explored the initiation of foreigners into Vodún, she almost completely ignores the politics of race in her analysis.

4. The Haitian Kreyol word "manbo" (also written as "mambo"), used to denote a female Vodou priest, also comes from Fɔngbè (*nana* = mother; *bǒ* = charm/sorcery).

5. In Fonland, an azɔgwé, sometimes as large as a basketball, is typically much larger than the small, handheld asɔ̀, which more closely resembles the handheld asson of Haitian Vodou.

6. While initiation into most spirit cults does not depend on one's membership in a specific lineage or kin group, some spirits are controlled by specific families. Most notably, the Ouidah region of Bénin is associated with the restricted cult of Dangbé, the royal python. One evening when speaking to the *Dangbénɔ* (the priest of Dangbé) about foreign initiation, he told me, "I don't have a problem with foreigners initiating into Vodún but they could never be initiated into the cult of Dangbé because it's only for our family." However, later in the same conversation he qualified his statement by saying, "I suppose we could initiate a foreigner if they married into the family. But that's the only possibility."

7. There is a sense among Béninois that "real Vodún" is found farther north, away from tourist centers. Most Béninois who expressed this sentiment pointed to Savalou, a small town in the extreme north of Fonland, as being the seat of "real Vodún" in Bénin.

WORKS CITED

Abimbọla, Wande. 1997. Ifá Will Mend Our Broken World: Thoughts on Yoruba Religion and Culture in Africa and the Diaspora. Roxbury, Mass.: Aim Books.

Abiodun, Rowland. 1994. Àṣẹ: Verbalizing and Visualizing Creative Power Through Art. Journal of Religion in Africa 24(4):309–22.

Adeola, Moses Olanre. 1992. Importance of Wild Animals and Their Parts in the Culture, Religious Festivals, and Traditional Medicine, of Nigeria. Environmental Conservation 19(2):125–34.

Airewele, Peyi Soyinka, and Rita Kiki Endozie, eds. 2009. Reframing Contemporary Africa: Politics, Economics, and Culture in the Global Era. Washington, D.C.: CQ Press.

Anderson, Benedict. 2006 [1983]. Imagined Communities: Reflections on the Origin and Spread of Nationalism. New York: Verso.

Appadurai, Arjun. 1995. The Production of Locality. In Counterworks: Managing the Diversity of Knowledge. Richard Fardon, ed. Pp. 204–25. London: Routledge.

———. 1996. Modernity at Large: Cultural Dimensions of Globalization. Minneapolis: University of Minnesota Press.

Araujo, Ana Lucia. 2010. Public Memory of Slavery: Victims and Perpetrators in the South Atlantic. New York: Cambria Press.

Aronson, Lisa. 2007. Ewe Ceramics as the Visualization of Vodun. *African Arts* 40(1):80–85.

Asad, Talal. 1986. The Idea of an Anthropology of Islam. Washington, D.C.: Center for Contemporary Arab Studies, Georgetown University.

———. 1993. Genealogies of Religion: Discipline and Reasons of Power in Christianity and Islam. Baltimore: Johns Hopkins University Press.

Augé, Marc. 1988. Le Dieux Objet. Paris: Flammarion.

Babatunde, Lawal. 1985. Orí: The Significance of the Head in Yoruba Sculpture. Journal of Anthropological Research 41(1):91–103.

Badone, Ellen, and Sharon R. Roseman, eds. 2004. Intersecting Journeys: Anthropology of Pilgrimage and Tourism. Urbana: University of Illinois Press.

Barnes, Sandra T., ed. 1997. Africa's Ogun: Old World and New. Bloomington: Indiana University Press.

_____. 2008. Meta-Cultural Processes and Ritual Realities in the Precolonial History of the Lagos Region. In Òrìṣà Devotion as World Religion: The Globalization of Yorùbá Religious Culture. Jacob K Olupona and Terry Rey, eds. Pp. 164–90. Madison: University of Wisconsin Press.

Barthkowski, John P. 1998. Claims-Making and Typifications of Voodoo as a Deviant Religion: Hex, Lies, and Videotape. Journal of the Scientific Study of Religion 37(4):559–79.

Bascom, William W. 1980. Sixteen Cowries: Yoruba Divination from Africa to the New World. Bloomington: Indiana University Press.

———. 1991. Ifa Divination: Communication Between Gods and Men in West Africa. Bloomington: Indiana University Press.

Bay, Edna G. 1998. Wives of the Leopard: Gender, Politics, and Culture in the Kingdom of Dahomey. Charlottesville: University of Virginia Press.

———. 2008. Asen, Ancestors, and Vodun: Tracing Change in African Art. Urbana: University of Illinois Press.

Beck, Ulrich. 1999. What Is Globalization? Cambridge: Polity Press.

Beidelman, T. O. 1997. The Cool Knife: Imagery of Gender, Sexuality, and Moral Education in Kaguru Initiation Ritual. Washington, D.C.: Smithsonian Institution Press.

Beliso-De Jesús, Aisha. 2015. Electric Santería: Racial and Sexual Assemblages of Transnational Religion. New York: Columbia University Press.

Bell, Catherine M. 1997. Ritual: Perspectives and Dimensions. New York: Oxford University Press.

Bellman, Beryl L. 1984. The Language of Secrecy: Symbols and Metaphors in Poro Ritual. New Brunswick, N.J.: Rutgers University Press.

Blier, Suzanne Preston. 1993. Art and Secret Agency: Concealment and Revelation in Artistic Expression. *In* Secrecy: African Art That Conceals and Reveals. Mary H. Nooter, ed. New York: Museum for African Art.

———. 1995. African Vodun: Art, Psychology, and Power. Chicago: University of Chicago Press.

Boas, Franz. 1940. [1896] The Limitations of the Comparative Method of Anthropology. *In* Race, Language, and Culture. Pp. 270–80. Chicago: University of Chicago Press.

Bond, Patrick. 2006. Looting Africa: The Economics of Exploitation. Pietermartizburg: University of KwaZulu-Natal Press.

Bourdieu, Pierre. 1980. Le Sens Pratique. Paris: Les Editions de Minuit.

Brautigam, Deborah. 2009. The Dragon's Gift: The Real Story of China in Africa. Oxford: Oxford University Press.

Brown, Karen McCarthy. 2001 [1991]. Mama Lola: A Vodou Priestess in Brooklyn. Berkeley: University of California Press.

Bruner, Edward M. 2005. Culture on Tour: Ethnographies of Travel. Chicago: University of Chicago Press.

Butler, Stuart. 2006. Benin: The Bradt Travel Guide. London: Bradt Travel Guides.

Carr, C. Lynn. 2015. A Year in White: Cultural Newcomers to Lukumi and Santería in the United States. London: Routledge.

Caulder, Sharon. 2002. Mark of Voodoo: Awakening to My African Spiritual Heritage. St. Paul, Minn.: Llewellyn Publications.

Cheru, Fantu. 2010. The Global Economic Order and Its Socioeconomic Impact. *In* Reframing Contemporary Africa: Politics, Economics, and Culture in the Global Era. Peyi Soyinka Airewele and Rita Kiki Endozie, eds. Pp. 195–217. Washington, D.C.: CQ Press.

Chidili, Bartholomew. 2007. Is African Religion a Religion? Asia Journal of Theology 21(2):325–44.

Churchill, Ward. 1994. Indians Are Us? Culture and Genocide in Native America. Toronto: Between the Lines.

Clarke, Kamari Maxine. 2004. Mapping Yorùbá Networks: Power and Agency in the Making of Transnational Communities. Durham, N.C.: Duke University Press.

Coats, Curtis. 2011. Spiritual Tourism—Promise and Problems: The Case of Sedona, Arizona. *In* Media, Spiritualities and Social Change. Stewart M. Hoover and Monica Emerich, eds. Pp. 117–26. New York: Continuum International Publishing Group.

Comaroff, Jean, and John Comaroff. 1991. Of Revelation and Revolution, Volume One: Christianity, Colonialism, and Consciousness in South Africa. Chicago: University of Chicago Press.

———. 1993. Modernity and Its Malcontents: Ritual and Power in Postcolonial Africa. Chicago: University of Chicago Press.

———. 1999. Occult Economies and the Violence of Abstraction. American Ethnologist 26(2):279–303.

———. 2009. Ethnicity, Inc. Chicago: University of Chicago Press.

———. 2012. Theory from the South: Or How Euro-America Is Evolving Toward Africa. Boulder, Colo.: Paradigm Publishers.

Coy, Michael W. 1989. Apprenticeship: From Theory to Method and Back Again. Albany: State University of New York Press.

D'Alisera, JoAnn. 2004. An Imagined Geography: Sierra Leonean Muslims in America. Philadelphia: University of Pennsylvania Press.

———. 2001. I ♡ Islam: Popular Religious Commodities, Sites of Inscription, and Transnational Sierra Leonean Identity. Journal of Material Culture 6(1):91–110.

Desforges, Luke. 2001. Tourism Consumption and the Imagination of Money. Transactions of the Institute of British Geographers 26(3):353–64.

Desjarlais, Robert R. 1992. Body and Emotion: The Aesthetics of Illness and Healing in the Nepal Highlands. Philadelphia: University of Pennsylvania Press.

Dilley, Roy. 2005. Islamic and Caste Knowledge Practices Among Haalpulaaaren in Senegal: Between Mosque and Termite Mound. Edinburgh: Edinburgh University Press.

Dominguez, Virginia. 1993. White by Definition: Social Classifications in Creole Louisiana. New Brunswick, N.J.: Rutgers University Press.

Doris, David T. 2011. Vigilant Things: On Thieves, Yoruba Anti-Aesthetics, and the Strange Fates of Ordinary Objects in Nigeria. Seattle: University of Washington Press.

Douglas, Mary. 1966. Purity and Danger. New York: Routledge.

Drewal, Henry John. 1998 Yorùbá Beadwork in Africa. African Arts 31(1):18–27+94.

———, ed. 2008. Sacred Waters: Arts for Mami Wata and Other Divinities in Africa and the Diaspora. Bloomington: Indiana University Press.

Drewal, Margaret T., and Henry J. Drewal. 1983. An Ifa Diviner's Shrine in Ijebuland. *African Arts* 16(2):60–67.

Durkheim, Emile. 1965 [1912]. The Elementary Forms of Religious Life. London: Allen & Unwin.

Eco, Umberto. 1983 [1973]. Travels in Hyperreality. Orlando, Fla.: Harcourt Brace and Company.

Ekholm-Friedman, Kajsa, and J. Friedman. 1995. Global Complexity and the Simplicity of Everyday Life. *In* Worlds Apart: Modernity Through the Prism of the Local. Daniel Miller, ed. Pp. 134–68. London: Routledge.

Elwert-Kretschmer, Karola. 1995. Vodun et controle social au village. Politique Africaine 59:102–20.

Evans-Pritchard, E. E. 1976 [1937]. Witchcraft, Oracles, and Magic Among the Azande. Oxford: Oxford University Press.

Fabian, Johannes. 1983. Time and the Other: How Anthropology Makes Its Object. New York: Columbia University Press.

Fairhead, James, and Melissa Leach. 2003. Termites, Society and Ecology: Perspectives from West Africa. In Les insectes dan la tradition orale. Élisabeth Motte-Florac and Jacqueline M. C. Thomas, eds. Pp. 197–219. Paris: Peeters-SELAF.

Falen, Douglas J. 2007. Good and Bad Witches: The Transformation of Witchcraft in Bénin. West Africa Review 10(1):1–27.

Ferme, Mariane C. 1994. What "Alhaji Airplane" Saw in Mecca, and What Happened When He Came Home: Ritual Transformation in a Mende Community (Sierra Leone). In Syncretism/Anti-Syncretism: The Politics of Religious Synthesis. Charles Stewart and Rosalind Shaw, eds. Pp. 27–44. London: Routledge.

———. 2001. The Underneath of Things: Violence, History, and the Everyday in Sierra Leone. Berkeley: University of California Press.

Forte, Jung Ran. 2007. "Way of Remembering": Transatlantic Connections and African Diasporas Homecoming in the Republic of Benin. Social Dynamics 33(2):123–43.

———. 2010. Black Gods, White Bodies: Westerners' Initiations in Contemporary Benin. Transforming Anthropology 18(2):129–45.

Frow, John. 1991. Tourism and the Semiotics of Nostalgia. October 57:123–51.

Fuller, Robert C. 2001. Spiritual, but Not Religious: Understanding Unchurched America. Oxford: Oxford University Press.

Gabail, Laurent. 2012. Performing Opacity: Initiation and Ritual Interactions Across the Ages Among the Bassari of Guinea. HAU: Journal of Ethnographic Theory 2(2):138–62.

Geary, David. 2008. Destination Enlightenment: Branding Buddhism and Spiritual Tourism in Bodhgaya, Bihar. Anthropology Today 24(3):11–14.

Geertz, Clifford. 1973. The Interpretation of Cultures. New York: Basic Books.

Gershon, Llana. 2011. Un-Friend My Heart: Facebook, Promiscuity, and Heartbreak in a Neoliberal Age. Anthropology Quarterly 84(4):865–94.

Geschiere, Peter. 1997. The Modernity of Witchcraft: Politics and the Occult in Postcolonial Africa. Charlottesville: University of Virginia Press.

———. 2013. Witchcraft, Intimacy, and Trust: Africa in Comparison. Chicago: University of Chicago Press.

Gilroy, Paul. 1993. The Black Atlantic: Modernity and Double-Consciousness. Cambridge, Mass.: Harvard University Press.

Goffman, Erving. 1959. The Presentation of Self in Everyday Life. New York: Doubleday Anchor.

Goody, Jack. 1977. The Domestication of the Savage Mind. Cambridge: Cambridge University Press.

Gottlieb, Alma. 1989. Witches, Kings, and the Sacrifice of Identity or the Power of Paradox and the Paradox of Power Among the Beng of Ivory Coast. In Creativity of Power: Cosmology and Action in African Societies. W. Arens and Ivan Karp, eds. Pp. 245–72. Washington, D.C.: Smithsonian Institution Press.

———. 1995. Of Cowries and Crying: A Beng Guide to Managing Colic. Anthropology and Humanism 20(1):20–28.

———. 2006. Packing a Cultural Suitcase: Anthropological Perspectives on the New African Migration to Europe and the US. Talk presented at the conference on New Contexts in Migration: When the Origin Transforms the Destination, Instituto Superior de Ciências do Trabalho e das Empress, Lisbon, October 9.

————. 2008. Loggers vs. Spirits: Competing Models of the Beng Forest. *In* African Ethnoforests: Sacred Groves, Culture, and Conservation. Celia Nyamweru and Michael Sheridan, eds. Pp. 149–63. Oxford: James Currey.

————. 2000. Secrets and Society: The Beng of Côte d'Ivoire. Mande Studies 2:129–51.

Gottlieb, Alma, and Philip Graham. 1994 Parallel Worlds: An Anthropologist and a Writer Encounter Africa. Chicago: University of Chicago Press.

————. 2012. Braided Worlds. Chicago: University of Chicago Press.

Gregory, C. A. 1996. Cowries and Conquest: Towards a Subalternate Quality Theory of Money. Comparative Studies in Society and History 38(2):195–217.

Griaule, Marcel. 1975 [1948]. Conversations with Ogotemmeli: An Introduction to Dogon Religious Ideas. New York: Oxford University Press.

Gujar, Bhouju Ram, and Ann Grodzing Gold. 1992. From the Research Assistant's Point of View. Anthropology and Humanism 17(3/4):72–84.

Haas, Brian, and Macolivie Jean-Francois. 2006. Woman Arrested at Airport with Human Skull in Her Carry-on. Seattle Times, February 11, http://seattletimes.com/html/nationworld/20 02798052_webskull10.html, accessed January 22, 2013.

Hannerz, Ulf. 1990. Cosmopolitans and Locals in World Culture. *In* Global Culture: Nationalism, Globalization, and Modernity. Mike Featherstone, ed. Pp. 237–52. Liverpool, U.K.: Sage.

Harris, Cheryl. 1993. Whiteness as Property. Harvard Law Review 106(8):1710–69.

Held, David. 2004. A Globalizing World? Culture, Economics, Politics. London: Routledge.

Herskovits, Melville J. 1938. Dahomey: An Ancient West African Kingdom. 2 vols. New York: J. J. Augustin.

————. 1971 [1937]. Life in a Haitian Valley. New York: Anchor Books.

Herzfeld, Michael. 2009 The Performance of Secrecy: Domesticity and Privacy in Public Spaces. Semiotica 175:135–62.

Hesse, Barnor. 2007. Racialized Modernity: An Analysis of White Mythologies. Ethnic and Racial Studies 30(4):643–63.

Human Fetuses Found in Luggage from Cuba at Miami International Airport. 2012. Huffington Post, March 22, https://www.huffingtonpost.com/2012/03/22/human-fetuses-found-in-jar -luggage-miami-santeria-cuba_n_1374345.html.

Humphrey, C., and J. Laidlaw. 1994. The Archetypical Actions of Ritual: A Theory of Ritual Illustrated by the Jain Rite of Worship. Oxford: Clarendon Press.

Hurston, Zora Neale. 2008a [1935]. Mules to Men. New York: HarperCollins.

————. 2008b [1938]. Tell My Horse: Voodoo and Life in Haiti and Jamaica. New York: HarperCollins.

Hüwelmeier, Gertrud, and Kristine Krause, eds. 2010. Traveling Spirits: Migrants, Markets and Mobilities. London: Routledge.

Iroko, A. F. 1982. Le rôle des termitières dan l'histoire des peuples de la République Populaire du Bénin des origines à nos jours. Bulletin de l'I.F.A.N. 44(1/2):50–75.

Jackson, Michael. 1975 Structure and Event: Witchcraft Confession Among the Kuranko. Man 10(3):387–403.

Jackson, Peter. 2004. Local Consumption Cultures in a Globalizing World. Transactions of the Institute of British Geographers 29(2):165–78.

Jocks, Christopher Ronwanièn:Te. 1996 Spirituality for Sale: Sacred Knowledge and the Consumer Age. American Indian Quarterly 20(3/4):415–31.

Joharifard, Shahrzad. 2005. Traditional Culture and the Problem of Dual Authority in the People's Republic of Benin. Senior honor's thesis, Department of History, Princeton University.

Johnson, Marion. 1970a. The Cowrie Currencies in West Africa, Part I. Journal of African History 11(1):17–49.

———. 1970b. The Cowrie Currencies in West Africa, Part II. Journal of African History 11(3):331–53.

Johnson, Paul Christopher. 2002. Secrets, Gossip, and Gods: The Transformation of Brazilian Candomblé. Oxford: Oxford University Press.

———. 2007. Diasporic Conversions: Black Carib Religion and the Recovery of Africa. Berkeley: University of California Press.

———, ed. 2013. Spirited Things: The Work of "Possession" in Afro-Atlantic Religions. Chicago: University of Chicago Press.

Jordan, Glenn, and Chris Weedon. 1995. Cultural Politics: Class, Gender, Race, and the Postmodern World. Cambridge, Mass.: Blackwell.

Jules-Rosette, Bennetta. 1975. Ritual and Conversion in the Church of John Maranke. Journal of Religion in Africa 7(2):132–64.

———. 1984. The Messages of Tourist Art: An African Semiotic System in Comparative Perspective. New York: Springer.

Kaplan, Steven. 2004. Themes and Methods in the Study of Conversion in Ethiopia: A Review Essay. Journal of Religion in Africa 34(3):373–92.

Keller, Charles M., and Janet Dixon Keller. 1996. Cognition and Tool Use: The Blacksmith at Work: Cambridge: Cambridge University Press.

Keller, Janet Dixon, and Takaronga Kuautonga. 2007. Nokonoto Kitea: We Keep Living this Way. Honolulu and Adelaide: University of Hawai'i and Crawford House.

Kirsch, Thomas G. 2004. Restaging the Will to Believe: Religious Pluralism, Anti-Syncretism, and the Problem of Belief. American Anthropologist 106(4):699–709.

Kluckhohn, Clyde. 1944. Navaho Witchcraft. Boston: Beacon Press.

Kohn, Eduardo. 2013. How Forests Think: Toward an Anthropology Beyond the Human. Berkeley: University of California Press.

Kriebel, David W. 2007. Powwowing Among the Pennsylvania Dutch: A Traditional Medical Practice in the Modern World. University Park: Pennsylvania State University Press.

Landau, Paul. 1999. Religion and Christian Conversion in African History: A New Model. Journal of Religious History 23(1):8–36.

Landry, Timothy R. 2008. Moving to Learn: Performance and Learning in Haitian Vodou. Anthropology and Humanism 33(1/2):53–65.

———. 2011. Touring the Slave Route: Inaccurate Authenticities in Bénin, West Africa. In Contested Cultural Heritage: Religion and Nationalism in a Globalized World. Helaine Silverman, ed. Pp. 205–31. New York: Springer.

———. 2015. Vodún, Globalization, and the Creative Layering of Belief in Southern Bénin. Journal of Religion in Africa 45(2):170–99.

———. 2016. Incarnating Spirits, Composing Shrines, and Cooking Divine Power in Vodún. Material Religion 12(1):3–26.

Lash, Scott, and John Urry. 1994. Economics of Signs and Space. London: Sage.

Launay, Robert. 2004. Beyond the Stream: Islam and Society in a West African Town. Long Grove, Ill.: Waveland Press.

Lave, Jean. 2011. Apprenticeship in Critical Ethnographic Practice. Chicago: University of Chicago Press.

Law, Robin. 1985. Human Sacrifice in Pre-Colonial West Africa. African Affairs 84(334):53–87.

———. 1997. Ethnicity and the Slave Trade: "Lucumi" and "Nago" as Ethnonyms in West Africa. History of Africa 24:205–19.

———. 2004. Ouidah: The Social History of a West African Slaving Port, 1727–1982. Athens: Ohio University Press.

Le Hérissé, Auguste. 1911. L'Ancien royaume du Dahomey, moeurs, religion,hHistoire. Paris: Émile Larose.

LeMay-Boucher, Philippe, Joël Noret, and Vincent Somville. 2011. Double, Double, Toil and Trouble: Investigating Expenditures on Protection Against Occult Forces in Benin. University of Namur, Department of Economics, Working Paper 1105:1–20.

Lindholm, Charles. 2012. "What Is Bread?" The Anthropology of Belief. Ethos 40(3): 341–57.

Lindquist, Galina, and Simon Coleman

2008 Introduction: Against Belief? Social Analysis 52(1):1–18.

Lugo, Alejandro. 2008. Fragmented Lives, Assembled Parts: Culture, Capitalism, and Conquest at the U.S.-Mexican Border. Austin: University of Texas Press.

Luhrmann, T. M. 1989. Persuasions of the Witch's Craft: Ritual Magic in Contemporary England. Cambridge, Mass.: Harvard University Press.

MacCannell, Dean. 1973. Staged Authenticity: Arrangements of Social Space in Tourist Settings. American Journal of Sociology 79(3):589–603.

———. 1999 [1976]. The Tourist: A New Theory of the Leisure Class. Berkeley: University of California Press.

MacLeod, Donald V. 1999. Tourism and the Globalization of a Canary Island. Journal of the Royal Anthropological Institute 5(3):443–56.

Martin, Emily. 2000. Mind-Body Problems. American Ethnologist 27(3):569–90.

Marwick, M. G. 1965. Sorcery in Its Social Setting: A Study of the Northern Rhodesian Cewa. Manchester: Manchester University Press.

Matory, Lorand J. 2005. Black Atlantic Religion: Tradition, Transnationalism, and Matriarchy in the Afro-Brazilian Candomblé. Princeton, N.J.: Princeton University Press.

Maupoil, Bernard. 1943. La géomancie à l'ancienne Côte des Esclaves. Paris: Institute d'Ethnologie.

Mauss, Marcel. 1990. [1950] The Gift: The Form and Reason for Exchange in Archaic Societies. W. D. Halls, trans. New York: W. W. Norton.

McDannell, Colleen. 1995. Material Christianity: Religion and Popular Culture in America. New Haven: Yale University Press.

McGee, Adam. 2012. Haitian Vodou and Voodoo: Imagined Religion and Popular Culture. Studies in Religion/Sciences Religieuses 42(2):231–56.

Mercier, Paul. 1954. The Fon of Dahomey. In African Worlds: Studies in the Cosmological Ideas and Surreal Values of African Peoples. Daryll Forde, ed. Pp. 210–34. Oxford: Oxford University Press.

Meyer, Birgit. 1999. Translating the Devil: Religion and Modernity Among the Ewe in Ghana. Edinburgh: Edinburgh University Press.

Miller, Daniel. 2010. Stuff. Cambridge: Polity Press.

———. 2011. The Comfort of Things. Cambridge: Polity Press.

Mills, Charles. 1998. Blackness Visible: Essays on the Philosophy of Race. Ithaca, N.Y.: Cornell University Press.

Moi, Toril. 1985. Sexual/Textual Politics: Feminist Literary Theory. London: Routledge.

Moreman, Christopher M., and Cory James Rushton, eds. 2011. Race, Oppression, and the Zombie: Essays on Cross-Cultural Appropriations of the Caribbean Tradition. Jefferson, N.C.: McFarland.

Morinis, Alan, ed. 1992. Sacred Journeys: The Anthropology of Pilgrimage. Westport: Greenwood Press.

Mossière, Géraldine. 2007. Sharing in Ritual Effervescence: Emotions and Empathy in Fieldwork. Anthropology Matters Journal 9(1):1–13.

Mudimbe, V. Y. 1988. The Invention of Africa: Gnosis, Philosophy, and the Order of Knowledge. Bloomington: Indiana University Press.

Mulcock, Jane. 2001. Ethnography in Awkward Spaces: An Anthropology of Cultural Borrowing. Practicing Anthropology 23(1):38–42.

Murphy, Joseph M., and Mei-Mei Sanford, eds. 2001. Osun Across the Waters: A Yoruba Goddess in Africa and the Americas. Bloomington: Indiana University Press.

Nash, Dennison. 1989 [1978]. Tourism as a Form of Imperialism. In Hosts and Guests: The Anthropology of Tourism. Valene L. Smith, ed. Pp. 37–54. Philadelphia: University of Pennsylvania Press.

Needham, Rodney. 1972. Belief, Language, and Experience. Oxford: Oxford University Press.

Newell, Sasha. 2012. The Modernity Bluff: Crime, Consumption, and Citizenship in Côte d'Ivoire. Chicago: University of Chicago Press.

———. 2013. Brands as Masks: Public Secrecy and the Counterfeit in Côte d'Ivoire. Journal of the Royal Anthropological Institute 19(1):138–54.

Nikolaus, G. 2011. The Fetish Culture in West Africa: An Ancient Tradition as a Threat to Endangered Birdlife? In Tropical Vertebrates in a Changing World. Karl-Ludwig Schuchmann, ed. Pp. 145–50. Bonn: Zoologisches Forschungsmuseum Alexander Koenig.

Nock, Arthur Darby. 1933. Conversion. Oxford: Clarendon Press.

Noret, Joël. 2010. En finir avec les croyances? Croire aux ancêtres au Sud-Bénin. In Corps, Performance, Religion. Joël Noret and P. Petil, eds. Paris: Publibook.

Norman, Neil L. 2009. Powerful Pots, Humbling Holes, and Regional Ritual Processes: Towards an Archaeology of Huedan Vodun, ca. 1650–1727. African Archaeological Review 26(3):187–218.

Offiong, David A. 1983. Witchcraft Among the Ibibio of Nigeria. African Studies Review 26(1):107–24.

Ogundiran, Akinwumi. 2002. Of Small Things Remembered: Beads, Cowries, and Cultural Translations of the Atlantic Experience in Yorubaland. International Journal of African Historical Studies 35(2/3):427–57.

Olupona, Jacob K., and Terry Rey, eds. 2008. Òrìṣà Devotion as World Religion: The Globalization of Yorùbá Religious Culture. Madison: University of Wisconsin Press.

Ong, Aihwa. 1999. Flexible Citizenship: The Cultural Logics of Transnationality. Durham, N.C.: Duke University Press.

Orsi, Robert A. 1999. Gods of the City: Religion and the American Urban Landscape. Bloomington: Indiana University Press.

Orta, Andrew. 2004. Catechizing Culture: Missionaries, Aymara, and the "New Evangelization." New York: Columbia University Press.

Ortner, Sherry. 1973. On Key Symbols. American Anthropologist 75(5):1338–46.

Parish, Jane. 2011. West African Witchcraft, Wealth and Moral Decay in New York City. Ethnography 12(2):247–65.

Pérez, Elizabeth. 2016. Religion in the Kitchen: Cooking, Talking, and the Making of Black Atlantic Traditions. New York: New York University Press.

Pierre, Jemima. 2013. The Predicament of Blackness: Postcolonial Ghana and the Politics of Race. Chicago: University of Chicago Press.

Piot, Charles. 1999. Remotely Global: Village Modernity in West Africa. Chicago: University of Chicago Press.

Prince, Ruth, and David Riches. 1999. Back to the Future: The New Age Movement and Hunter-Gatherers. Anthropos 94(1):107–20.

Rassinoux, Père Jean. 2000. Dictionnaire Français-Fon. Madrid: Société des Missions Africaines.

Reed, Anne. 2014. Pilgrimage Tourism of Diaspora Africans to Ghana. London: Routledge.

Rey, Terry, and Alex Stepick. 2013. Crossing the Water and Keeping the Faith: Haitian Religion in Miami. New York: New York University Press.

Richman, Karen E. 2005. Migration and Vodou. Gainesville: University Press of Florida.

Rodney, Walter. 1981. How Europe Underdeveloped Africa. Washington, D.C.: Howard University Press.

Rogers, Richard A. 2006. From Cultural Exchange to Transculturation: A Review and Reconceptualization of Cultural Appropriation. Communication Theory 16:474–503.

Rose, Wendy. 1992. The Great Pretenders: Further Reflections on White Shamanism. In The State of Native America: Genocide, Colonization, and Resistance. M. Anette James, ed. Pp. 403–21. Boston: South End Press.

Rosenthal, Judy. 1998. Possession, Ecstasy, & Law in Ewe Voodoo. Charlottesville: University of Virginia Press.

Ruel, Malcolm J. 1982. Christians as Believers. In Religious Organization and Religious Experience. J. Davis, ed. Pp. 9–31. London: Academic Press.

Rush, Dana. 1997. Vodun Vortex: Accumulative Arts, Histories, and Religious Consciousnesses Along Coastal Benin. Ph.D. dissertation, University of Iowa.

———. 2001. Contemporary Vodun Arts of Ouidah, Benin. African Arts 34(4):32–47, 94–96.

_____. 2010. Ephemerality and the "Unfinished" in Vodun Aesthetics. African Arts 43(1):60–75.

———. 2013. Vodun in Coastal Bénin: Unfinished, Open-ended, Global. Nashville, Tenn.: Vanderbilt University Press.

Şaul, Mahir. 2008. Money in Colonial Transition: Cowries and Francs in West Africa. American Anthropologist 106(1):71–84.

Scheld, Suzanne. 2007. Youth Cosmopolitanism: Clothing, the City and Globalization in Dakar, Senegal. City & Society 19(2):232–53.

Segurola, B., and J. Rassinoux. 2009. Dictionnaire Fon-Français. Madrid: Société des Missions Africaines.

Shapin, Steven. 1996. The Scientific Revolution. Chicago: University of Chicago Press.

Smith, Andrea. 2005. Spiritual Appropriation as Sexual Violence. Wičazo Ša Review 20(1):97–111.

Sperber, Daniel. 1985. On Anthropological Knowledge. Cambridge: Cambridge University Press.

Steiner, Christopher B. 1994. African Art in Transit. New York: Cambridge University Press.

Stewart, Kathleen. 1996. A Space on the Side of the Road. Princeton, N.J.: Princeton University Press.

Stewart, Susan. 2007 [1984]. On Longing: Narratives of the Miniature, the Gigantic, the Souvenir, the Collection. Durham, N.C.: Duke University Press.

Stoller, Paul. 2004. Stranger in the Village of the Sick. Boston: Beacon Press.

———. 2009. The Power of the Between: An Anthropological Odyssey. Chicago: University of Chicago Press.

Stoller, Paul, and Cheryl Olkes. 1987. In Sorcery's Shadow: A Memoir of Apprenticeship Among the Songhay of Niger. Chicago: University of Chicago Press.

Strandsberg, Camilla. 2000. Kérékou, God and the Ancestors: Religion and the Conception of Political Power in Benin. African Affairs 99(396):395–414.

Tall, Emanuelle Kadya. 1995. Dynamique des cultes Voduns et du Christianisme Céleste au Sud-Bénin. Cahiers des Sciences Humaines 31(4):797–832.

Taussig, Michael T. 1999. Defacement: Public Secrecy and the Labor of the Negative. Stanford, Calif.: Stanford University Press.

Taylor, Bron. 1997. Earthen Spirituality or Culture Genocide? Radical Environmentalism's Appropriation of Native American Spirituality. Religion 27:183–215.

Thompson, Robert Farris. 2011. Aesthetic of the Cool: Afro-Atlantic Art and Music. New York: Periscope Publishing.

Tsing, Anna. 2005. Friction: An Ethnography of Global Connection. Princeton, N.J.: Princeton University Press.

Turner, Victor. 1967. The Forest of Symbols: Aspects of Ndembu Ritual. Ithaca, N.Y.: Cornell University Press.

———. 1969. The Ritual Process: Structure and Anti-Structure. Chicago: Aldine Transaction.

———. 1980. Social Dramas and Stories About Them. Critical Inquiry 7(1):141–68.

———. 1996 [1957]. Schism and Continuity in an African Society: A Study of Ndembu Village Life. London: Berg Publishers.

Turner, Victor, and Edith L. B. Turner. 1978. Image and Pilgrimage in Christian Culture. New York: Columbia University Press.

Urry, John. 2002. The Tourist Gaze. London: Sage.

Van Gennep, Arnold. 1909. Les rites de passage. Paris: Nourry.

Verger, Pierre Fatumbi. 1995a. Ewé: The Use of Plants in Yoruba Society. São Paulo: Editora Schwarcz.

———. 1995b. Dieux d'Afrique: Culte des Orishas et Vodouns à l'ancienne Côte des Esclaves en Afrique et à Bahia, la Baie de tous les Saints au Brésil. Paris: Revue Noire.

Vertovec, Steven. 2007. Super-Diversity and Its Implications. Ethnic and Racial Studies 30(6): 1024–54.

Washington, Teresa N. 2005. Our Mothers, Our Powers, Our Texts: Manifestations of Àjẹ́ in Africana Literature. Bloomington: Indiana University Press.

Wittgenstein, Ludwig. 1980 [1977]. Culture and Value. Peter Winch, trans. Chicago: University of Chicago Press.

Young, James O., and Conrad G. Brunk, eds. 2009. The Ethics of Cultural Appropriation. Malden, Mass.: Blackwell.

INDEX

ACKNOWLEDGMENTS

Acknowledging those people who helped or supported me during this process seems like an impossible task—one that, no matter how exhaustive, will always be incomplete. Even so, I endeavor to extend my gratitude to those people who made writing this book possible.

First and foremost, I would like to thank my mother and father, Catherine and Tim S. Landry, for the years of emotional support they freely gave as I followed my intellectual dreams. To my brother, Kevin, his wife, Kim, and their daughters, Dakota and Logan: thank you for being the most personally supportive people I know. You will never know how much your simple understanding has affected me.

To Virginia Dominguez, you always found the right way to challenge me and make me think about things differently; to Janet Dixon Keller, thank you for the enriching experiences and valuable lessons you imparted to me over the years. To Helaine Silverman, you always made me feel as though my work was valuable. You served as one of my greatest fans and one of my most profound allies. Your support and enthusiasm for this will forever be remembered.

To Alma Gottlieb, your guidance and support made me a better scholar and a better writer. You taught me that one's writing is just as important as one's research, and you always encouraged and nurtured my determination to be not just an anthropologist but also a humanist. My success has been in large part thanks to your tireless editorial and practical support.

To Paul Stoller, your work inspired me not to just be an anthropologist but to also tread down the somewhat controversial path of religious apprenticeship. From your groundbreaking work on sorcery you gave me the courage to forge ahead with my intentions to become initiated and embody the "between" in profound but challenging ways. Your continued support has been encouraging. Thank you.

To Dana Rush, who quite literally introduced me to Bénin, I appreciate your early guidance more than you realize. To Douglas Falen, I have gained incredibly from our conversations, e-mail exchanges, and our brief time in Bénin together. I look forward to many years of continued dialogue and collaboration. To Micha Boyer, Nathan Hedges, and James Kennell, thank you for making the small field of Bénin studies a collegial and fertile intellectual community; I look forward to many years that await us all. To Daniel Miller and Beatriz Zengotitabengoa, thank you for your company while we all conducted research in Bénin. You both made my time there that much more enjoyable.

To Lauren Anaya, Jamie Arjona, Sophia Balakain, Junjie Chen, JoAnn D'Alisera, Angela Glaros, Michele Hanks, Lance Larkin, Krista Milich, Nancy Phaup, and Batamaka Somé, thank you all for reading and commenting on my writing—the good, the bad, and the hurried; without all of you this journey would have been much less bearable. Over the years you have all become some of my closest friends. I look forward to our futures. Your support has meant the world to me.

To my colleagues in anthropology and religious studies at Trinity College, Leslie Desmangles, Elli Banks Findly, Gabriel Hornung, Shafqat Hussain, Tamsin Jones, Ron Kiener, Mareike Koertner, Jane Nadel-Klein, Beth Notar, Mark Silk, and Jim Trostle, thank you for making time in the office both productive and enjoyable.

To my friends in Bénin, especially Adjos Adjovi, Thomas Agbodjan, Anatase Bataku, Hyppolite Behanzin, Meme Dagba, Martine de Souza, Hughes de Souza, Laura de Souza, Marie-Anne de Souza, Manitos de Souza, Marc Esse. Boniface Egnile, Jean Egnile, Joël Egnile, Rodrigue Egnile, Romaric Egnile, Jeanne-Paule Guvide, Bernard Lima, Momo Lima, Delphin Nouatin, and Hector Zogo, and to the countless others who shared with me their homes, their lives, and sometimes even their secrets: thank you, this book is just as much yours as it is mine—*merci beaucoup pour tout! Mǎwǔ ná gɔ́ alɔ nú wè!*

My thanks to Brill and the *Journal of Religion in Africa* for allowing me to republish a version of my article "Vodún, Globalization, and the Creative Layering of Belief in Southern Bénin" (Landry 2015) here as Chapter 4, "Belief, Efficacy, and Transnationalism."

Finally, I would like to extend my deepest thanks to those institutions that believed in this project enough to fund my research in Bénin. I would like to thank the Wenner-Gren Foundation, the Fulbright Institute for International Education, the UIUC Nelle M. Signor Scholarship of International Relations, the West African Research Association, and the Department of Anthropology at the University of Illinois at Urbana-Champaign for their financial support. Without the generous funding from these institutions, this book would have not been possible. Thank you.